Allan Massie

Allan Massie is a celebrated novelist and biographer. He is also a leading columnist for the *Daily Mail*, *Daily Telegraph*, *Sunday Times* and the *Scotsman*. After reading history at Trinity College, Cambridge, he spent some years in Rome before returning to live in the Scottish borders. He is a Fellow of the Royal Society of Literature.

D0879305

Other books by the author

NON-FICTION

Muriel Spark

Ill-Met by Gaslight

The Caesars

Portrait of Scottish Rugby

Colette

101 Great Scots

Byron's Travels

Glasgow: Portrait of a City

The Novel Today 1970–89

Edinburgh

FICTION

Change and Decay in All Around I See

The Last Peacock

The Death of Men

One Night in Winter

Augustus

A Question of Loyalties

Tiberius

The Hanging Tree

The Sins of the Father

Caesar

The Ragged Lion

These Enchanted Woods

King David

Shadows of Empire

Antony

Nero's Heirs

The Evening of the World

Arthur the King

Caligula

The Thistle and the Rose

*Six Centuries of Love and Hate between
the Scots and the English*

ALLAN MASSIE

JOHN MURRAY

© Allan Massie 2005

First published in Great Britain in 2005 by John Murray (Publishers)
A division of Hodder Headline

Paperback edition 2006

The right of Allan Massie to be identified as the Author of the Work has been asserted by him in accordance with the Copyright, Designs and Patents Act 1988.

2

All rights reserved. Apart from any use permitted under UK copyright law no part of this publication may be reproduced, stored in a retrieval system, or transmitted, in any form or by any means without the prior written permission of the publisher, nor be otherwise circulated in any form of binding or cover other than that in which it is published and without a similar condition being imposed on the subsequent purchaser.

A CIP catalogue record for this title is available from the British Library

ISBN-13 978-0-7195-6596-0
ISBN-10 0-7195-6596-0

Typeset in Monotype Bembo by Servis Filmsetting Ltd, Manchester

Printed and bound by Clays Ltd, St Ives plc

Hodder Headline policy is to use papers that are natural, renewable and recyclable products and made from wood grown in sustainable forests. The logging and manufacturing processes are expected to conform to the environmental regulations of the country of origin.

John Murray (Publishers)
338 Euston Road
London NW1 3BH

In memory of Giles Gordon

Contents

Acknowledgements

There has been a fashion in recent years for authors to compile a very long list of acknowledgements extending in some cases to the family cat. This shows what decent fellows they are and may lend their work a spurious authority. It is not a fashion I care for. I have talked to many people about the topics covered in this book, and read widely, but my opinions and mistakes are my own.

I am however grateful to my agents, the late Giles Gordon, and his successor at Curtis Brown, John Saddler, for their encouragement. I am also grateful to John Murray for publishing the book, and to my editors there: first, Caroline Knox who commissioned it and continued to support and encourage me when I failed to meet deadlines, and Gordon Wise who urged me forward to the finishing line.

Introduction

A BOOK SUCH as this, essays about the relations between Scotland and England, Scots and English, and the varieties of British experience – what indeed being British has meant – may benefit from an autobiographical note, which at least must reveal the author's point of view, his point indeed of departure.

I was born in Singapore, which makes me quite a typical Scot, a child of the British Empire. My father had gone to Malaya in 1926, at the age of nineteen, to a job as a rubber planter. He went there because he was poor. He would have preferred to farm in Aberdeenshire, but he had no capital. His own father had died young, when mine was only a year old, leaving a widow and four children. So, being in Walter Scott's phrase 'born a Scotsman and a bare one', my father had to make his way in the world. His experience was common enough. Scots had been emigrating in search of fortune since the Middle Ages: to Europe, to England and to the Empire. Many stayed where they settled. There were said, for instance, to be 30,000 Scots families resident in Poland in the early seventeenth century.

In another respect I am less typical. I can name my eight great-grandparents, who were all Scots, born and passing their whole lives in the north-east, in Aberdeenshire or Banffshire. I can follow some of them a generation or two further back, without coming on any who weren't themselves Scottish. There may have been foreigners among my more remote ancestors, but I don't know of them.

Most of those I do know of were farmers, though not on any considerable scale. Some were ministers of religion, Presbyterians; one or two were village schoolmasters. My paternal grandfather combined

the tenancy of a farm with work as a salesman for a firm of agricultural merchants. His brother became a successful lawyer in Aberdeen.
Earlier generations of Massies farmed in a number of different places,
some only crofts, all within thirty miles of Aberdeen. Massie is quite
a common name in the north-east; not in other parts of Scotland.
There is, I think, no connection with the Cheshire family Massey, one
member of which was a Civil War general, fighting first for the
Royalists, then for the Parliament, and then again for the king.

My mother's father was a Forbes, the name pronounced till quite
recently as two syllables. The Forbeses were one of the two chief families of Aberdeenshire, the Gordons the other. Donside was Forbes
country and the head of the family is the premier baron of Scotland;
but we have to my knowledge no connection. Gordons tended to be
Roman Catholic, Episcopalian, Cavalier, Tory, Jacobite; Forbeses
were mostly Presbyterian and Whig, though Alexander Forbes, the
4th and last Lord Pitsligo, was out in both the principal Jacobite
Risings, despite being almost seventy in the '45, and Robert Forbes,
author or editor of the records of Jacobitism, *The Lyon in Mourning*,
was an Episcopalian who became Bishop of Ross & Cromarty. As a
child I liked to think that my Forbes ancestors were Jacobites, but did
so without evidence.

The other side of my mother's family is better documented. My
Forbes grandfather was an only child; his wife Mary Allan one of seven
children. We can trace the Allan family back to the poll-book of
Aberdeenshire of 1696. There are numerous collateral branches, partly
because my great-great-great-grandmother Mary Martin married
three times, John Allan being her second husband. Through the
Martins we are connected in some remote cousinship to the
Norwegian composer Edvard Grieg. A nephew of Mary Martin's was
Theodore Martin, biographer of the Prince Consort, and husband of
the Shakespearean actress Helen Faucit, a close friend of Thackeray's
daughter Minnie who married Leslie Stephen, father of Virginia
Woolf. The Allans give us another interesting but fairly distant connection: a first cousin once removed of my Allan grandfather – her own
father being an Aberdeen shipmaster – married William Alexander,

editor of the *Aberdeen Free Press* and author of the classic novel of north-east rural life, *Johnny Gibb of Gushetneuk*. These relationships, mildly distinguished, are distant; I knew almost nothing of them when young.

An obituary published in the *Aberdeen Free Press* in June 1910 tells me more about my great-grandfather, Alexander Allan: 'a kind and helpful neighbour, a real friend and adviser to many, readily giving his skilful service in the care of farm stock' – he seems to have been a successful cattle breeder, rearing 'animals of cross character for commercial purposes'. Aberdeenshire was by the mid-nineteenth century cattle country, supplying the London market, this made possible by the railway. 'In matters pertaining to the public welfare he took a keen and active interest,' serving on a school board and parish council. He was a member of the Free Church; and indeed after the disruption of 1843 Free Kirk services had been held in his father's barn till a distillery in the neighbouring village was converted to a church. Alexander Allan himself was successively precentor, deacon and elder in the Blackburn Free Church. 'He was a staunch Liberal in politics and was active in his efforts to secure the return of the Liberal candidate for the time being.' This doesn't make it clear whether he remained a Gladstonian Liberal (as I suspect he did), or like many Scottish Liberals followed Joseph Chamberlain, breaking with the party over the issue of Irish Home Rule; and so became a Liberal Unionist.

I record this in some detail, partly because he is the only ancestor of that generation for which this is possible, but also, and more importantly, because I judge that in his character, interests and activities he is the type of others. Certainly a very similar brief obituary could have been written, and doubtless was written, of innumerable north-east farmers, who worked diligently and were active in discharging obligations to society. I can remember many such.

Scotland is now usually described, happy to be described, as a Celtic nation, and Gaelic was still spoken in upland Aberdeenshire – in upper Deeside and upper Donside – till late in the nineteenth century, even into the twentieth in a few glens. But I don't think any of the forefathers of whom I have record spoke it. Certainly the names that crop up in the various branches of the family tree such as Fordyce, Birnie, Wilson, Hill, Johnston, Troup, are none of them Highland. Scots rather than Gaelic has been spoken in Lowland Aberdeenshire since the early Middle Ages, and even today the Scots of Buchan and the Garioch is rich and vigorous – and as incomprehensible to Scots from other parts as it is to Englishmen. Late in his life, a young woman asked my father if he would be wearing the kilt to a grandson's wedding. He replied, 'I'm a Lowlander. I've never worn a kilt in my life.' In another context, interviewing him for a television programme I was making, I asked whether, in Malaya, they had thought of themselves as Scots or British. 'Oh,' he said, 'we were British, except on St Andrew's Night.' Yet before he sailed for Malaya I doubt if he had ever been south of Perth. He certainly hadn't then visited Edinburgh, and he never knew Glasgow at all.

He had left school at fourteen, as so many, the majority indeed, did then. But he had inherited the Scots' respect for education, knew its value, and indeed educated himself in the evenings of lonely years on a rubber estate, having boxes of books sent to him from a library in Kuala Lumpur. He married in 1935 in the course of his second leave home, having become engaged on the first four years earlier. We were fortunate that his next leave fell in 1939. My mother remained behind with us children. Father returned to work and was taken prisoner at Singapore. He spent almost four years in a Japanese POW camp, and very nearly died there.

At first he didn't intend to return to Malaya after the war. My mother had inherited a farm in Aberdeenshire from her father and he was eager to run it. But his company held out attractive prospects. His immediate superior reminded him that he had always said he wanted to give his children the best education possible, and this was his opportunity to do so.

His decision had a great influence on my life. Had he held to his intention of farming on Donside, my brother and I would probably have been sent to school in Aberdeen, either to that ancient foundation Aberdeen Grammar School or to Robert Gordon's College. It is probable that from either I would have proceeded to university in

Aberdeen, and then, I sometimes think, to a career in the law, perhaps in the firm of advocates (as solicitors are called in Aberdeen) of which my father's uncle had been a partner, as that uncle's son-in-law then was. When the discovery of North Sea oil made Aberdeen a boom town in the 1970s, I might, like other lawyers there, have seized the opportunity to make myself rich.

Instead we were sent to boarding-school, first to a preparatory school, Drumtochty Castle, in Kincardineshire, and then to Trinity College, Glenalmond in Perthshire. I have nothing to complain of in either.

Glenalmond, as it was generally known to outsiders, was a nine-teenth-century foundation, closely connected with the Episcopal Church of Scotland, then recovering from the effects of its adherence to the Jacobite cause, and displaying a renewed vitality and vigour, partly inspired by the Oxford or Tractarian Movement in England. Originally indeed the school was coupled with a theological college, but this was soon removed to Edinburgh. The guiding spirits in the enterprise were the future prime minister William Gladstone and James Hope, who later took the name of Hope-Scott when he married Sir Walter Scott's granddaughter and they inherited Abbotsford.

The author of a history of Glenalmond, George St Quentin, wrote:

> The beginnings of the College date from a time when Dr Arnold had restored the prestige of large boarding-schools. Several famous English schools were started between 1840 and 1865, designed to make board-ing-school education accessible to those of the middle class who could not afford the fees of the older and more expensive Public Schools such as Winchester, Eton and Rugby. Trinity College, Glenalmond, was one of a group of three schools founded contemporaneously by Churchmen to provide education with special attention to the incul-cation of Church principles. The other two were Radley in England and St Columba's, Rathfarnham in Ireland.

When I was at Glenalmond, the seven bishops of the Scottish Episcopalian Church were still, *ex officio*, members of the college's governing Council. The then warden's predecessor, appointed in 1938, had been the first not to be a clergyman.

Gladstone, in advocating the scheme, pointed out that there wasn't in Scotland a single establishment where the sons of Scottish Episcopalian gentry could be educated according to their own faith. Glenalmond would make it unnecessary for such to send their sons to school in England.

The Scottish public or independent schools have been often regarded with suspicion by other Scots, Glenalmond perhaps most of all, since many Scots, ignorant of history, call the Episcopal Church 'the English Church'. A quarter of a century ago, asked to contribute to a book of essays about a Scottish childhood, I wrote, somewhat pompously, that by going to Glenalmond I was committed to the United Kingdom. On the other hand, 'it never occurred to me that Glenalmond was anything but a Scottish school'. Yet:

> the Scottish public schools have often enough and justifiably enough been seen as an alien element – the fifth column of England. Since the aristocracy in the early nineteenth century had accepted anglicization and were already flocking to Eton, Harrow, Winchester and possibly Rugby, it became necessary at home to provide comparable institutions for the sons of their professional men of business and the lesser gentry, so that some social contact might be maintained.

I seem not to have been entirely convinced by this quasi-sociological interpretation, for I continued:

> This misses however the degree of commitment to the imperial idea and the United Kingdom; in the fruition of the Empire, the characteristic ideology was centripetal. Separatism in the Victorian noon-day was a crank's game, suitable only to the Irish. The Scottish Public Schools – Fettes, Loretto, Glenalmond, Merchiston – were not an indigenous growth. They were planted, like colonies. But they took root. Others might resent them. Those educated at the older city schools might condemn them as alien, apart from the Scottish tradition. They didn't feel that way to those within the community. We were sufficiently intense at Murrayfield. The few English boys were treated with a hostility that strove to be off-hand and contemptuous, but never quite managed it . . .

That was written in 1977 when I was living in Edinburgh and was caught up, to some extent anyway, in the fervid atmosphere created by anticipation of devolution. It now seems a touch snide, also unnecessarily defensive.

Nevertheless Glenalmond, however Scottish our sentiments may have been, was unquestionably British. More than half the masters were themselves English, and almost all graduates of Oxford or Cambridge. It was assumed that intelligent boys would be directed there. The effect was to reinforce Johnson's observation about the fairest prospect open to a Scotsman. Its truth couldn't be denied. To look elsewhere would have been taken as evidence of provincialism. There was never any question of going to a Scottish university unless you had first failed to get into either Oxford or Cambridge, or had been deemed unworthy to make the attempt to do so. 'Nothing', I wrote in 1977, 'shows more clearly how Scotland was regarded as a home for the second-rate than this assumption that the best should seek their future outwith it.'

Perhaps as a corollary I then saw London, not Edinburgh, as the capital. London was where I expected to make my career, and indeed till I was in my thirties I spent more time in London than in Edinburgh and certainly knew it better. On the other hand, precisely because London was the capital of the United Kingdom, and still, just, of the Empire, I never thought of it as an English city, as Manchester, Leeds and Birmingham were very evidently English. London was British.

And so was Cambridge when I arrived there. The town itself was certainly English, agreeably English in the dingy pubs around the Lion Yard where you might drink Tolly's weak bitter with warned-off jockeys and decayed stable-lads, small businessmen and slightly disreputable retired solicitors. So was the countryside around, English and foreign. The college servants – the porters and bedmakers – were certainly, and to a young Scot interestingly, English. But the university wasn't. It was British.

This was doubtless in part because among my friends, mostly products of English public schools – Eton, Westminster, Winchester,

Repton, Rugby – few turned out to be 100 per cent English, few had two English parents. Some were authentic Scots, schooled in England but at home in Scotland. Some were Anglo-Scots, with names such as Dewar, Macleod, Guthrie, Gray, McGibbon, or Glasgow–Irish Anglo-Scots (Brogan); some were Scots on the distaff side so that the surname – Roberts, Davies, for instance – concealed this heredity. Others who, as far as I know, had no Scots ancestors were nevertheless not pure English, having an American, or Russian, or Ulster Protestant or central European parent. Many of them would have called themselves English, thought of themselves as English, but they were not English as the porters and bedmakers were. This was not just a question of class, though class came into it. There was another difference; they couldn't, correctly, have been described as anything but British.

At the same time I came to know, respect, even love rural England: the great arching skies of East Anglia, the lonely placidity of the Fenland, the little villages with their churches centuries older than most Scottish places of worship. My father, then divorced from my mother, had retired from Malaya and taken a farm on the Hampshire–Berkshire border, at Silchester. The wall of the old Roman city divided the farmhouse garden from the fields; and you felt there the timelessness of southern England, beautiful, tranquil, undisturbed by war for hundreds of years. It was a country at once foreign and familiar, foreign because so unlike my Scotland, familiar from the work of English poets and novelists. England, it seemed, was a country where there were no live questions of identity, where there was no unfinished historical business. This accounted for the gentleness and tolerance that then seemed characteristic of the English people.

In the middle 1970s, my wife and I returned from Italy, where I had been living, teaching English, for some years, and settled in Edinburgh. I had published some short stories – in England, in Alan Ross's *London Magazine* – was working on a novel, and, by way of book-reviewing, freelance journalism, eventually graduated (if that is the right word) to the position of a political columnist. For the first time I found myself caught up in the public life of Scotland, and for a few years shared the enthusiasm for devolution. In time I turned against it, partly because it seemed to engender unrealistic hopes and assumptions, partly because I was disturbed by an undercurrent of anglophobia, partly because I thought it likely to lead to independence, which I did not desire, and partly because the implicit denial of Britishness was distasteful.

Looking back over that book of essays published in 1977 I find much of interest and enduring relevance. It was conceived and edited, with a light hand, by my friend Trevor Royle, then the Literature Director of the Scottish Arts Council, now a successful journalist and military historian. Trevor himself is, or was born, an Englishman (though in India), and was brought up in St Andrews, going to school there and then to university in Aberdeen. He is the reverse of the Anglo-Scot, that less common being, the Scots Englishman, the Sassenach who has identified himself with Scotland. He wrote of 'the terrible sense of paradox in Scotland'. He felt empathy 'with a small country with its own indigenous culture being threatened by the processes of international big business', but there were other times when he 'bitterly resented the shame of being on the outside and cursed the Scots bigotry towards the English and all that they stood for'.

Another friend who contributed to the book, Giles Gordon, was soon to become my literary agent. He was then living in London where he had gone to work in publishing as a very young man, taking, like so many, that high road to fortune. In the middle 1990s he would return to Scotland to set up a Scottish branch of the literary agency in which he was a partner, but in 1977 he was a Londoner, married to a Londoner, and revelling in the cultural life of the capital, its theatres, its restaurants, and the Garrick Club.

Yet, he wrote in 1977, it was in London that he realized:

there was no escape from the fact that I was as Scottish as my father. And yet, considered in another way, I regard myself as being the nationality my passport has always proclaimed me to be: British . . . I'd surmise that relatively few people think of themselves as indigenously British. Certainly most of the English don't; they know they are English; the Welsh are Welsh and the Scots are Scots. I do not feel British because I live in London. I feel British because my Scottish education [at the Edinburgh Academy, a school that numbers among its founders Lord Cockburn and Sir Walter Scott] – my education in Scotland wittingly or unwittingly inculcated upon me the assets of being British. I believe fundamentally that it's a privilege to be British today and certainly my bones and flesh and spirit are Scottish–British; and I repudiate any suggestion of being English–British . . .

'It is', Giles concluded, 'those Scots who have been able to get over their superficial allegiance to the idea of their country, the high-brow haggis-bashing, who have attained – most usually without being aware of the fact – a real Scottishness.'

The arguments Trevor Royle and Giles Gordon then deployed continue still to turn and twist. They are doubtless of more importance to Scots than to the English, who mostly indeed are indifferent to them – which is why this book on relations between the two countries, the two peoples that are so nearly one, and who have in war at least attained that unity, is, superficially at least, more concerned with Scots' attitudes to England and Britain than with English ones to Scotland and the United Kingdom. The questions matter more to us.

A few years ago I wrote a novel with the title *Shadows of Empire*. It's about a family that made its money in the west of Scotland in the nineteenth century and then became part of the British Establishment. It covers the middle years of the twentieth century, years cursed with the dominance of ideology and war. Near the end the narrator is speaking with his oldest friend, an Edinburgh doctor, Toby Macrae, who was intended, though few reviewers recognized it, to be the moral centre of the novel. They have been discussing the narrator's younger brother, Alastair, a Fascist, perhaps a traitor:

Toby said: 'You must remember, we, unlike the English, have an innate tendency to take things to extremes for the sake of an idea. Revert to the seventeenth century. Have you ever thought how it was that in England, Puritanism, after the Restoration, so quickly transformed itself into a decent civic dissent and nonconformity, while here we had the Covenanters, obstinately, blindly, fanatically still setting themselves to establish God's kingdom on earth, and absolutely indifferent to suffering caused and endured?'

'You're not suggesting that Alastair's conduct is explained by ancestral Covenanting zeal. That's too ridiculous. He scarcely thinks of himself as a Scot.'

'No, I grant you that would be naive, but I do suggest that he is, in spite of Eton, Oxford, and an upbringing in salad country, enough of a Scot to feel the magnetic attraction of an Idea – whatever its relation to reality. As a race we're an odd mixture, Alec. We like to think of ourselves as hard-headed practical men, building the railways and bridges of Africa and Asia and America, traders, manufacturers, and engineers, servants of the Empire and the rest – though that last one is a giveaway, for the Empire has been important as an Idea as much as a Thing. But there's the other side of it – the madness for theology and disputation concerning matters that no Englishman would give the time of day to considering.'

There's something in the distinction I had Toby Macrae make, one that Stevenson made also; but, like all generalizations about national character, it's also specious. It leaves too much out, and not only because there have been Englishmen who argued theological questions with as much fervour and hair-splitting as any Scot or Jew.

The significant omission is the central question of influence: the degree to which both Scots and English have been formed by the British experience: Anglicization and Scotification, Englished Scotland and Scotched England. That interplay is the central theme of this book of essays, as it has been in my own life, and is still in the life of the nation or nations.

Part One

Prelude

~

IN 1802 WALTER Scott published his *Minstrelsy of the Scottish Border*, consisting of 'Historical and Romantic ballads collected in the Southern Counties of Scotland, with a few of modern date, founded upon local tradition'. Some of these modern ballads were his own work, and the *Minstrelsy* also included some poems and ballads which originated in the north of England. That was fair enough. Borderers, either side of the line dividing England from Scotland, had more in common with each other than either had with their fellow-nationals to the south or north. Some families – Grahams, Rutherfords, Armstrongs, for instance – were to be found on both sides of the Border.

Scott was a young man, only thirty-one then, not yet known as either poet or novelist. His purpose was, in part at least, patriotic. He hoped that his collection of ballads 'might contribute somewhat to the history of my native country; the peculiar features of whose manners and character are daily melting and dissolving into those of her sister and ally. And, trivial as may appear such an offering to the *manes* of a kingdom, once proud and independent, I hang it upon her altar with a mixture of feelings which I shall not attempt to describe.'

Despite this disclaimer, he appended a verse, to some extent descriptive of these same deep and disturbing feelings:

> – Hail, land of spearmen! Seed of those who scorned
> To stoop the proud crest to Imperial Rome!
> Hail! dearest half of Albion, sea-wall'd!
> Hail! state unconquer'd by the fire of war,

Red war, that twenty ages round thee blaz'd!
To thee, for whom my purest raptures flow,
Kneeling with filial homage, I devote
My life, my strength, my first and latest song.

There is an ambivalence here wholly characteristic of Scott, characteristic too of so many of his fellow-countrymen. That term itself had two meanings. Scott was a British patriot, ardent supporter of the war against revolutionary France. But for his lameness he would have been a soldier. As it was, he enlisted in a militia regiment, the Edinburgh Light Horse. But at the same time he regretted what he saw as the 'melting and dissolving' of the 'peculiar features' of Scotland. Nevertheless England, into whose manners and character these features seemed to be dissolving, was Scotland's 'sister and ally'.

It was Scotland that had 'scorned to stoop the proud crest to Imperial Rome'. It was Scotland that was to him 'the dearest half of Albion', but it was Albion, the whole island of Britain, that was 'sea-wall'd'; and it was Albion, not Scotland, that was engaged in a war against the France of the Revolution and Napoleon, in defence of its liberties.

Scott consented to the Union with England. It was a reality, and he was far too sensible a man to fly in the face of reality. He liked and admired England and the English. At the same time he was a jealous guardian of all that was Scottish. He hated and feared that 'melting and dissolving', and by his own work arrested it. So he gave his fellow-Scots a renewed sense of their identity and history, and at the same time brought their 'sister and ally' to a better understanding of the nation to which they were joined.

This book is not primarily about Scott, though he permeates it. The subject is the relations through history of Scots and English, how each impacted on the other. So it is also about being British.

But I also hope to show that if, to some degree, the 'peculiar features' of Scotland have indeed 'melted and dissolved' into those of our 'sister and ally', England too has been profoundly influenced by the

Scottish connection, so much so indeed that in certain respects modern England may be held to be a Scottish creation.

I

Two Nations

⁓

THE 8TH OF August 1503 is not a date the significance of which will be readily remarked by many; and yet it should be, for it was then that a marriage was celebrated which made the future union of the kingdoms of England and Scotland possible. The bridegroom was James IV, King of Scots, and the bride Margaret Tudor, daughter of Henry VII of England and Elizabeth of York.

William Dunbar, the greatest of Scottish Renaissance writers, celebrated the union of the Thistle and the Rose in a poem. The Thistle, 'keepit with a bush of spears', is told by Dame Nature that it is his duty to love and protect 'the fresshe Rose, of colour reid and whyte' – Margaret herself being the daughter of a marriage which had joined the Red Rose of Lancaster to the White Rose of York. Dunbar acclaims the Rose as being of more illustrious lineage than the Lily, which was the emblem of France. Performing his duty as a Court poet, he thus advises that Scotland's proper future lies in marriage with England and the abandonment of the 'Auld Alliance' with the Lily, France.

Henry himself had no thought of union. It was unlikely that any child of the Thistle and the Rose would inherit the English throne – he had after all two sons. He hoped to secure his northern frontier and deter his new son-in-law from any hostile adventures. It was only a few years since James had acknowledged and supported the young man, Perkin Warbeck, who claimed to be Richard of York, the younger of the princes in the Tower and brother of Henry's wife Elizabeth.

As for James, he was reluctant to follow his poet's advice. Though he signed a Treaty of Perpetual Peace with England, he resisted his new father-in-law's urging to renounce the French alliance. That indeed would hold for another sixty years.

The Treaty of Perpetual Peace, on the other hand, was broken in ten. When Margaret's brother Henry VIII invaded France in 1513, James, loyal to the French alliance, launched a diversionary attack on the north of England. It resulted in the disaster of Flodden, where the king himself was killed. It seemed as if the new policy of Anglo-Scottish friendship, promoted by Henry VII, the first English king formally to recognize Scottish independence since Edward III reluctantly did so in the Treaty of Northampton in 1328, was also dead. And indeed the next forty years would see several renewals of the old intermittent cross-Border warfare.

This was not surprising. Though relations between Scotland and England had been good, even friendly, in the early Middle Ages, Edward I's attempt to conquer Scotland and incorporate it, like Wales, in an English empire, had stirred up an enmity which could not be easily laid to rest. Yet there were some who understood that this hostility benefited neither country. In 1521, the Scottish scholar John Mair, theologian, philosopher and historian, who had studied at Oxford, Cambridge and Paris, and taught at the universities of Glasgow, St Andrews and Paris, published his *Historia Majoris Britanniae, tam Angliae quam Scotiae*, in which he wrote:

> It would be to the utmost advantage to both kingdoms that they should be under the rule of one monarch, who should be called King of Britain, always provided he had a just and honourable title thereto . . . and any man, be he Englishman or Scot, who will deny this, has, I say, no love for the welfare of his country and the common good . . . I pray to God, the Ruler of all, that He may grant such a peace to the Britons that one of their kings in a marriage union may possess both kingdoms by just title.

No further marriage was to be necessary. Mair's prayer was answered in 1603 when James VI of Scotland, the great-grandson of James IV and Margaret Tudor, inherited the crown of England, peacefully and without opposition to his 'just title', on the death of Queen Elizabeth, herself the granddaughter of Henry VII.

The union thus effected might have taken place in similar fashion 300 years earlier. The opportunity arose as a result of accident, and disappeared thanks equally to chance. In 1286 Alexander III of Scots rode his horse over a cliff in Fife, and left as his heir only a granddaughter Margaret. Known to history as the Maid of Norway, she was herself the child of a dynastic marriage between Alexander's daughter and the King of Norway. Edward I of England now proposed that the little Queen of Scots should be married to his son Edward, Prince of Wales. The proposal was accepted. The union of the two kingdoms seemed likely, and, since many of the greater Scottish barons, themselves of Norman or part-Norman origin, held estates in England as well as in Scotland, and were therefore vassals of both the English and the Scottish crowns, a peaceful union by way of a marriage alliance and inheritance might have proved acceptable and worked satisfactorily.

It is difficult now to know what there was of national feeling in the thirteenth century. Certainly foreigners were often resented. In England, in the reign of Edward's father Henry III, dislike of the king's French councillors was vigorously expressed and provoked rebellion. Yet the leader of that rebellion, Simon de Montford, himself belonged to a family which had acquired great estates in Languedoc. But, though immigrants and interlopers might be resented, medieval society was stratified horizontally, according to class and occupation, rather than being divided vertically by nationality. The Church was an international body, employing an international language, Latin. The links between monastic orders took no heed of political frontiers. Nobles and knights too had loyalties and interests that may be styled transnational.

Nor were these political frontiers themselves settled. That between Scotland and England had moved north and south frequently in the preceding centuries, and would continue to do so for some time to come. The great port of Berwick-on-Tweed changed hands no fewer than thirteen times between 1147 and 1482. Eventually the line of the frontier was fixed, but it might have been fixed elsewhere. In which case the present-day inhabitants of Northumberland and Cumberland might call themselves Scots, or today's Scottish Borderers might be English. Certainly, throughout the Middle Ages, there was little to distinguish the people either side of the modern Border. They spoke the same language, the northern variety of Old English or Anglo-Saxon. (When in 1802 Scott published his *Minstrelsy of the Scottish Border* he included some poems, 'The Lyke-Wake Dirge' for instance, which originated in the north of England.) They practised the same religion and lived very similar lives. That the inhabitants of Northumberland today are English and the inhabitants of Berwickshire and Roxburgh are Scots is the result merely of the historical accidents that fixed the Border on its present line.

A note on language is necessary here, since linguistic differences are commonly one of the determining characteristics of nationality.

Thirteenth-century England had three languages. The first was Latin, which was the written language of educated men, all of whom were clerics. It was the language of the Church, of the universities and of intellectual discourse throughout western Europe. The second was Norman-French, the language of the Court, the nobility and the royal law-courts. The third was English, the tongue of the common people – the peasantry and all but the richest burgesses. By the end of the fourteenth century it would have ousted Norman-French.

This English language was in a state of rapid transition, the consequence of its dislodgement from use for all high purposes after the Norman Conquest. Its grammar was losing its inflections and its vocabulary admitting many words of French origin. In *Ivanhoe* Scott has a Saxon peasant remark that the living domestic animals have good Saxon names – ox, calf, sheep, swine – but when they appear on the table to be eaten they have become Norman-French – beef, veal, mutton, pork. However, this English, which philologists term Middle English and which can be read, if with some difficulty yet without special study, by us today, as Anglo-Saxon cannot, took different forms in different parts of the country.

There were three distinct varieties: the English of the south-west which was to dwindle into a dialect; the English of London, Oxford and Cambridge, and the midlands, which evolved into what we now recognize as Standard English; and the tongue spoken north of the Humber, and up the east coast of Scotland, in the Lothians, and at least as far north as Aberdeen. In England, the northern branch of the language would also decline to dialect status, but in Scotland, where it came to establish itself as the language of the Court, it showed signs by 1500, at the time of the marriage of James IV and Margaret Tudor, of becoming a distinct language, capable of being used for all purposes as dialects are not; by then it stood in relation to English much as Catalan does to Castilian, or Neapolitan to Tuscan or standard Italian. Nevertheless William Dunbar still called the language in which he wrote 'Inglis', and it was Gavin Douglas, translator in the next generation of Virgil's *Aeneid*, who seems to have been the first to call his tongue 'Scottis'.

In the thirteenth century however the linguistic map of Scotland was even more varied than that of England. Whereas there the tongue spoken by the pre-Saxon inhabitants, the Britons, had either died or was now confined to the west where it survived as Welsh or Cornish, the Saxon, Anglian or English language had not achieved a like dominance in Scotland. British (or Welsh) long survived in Galloway and parts of Strathclyde, while except in the Borders, the Lothians and up the eastern seaboard the common tongue was another variety of what we now agree to call the Celtic languages, Gaelic. (Scots and English-speakers would usually call this 'Erse' till the early nineteenth century.) Moreover in the Northern Isles (Orkney and Shetland) which would not be subject to the Scottish Crown till the late fifteenth century, and perhaps also in the Western Isles, the common tongue was Norse (Old Norse or Norn).

Linguistically therefore Scotland was deeply divided, and though its medieval kings knew three languages – Gaelic, Inglis and Norman-French – the Inglis-speaking people of the south and east of Scotland had more in common, linguistically, with the men of Northumberland and Yorkshire than with Scots north of the Forth.

★

Edward I's hope of uniting the two kingdoms peacefully was dashed when the Maid of Norway died in Orkney on the voyage back to Scotland. There was no obvious or agreed successor. This gave Edward a new opportunity. He was asked by the Scots barons to adjudicate between the claimants to the throne. From each competitor he extracted a promise that he would acknowledge him as overlord. This was reviving an old English claim. William the Lion, King of Scots, had agreed to become Henry II's vassal by the Treaty of Falaise (1174). That submission was made under duress, William then being Henry's prisoner, and was soon rescinded.

In 1290 the two chief competitors were John Balliol and Robert Bruce. Both belonged to Anglo-Norman families resident in Scotland for several generations, and both were descended in the female line from David I (1124–53). Both held estates in England as well as Scotland, and were therefore already Edward's vassals there. Balliol also had estates in Picardy, for which he owed allegiance to the King of France. Edward selected him and, in accordance with his promise, the new King of Scots accepted the King of England as his overlord.

He may have thought this a mere formality, to be cast aside. Edward soon showed it wasn't. His demands became intolerable, and Balliol resisted them. Asserting his independence, he made an alliance with France. This was the beginning of that Auld Alliance which was to be the cornerstone of Scottish foreign policy till the mid-sixteenth century. Edward responded by invading Scotland. He met little resistance. Balliol surrendered and was stripped, humiliatingly, of his crown and royal robes. Edward carried the Stone of Scone (Stone of Destiny), on which Scottish kings were traditionally crowned, back to London, and proceeded to treat Scotland as a conquered province, controlled by an army of occupation. Before long the demands of English tax-collectors provoked resistance, which found leaders in a northern baron Andrew Murray and a Renfrewshire knight, William Wallace. The Wars of Independence had begun.

They would last for more than thirty years till that Treaty of Northampton by which the English Crown was constrained to recognize Scottish independence. It was from this time of trial that the

Scottish nation, as a self-conscious entity, was formed. The wars gave Scotland their two necessary national heroes in Wallace and the younger Robert the Bruce, grandson of the Competitor. Wallace defied the English king till he was betrayed, tried for treason and put to death in London with horrible brutality. Bruce made himself king in 1306, won the decisive battle, Bannockburn, in 1314, and expelled the English from Scotland. Some forty years after his death, his exploits were recounted in an epic poem, *The Brus*, written in the vernacular by John Barbour, Archdeacon of Aberdeen:

> A! Fredome is a noble thing!
> Fredome mayss man to haiff liking.
> Fredome all solace to man giffis;
> He levys at ess that frely levys.

'The Scots were the first people in all of Europe to set themselves apart as a nation,' one (nationalist) historian has declared. The extent to which national consciousness was felt may be debated, but for subsequent generations the memory of the Wars of Independence has been central to Scots' idea of themselves.

In 1320 the Scottish case for independence was set out in the Declaration of Arbroath, addressed to the pope. The document was probably written by Bruce's chancellor, Bernard de Linton, Abbot of Arbroath. In sonorous and muscular Latin, it recounted the wrongs Scotland had suffered at the hands of the English kings, and declared that:

> For as long as one hundred of us remain alive, we shall never under any conditions submit to the domination of the English. It is not for glory or riches or honour that we fight, but only for Liberty, which no good man will consent to lose but with his life.

In the preamble to the Declaration, the antiquity of the Scottish nation was affirmed. It derived 'from Greater Scythia across the Tyrrhenian Sea and beyond the Pillars of Hercules' until at last the Scots 'came to our abode in the West where we now dwell. The Britons were driven out. The Picts were utterly destroyed. We were attacked again and again by Norse, Angle, and Dane, but by many victories and ceaseless toil we established ourselves here, and ever since we have held our land free from servitude of every kind.'

This of course was nonsense, sublime romantic nonsense. The people of Scotland were formed from Picts, Britons, Scots, Angles and Norsemen. Bruce himself and Bernard de Linton were, in the male line, of Norman origin. So were many of the barons such as Roger Mowbray and Ingram Umfreville who appended their seals to the Declaration. They belonged to the same stock as the English barons against whom they had fought at Bannockburn.

Constructing elaborate pseudo-histories to justify immediate political positions was common in the Middle Ages (and is not unknown in our own time). In the twelfth century Geoffrey of Monmouth had written his *History of the Kings of Britain*, tracing their descent from Brutus, a mythical Trojan prince. Geoffrey himself was a Breton, brought up in Wales, and in receipt of patronage from Norman barons and bishops. His 'history' popularized the Arthurian legends, and he represented Arthur as a pattern of Anglo-Norman kingship. Moreover Arthur's status as king of all Britain made it clear that, historically – in Geoffrey's sense of the word – the whole island of Britain should properly be ruled by one monarch. Edward I was sufficiently impressed by the Arthurian legend to order the opening of a tomb in Glastonbury Abbey reputed to be Arthur's; and indeed the king's body was suitably discovered and identified. Edward III, who, despite the Treaty of Northampton, resumed the Scottish war before turning his attention to France and pursuing his flimsy claim to the French crown, was also an Arthurian enthusiast. Creating the Order of the Garter, he imitated the legendary chivalry of Arthur's Round Table.

Nevertheless, however the arguments might be pursued by pseudo-historians – and they would be elaborated with much fertile invention over the centuries that followed – the failure of the Edwardian attempt to conquer Scotland ensured that the two kingdoms would remain separate, and become more distinct in the later Middle Ages. The friendship and easy relations which had prevailed for most of the thirteenth century could not be restored, at least were not restored.

Scotland would never be, like Ireland, a conquered and colonized country.

The significance of this cannot be exaggerated. It has determined the nature of our relationship with England. Though since the Union there have been Scots who have resented England's preponderance and the tendency among the English to be unable to make a distinction between England and the United Kingdom, nevertheless Scots have had no cause to feel inferior, or to indulge in the understandable hatred of England that the English conquest and subsequent domination has inspired in many Irishmen.

Yet for centuries the Wars of Independence influenced the development of Scottish history. Edward's failure to conquer Scotland resulted in the substitution of French for English influence in Scotland. Whereas, at least from the reign of David I, Scottish kings had taken the Anglo-Norman organization of the southern kingdom as their model, and Lowland Scots had, in manner and speech, been scarcely distinguishable from the northern English, now, from the mid-fourteenth century onwards, French influence can be discerned in many aspects of Scottish life. In church and castle architecture, France not England was the model. Young noblemen were sent to France to further their education, and when they came home they organized their households according to the fashion they had learned in France. The lords' claret was poured from a 'gardevin' into a 'tassie'. Their food was served on an 'ashet'.

Though a common language preserved English influence in the vernacular literature, and poets such as James I, Robert Henryson and William Dunbar regarded Chaucer as their master, and were to be long known to literary historians as 'the Scottish Chaucerians', elsewhere English influence waned, French waxed. Scots law began its divergence from the English common law and the foundations were laid of a legal system, French–Roman, which, despite the vast accretion to statute law passed by the Parliament of the United Kingdom since 1707, survives to this day. When universities were established in the fifteenth century – St Andrews in 1412, Glasgow in 1451, King's College, Aberdeen in 1495 – the model was the Sorbonne, not

Oxford or Cambridge. Scottish soldiers fought in the armies of France in the long war against the England of Edward III and the Lancastrian kings. After a Scots army had defeated the English at the Battle of Baugé in 1420, its commander, the Earl of Buchan, was appointed Constable of France. Scots fought alongside Joan of Arc; a Scot, James Power or Polwart, painted her battle-standard. Around 1430 the French king, Charles VII, established the Scots Bodyguard of Archers, of which Sir Walter Scott's Quentin Durward was a member. Then, in 1513, the year of Flodden, Louis XII issued his *Concession de lettres de naturalité pour les Ecossais résidents en France*, which gave Scots in France the same legal rights and status as native Frenchmen.

Yet by this time the end of the Auld Alliance was near. It was no longer necessary.

After the last battle of the Hundred Years War, Châtillon (1453), there was never again a serious attempt by England to invade and defeat France. English kings still continued to style themselves Kings of France, as indeed the kings of Great Britain would do till the Treaty of Amiens in 1801, but their holding there was now confined to the port of Calais. Arguably the English wars had made France a nation, as the Wars of Independence had Scotland, and had greatly strengthened the French Crown. At the same time the concentration for more than a century of English effort on the French wars meant that from the 1330s there was no serious English attempt to conquer Scotland. Anglo-Scottish warfare had been fierce but sporadic, restricted mostly to the counties either side of the shifting Border. By the late fifteenth century that line had at last been fixed. In 1488 Berwick-on-Tweed finally became an English town, even though some modern Scottish nationalists may choose to regard it as *Scotia irredenta*.

In the first half of the sixteenth century Scotland was divided between the traditionalists who held to the French alliance, and those who saw advantage in friendship with England. Henry VIII and his minister Cardinal Wolsey, eager to play a major role in European politics, wished either to neutralize Scotland or to persuade or force Scots to agree to an alliance. They cultivated a pro-English party in Scotland, not scrupling to resort to bribery.

The death of James V in 1542 offered England an opportunity. He was succeeded by his daughter Mary, only a week old. Henry now resumed the old policy of Edward I, in its early apparently benign form. He proposed a marriage alliance between the infant Mary and his own young son, the future Edward VI, then aged nine. The Scots hesitated. Some approved the project. Others, notably the queen's mother, Marie de Guise, a French princess, and her chief minister Cardinal Beaton, opposed it, and favoured a French match. They would probably have done so in any case, but there was another consideration. These were the years of the Reformation in northern Europe. Henry had broken with the pope, though stopping short of committing England to Protestantism. Scotland, like France, was still Catholic: the most notable Scots Protestant, George Wishart, would be condemned as a heretic and burned at the stake in St Andrews in 1546.

Henry, old, stupid and impatient, tried to force the issue. He dispatched an army, commanded by the young prince's uncle the Earl of Hertford (later Duke of Somerset), to ravage the southern counties of Scotland. Hertford's campaigns, in which the beautiful Border abbeys of Melrose, Dryburgh, Kelso and Jedburgh were burned, seemed a rough way of wooing to the Scots, who responded by sending the little queen to France for safety. It looked as if Henry in his folly had merely reanimated the Auld Alliance.

But events took a different turn. First, the regency of Marie de Guise, supported by a French army to deter another English invasion, and then the engagement of the child queen to the dauphin, heir to the throne of France, seemed to some Scots an equal threat to independence: Scotland might become a French, rather than English, province. Second, and more important, the regency saw the emergence of the Protestant reforming movement in Scotland.

It rose with an alarming suddenness in 1558–9. An alliance between zealous Protestants and a section of the Scots nobility styled the Lords of the Congregation, some motivated by the desire to seize Church lands (as the English nobility, gentry and merchant class had so profitably done) rather than by religious enthusiasm, resulted in a revolution. This was a revolution in public policy as well as in Church government. England, just restored to Protestantism by the death of Mary Tudor and accession of her half-sister Elizabeth, came to the help of the Scots Reformers, with both money and troops. The French were expelled, and Protestantism established in Scotland. It was the end of the Auld Alliance. Many Scots who retain a sentimental affection for the memory of that alliance forget that it ended when the dominant party in Scotland called for English military assistance to get rid of the French.

When people talk today of the rigours and austerity of Scots Calvinism, they usually attribute this to John Knox, the animating spirit of the first stage of the Reformation in Scotland. He has become a symbol of all that is, or was, harsh, gloomy and life-denying in Scottish life. In the words of the historian Gordon Donaldson, 'Knox is commonly believed to have permanently impoverished Scottish culture by the introduction of a joyless asceticism antipathetic to all the arts, and to his influence is attributed all that is bleak in the Scottish scene.' In fact, as Donaldson argued, restrictive puritanism in the second half of the sixteenth century was by no means confined to Knox and Scotland. There was a puritanism of the Counter-Reformation in Rome as narrow and fanatical as the puritanism of Calvinist Scotland.

Moreover, even if the harshest view of Knox is accepted, Scotland owes much to him. It was Knox who set in motion the commitment to education for all which was to contribute so greatly in time to the eighteenth-century efflorescence of the Scottish Enlightenment. He was unable to translate into reality his intention that a school should be established in every parish. Indeed it was not till an Act of the Scottish Parliament in 1695 that this was on the way to being achieved. But Knox deserves the credit for that commitment to education which led to the Scottish idea of the 'Democratic Intellect' and spread literacy and at least elementary education more widely in Scotland than in England or indeed any European country.

One statue of Knox towers, magnificently, over Glasgow's Necropolis; it was erected by public subscription in the 1820s at the time of the movement for Catholic Emancipation and as evidence of Glasgow's stoutly Protestant faith. Another stands, forbiddingly, in the courtyard of the Church of Scotland's Assembly Hall in Edinburgh, used in 1999–2004 as the temporary home of the devolved Scottish Parliament. Its aspect would seem to confirm the popular twentieth-century image of Knox as the dourest and most censorious of our great men, the Scottish killjoy.

Yet Knox, a Catholic priest in early life, was in many respects thoroughly anglicized. When Scotland was still Catholic, he lived and preached in England during the reign of Edward VI. He was indeed so prominent among the English Reformers that he was offered a bishopric which he refused, not because he then had any objection to bishops – that came later, after his sojourn in Calvin's Geneva – but, prudently, 'in foresight of trouble to come'. The trouble he envisaged was the death of the tubercular young king and the succession of his half-sister Mary Tudor, an unreformed Roman Catholic. Had he accepted, he might well be numbered among the English Marian martyrs, along with Cranmer, Latimer and Ridley. Or perhaps not; Knox was, in personal matters, cautious to the point of timidity. He removed to the Continent where he associated chiefly with English exiles from Mary's persecution. He would have returned to England on Mary's death if he had not been barred by her successor Elizabeth. She was offended by his pamphlet, *A Blast of the Trumpet against the Monstrous Regiment* [rule] *of Women*. That blast was directed at Mary Tudor and Marie de Guise, both Catholics; but it was a failure of foresight not to have considered that Mary Tudor's successor would be a Protestant queen.

Despite this rebuff, Knox remained an anglophile. He had acquired an English accent, frequently remarked on by his critics in Scotland. His first wife was English, and he set the pattern for upper-class Scots of later generations by sending his sons to be educated in England.

Indeed Gordon Donaldson, a touch mischievously, went much further. 'Knox', he wrote, 'was perhaps the chief agent of all time in the anglicization of Scotland, in both its politics and its culture. The

Reformation to which he contributed did more than anything else to bring about the anglicization of the Scots language.'

This is undeniable. The Bible, the Psalter, the service book of the Scots Reformed Kirk were all in English, not 'Scottis'. No doubt all were read with a Scots accent, but the language was English. When in the seventeenth century Biblical passages were paraphrased and versified to be sung in the Scots Kirk, their language too was English:

> O God of Bethel by whose hand
> Thy people still are fed,
> Who through this weary pilgrimage
> Hast all our fathers led.

Or:

> Come, let us to the Lord our God
> With contrite hearts return;
> Our God is gracious, nor will leave
> The desolate to mourn.

Donaldson adds:

> But we have to remember that the choice of English by the reformers was to open to Scots, in the next generation, the riches of the Authorized Version, which, if it was a good thing for England, can hardly have been a bad thing for Scotland. Knox's preference for English ways, his admiration for England, are admitted. But the England which he admired was the England in which William Shakespeare was born eight years before Knox's death.

And Shakespeare has meant as much to Scots as to the English; there is no writer whom Walter Scott quoted more often.

Though Knox was an anglicizer, and though the success of the Reformation in Scotland was made possible by the support of the English Crown, by English arms and English money, the Church of Scotland, as instituted by Knox and formed by his successors, chief among them Andrew Melville, took a very different form from the Church of England, and acquired a very different character. This difference was such that, by the nineteenth century, it could be seen as that which principally distinguished the peoples of the two countries. Yet that distinction might never have been apparent if the Puritan Revolution of the seventeenth century had succeeded in England as it had already done, in Presbyterian guise, in Scotland.

2

Elizabeth and Mary

—◆—

THE STORY OF Mary Stuart and Elizabeth Tudor has been told so
often, in so many forms, that it scarcely needs to be rehearsed
here. Yet, because the two queens play so large a part in the mythology of both countries, some observations are desirable.

Elizabeth, coming to an uncertain throne at the age of twenty-five,
became inevitably the symbol of England's Protestant nationalism.
Whatever her personal inclination in religion, she represented
England's rejection of Rome. It was after all Henry VIII's determina-
tion to discard his first wife, Catherine of Aragon, and marry
Elizabeth's mother Anne Boleyn which precipitated the breach with
Rome and the creation of the independent national Church of
England. No devout Catholic could acknowledge that Elizabeth was
legitimate, since she was born when Catherine was still alive, and
Henry's marriage to Anne was in their eyes no marriage at all. Of
course many English Roman Catholics overcame their scruples and
accepted Elizabeth as their queen. The Catholic King Philip of Spain,
widower of her sister Mary Tudor, did so too. He had political reasons
– rivalry with France – and even thought for a time that he might
marry Elizabeth in turn. Political imperatives were sufficient to enable
Philip to persuade the pope to delay Elizabeth's excommunication till
1570, twelve years after her accession.

In Scotland Mary Stuart represented the French interest. Brought
up in France, where her Guise relatives were powerful, and married
to the dauphin who succeeded his father as Francis II in 1559, she was
in the eyes of many Catholics the legitimate Queen of England too.
Indeed, if Elizabeth was to be debarred on account of her presumed

illegitimacy, Mary was the first in the line of succession from Henry VII, though Henry VIII had excluded her in his will. There was however some doubt whether he had the right to do so. In any case Mary and her husband Francis assumed the arms of England as well as those of France and Scotland.

Francis, always sickly, died in 1560. Mary returned to Scotland the next year, the Catholic queen of a now Protestant country. Her years there were few and stormy. Recognizing that there was no hope of displacing Elizabeth in England, she now tried to persuade her to nominate her as heir-apparent to the English throne. Elizabeth declined; uncertainty about the succession was her protection. Even if she had been willing to do as Mary asked she was astute enough to realize that the English political establishment would not take kindly to another Catholic monarch. Besides she had not given up the idea that she would herself marry and might bear children.

Soon Mary had difficulties enough in Scotland. Elizabeth's attitude to these was ambiguous and inconsistent. Cautious in foreign policy, she supported the Protestant lords who favoured an English alliance, but only to the point of hoping that Mary would be guided by their counsel. When, after the mysterious murder of her second husband, Darnley, Mary married the Earl of Bothwell, whom many thought guilty of that murder, they lost patience with her and compelled her to abdicate in favour of her infant son James. Elizabeth could not be pleased to see a rightful queen treated in this manner. The following year Mary escaped from prison, raised an army, and was defeated by the rebel lords at Langside, just outside Glasgow. She fled across the Solway to England.

That flight was Mary's worst mistake. She should, somehow, have contrived to make for France where, as Antonia Fraser puts it, 'she had the inalienable estates and income of a queen-dowager', and where 'as a Catholic queen fleeing from a Protestant country, she had every reason to expect the support of her brother-in-law Charles IX and Queen Catherine [her mother-in-law], to say nothing of her Guise relations'. That was what her best friends advised; but 'the siren song of Elizabeth's friendship, the mirage of the English succession, were still strong enough in this moment of decision to blot out the stable image of the proven friendship with France'.

For Elizabeth her arrival posed a problem. It was impossible that she, a Protestant queen, could invade Protestant Scotland to restore her Catholic cousin to the throne. But she could not approve her demission. For some time she hoped to persuade the Scots to accept Mary back on conditions. When it became clear that there was no chance of this, Mary's confinement in England became inevitable. That confinement was to last almost twenty years till she was finally condemned to death on charges of complicity in plots against Elizabeth's life, therefore treason, and executed in 1587. Extreme Protestants in the English Parliament had been calling for her death since 1571, the year of the Ridolfi Plot, aimed at the deposition of Elizabeth, her replacement by Mary, who was to be married to the Duke of Norfolk, the leading Catholic nobleman in England. Norfolk went to the block, but Elizabeth resisted demands for Mary's head. When she finally acceded to them, it was with reluctance; she was ashamed and assailed by guilt.

Mary's confinement had been mild at first, no more than house arrest; she was permitted to go hunting and hawking. It became more severe as the years passed and Elizabeth's spymaster Sir Francis Walsingham sought to entrap her in conspiracies. Her imprisonment has made her a figure of romance – the beautiful doomed Scottish queen, subject of novels, plays and films. But in her lifetime her cause appealed to Englishmen rather than to Scots. It was young English Catholics who plotted to set her free and put her on the throne – of England, not Scotland. After 1573, when the civil war in Scotland between her supporters, 'the Queen's Men', and her enemies, 'the King's Men', ended in the utter defeat of her party, those who governed Scotland on behalf of her young son were indifferent to her fate. They were content as long as she was kept in an English prison, with no prospect of being returned to Scotland. When she was put on trial and condemned, King James requested the ministers of the Kirk to remember his mother in their prayers, asking 'that it might please God to illuminate her with the light of His truth, and save her from the apparent danger wherein she is cast'. The ministers of Edinburgh refused, on the grounds that to pray for her preservation implied a belief in her innocence and a condemnation of Elizabeth's conduct.

No wonder that two centuries later the Tory and High Church Englishman Dr Johnson should break out angrily when Boswell talked sadly of the loss of Scotland's independence as a result of the Union: 'Sir, never talk of your independency, who could let your Queen remain twenty years in captivity, and then be put to death, without even a pretence of justice, without your ever attempting to rescue her; and such a Queen too! as every man of any gallantry of spirit would have sacrificed his life for.'

During the years of her imprisonment such men of spirit were to be found in England, not Scotland. While Elizabeth's councillors were uniformly hostile to Mary – their hostility tempered only by their awareness that, should Elizabeth die, her claim to the throne might be hard to resist – she was, from her arrival in England, the hope of English Catholics, faithful to their religion, resentful of the reimposition of Protestantism, often debarred from positions of authority, and increasingly persecuted. Though Elizabeth had tried to steer a middle course between religious extremes, events on the Continent – wars of religion in France, and a Protestant revolt against Catholic Spain in the Netherlands – forced her unwillingly into the role of Protestant champion. The ideological division of Europe, which gave the sixteenth century some resemblance to the twentieth, compelled many to choose between loyalty to their faith and loyalty to the established government of their country. So ardent young English Catholics were drawn to the cause of the Scottish queen, plotted on her behalf, and, some of them, fell in love with her at a distance. If to English Protestants she was a wicked and dangerous woman, to some English Catholics she was an oppressed and ill-used queen, a figure of romance and a beacon of hope. So, long after she had lost all support in Scotland, her cause remained burningly alive in England.

The characters of the two queens have provoked argument from their time to ours. Few have found it easy to be fair to both. Politico-religious prejudices cut across national ones. The Elizabethan religious settlement determined the course of English history. The defiance of Catholic Spain became a necessary national myth, still powerful in the Victorian Age, vigorously expressed in Froude's *History*, Kingsley's novel *Westward Ho!*, poems by Tennyson and Newbolt. For them Elizabeth – 'Gloriana' – symbolized the formative and glittering age of English history. To be English was to be Protestant, and Elizabeth by her wise policy and determination had secured the liberties of Protestant England. How could she not be a great woman as well as a great queen? Macaulay was unusual among historians in deploring her failure to extend toleration to all in order to create a truly national Church. 'She had the happiest opportunity ever vouchsafed to any sovereign of establishing perfect freedom of conscience throughout her dominions, without danger to her government, without scandal to any large party among her subjects.' 'What', he asked, 'can be said of a ruler who is at once indifferent and intolerant?' The answer of course is that she was a creature of the sixteenth century, not a Holland House Whig like the historian. But even Macaulay was constrained to write that 'Of all the sovereigns who exercised a power which was seemingly absolute, but which in fact depended for support on the love and confidence of her subjects, she was by far the most illustrious.' In comparison, Mary, however tragic her fate, was a failure, one who had lost that love and confidence, and been accordingly rejected by her subjects. The chief among these subjects might have been scoundrels. Walsingham, Elizabeth's secretary of state, believed that 'money would do anything with that nation'. Nevertheless Mary's failure in Scotland was evidence of her incapacity.

Scotland was at least as devoutly Protestant as England. Scottish identity was expressed in the Kirk. Mary was, it may be, a victim of the passions which the Reformation had unleashed. She might be viewed with sympathy. But, for as long as Knox and all that he represented – Calvinism, the Kirk – were regarded as the makers of modern Scotland, the memory of Mary could be only an embarrassment to many Scots. The reverence for Knox survived well into the twentieth century. In *The Presbyterian Tradition* (1933) the Very Rev. Charles Warr, minister of St Giles in Edinburgh and also chaplain to King

George V, wrote that, for all his faults of character and lack of essential Christian virtues, Knox:

> remains as perhaps the most tremendous figure which has been thrown up by Scottish history, and . . . he achieved what he set out to do. His object was to make Scotland Protestant and free, and, titanic as were the forces arrayed against him, he succeeded in doing it. The principles of democracy and liberty which he thundered from the pulpit of St Giles have gone out to the ends of the earth.

Even in Scotland then many of those bred in that Presbyterian tradition have always evinced a preference for Elizabeth over Mary. The English queen helped, involuntarily certainly, the Reformation to triumph in Scotland, and Knox's work to endure.

3

One King, Two Kingdoms

MARY HAS ALWAYS attracted devotees. So has her grandson Charles I, the Martyr King. No such cult has attached itself to his father, James VI & I, though he has claims to have been the most successful of the Stewart (later Stuart) kings. The reason is obvious: he was often ridiculous and died in his bed, not on the scaffold. So, no glamour. Moreover his reign in England has generally been compared unfavourably with Elizabeth's, though much that is styled Elizabethan was also Jacobean, and though it was in his time and under his patronage that the Church of England came to its rich maturity. It was James himself who commanded the making and publication of the Authorized Version of the Bible. If not its only begetter, he was its patron, and the King James Bible is his richest legacy, a work such as Elizabeth never contemplated, and the great store-house of the English language.

James's reputation has suffered also because his reign may be seen to foreshadow the troubles that engulfed his son, and provoked the breakdown of order and the Civil War. Yet James, a far more astute politician than Charles, one who knew when to bend, compromise and yield, can scarcely be held responsible for his son's failure.

He was an unusual man to find on the throne, both a scholar and an intellectual – perhaps the only intellectual to be king of either Scotland or England. He delighted to instruct his subjects, often to their irritation. He called himself 'the great schoolmaster of the realm'. One can imagine him as a university don. He was king in Scotland before he was a year old, and his childhood was lonely, disagreeable and often dangerous. He never knew his parents and, himself affectionate by nature, was starved of affection in his youth. His tutor, George Buchanan, scholar, poet and Latinist, was the author of a book purporting to prove Mary's complicity in the murder of James's father, Darnley. He was a harsh master, severe and perhaps sadistic. In adult life, by his own account, James found himself trembling at the approach of a man who resembled his tutor. Yet he had much to be grateful to Buchanan for. He grew up to be the most erudite king in Europe, even though Henry IV of France called him 'the wisest fool in Christendom', a sobriquet that has stuck. Buchanan assembled a library of 600 volumes for the young king's use. James was studying Latin and Greek from the age of five. There was always something of the Scots pedant in him, well captured by Scott in *The Fortunes of Nigel*.

As King of Scots, poor, without military resources, bedevilled both by a fractious nobility and by arrogant Calvinist ministers, he nevertheless managed to impose his will on the kingdom, and bishops on the Kirk. His life was frequently threatened by conspiracies, and also, as he believed, by witchcraft practised by a demented and ambitious cousin, the Earl of Bothwell. Yet, after his translation to England, he could truthfully claim that he ruled Scotland more easily by his pen than his ancestors had by the sword.

It was his constant aim to inherit the English crown, and this ambition led him to acquiesce, with only a mild protest, even in his mother's execution. This was doubtless shameful, though extenuating circumstances have been found. He had never known Mary, and had been reared on tales of her wickedness. When he became King of England he made such amends to her memory as were possible, arranging for her reburial in Westminster Abbey.

Had James had his way, the Union of 1603 would have been more complete. Soon after arriving in England he tried to persuade the Parliaments of both kingdoms to consider such a union. He was the husband of both realms, he said, and, as a Christian monarch, it was not fitting he should have two wives. So English commissioners were asked to examine the means of creating a union 'convenient and necessary for the honour of His Majestie, and the weale and common good of both the said realmes', while the Scottish commissioners were told 'to confer, treate and consult upon a perfyte union of the realmes of Scotland and England . . . not derogating ony wayes one funda-mentall lawes, ancient privileges, offices, richtis, dignities and liberties of this kingdome'.

In these instructions one can see the difficulties of effecting, and subsequently maintaining, a perfect union, difficulties which would persist for the next hundred years, and which have indeed contrib-uted to the revival of Scottish nationalist feeling today. In any union between a large and rich country and its smaller and poorer neigh-bour, the former surrenders little of value, while the latter fears to lose much.

Nevertheless it was the English who jibbed at James's proposals. There seemed to Englishmen, already irritated by the number of needy Scots flocking to Whitehall, little to be gained by closer union. It was enough that James's accession should have rendered the Border peaceful and removed the danger to England always threatened by an independent Scotland's foreign policy. In contrast the Scots Parliament actually passed an Act of Union, as requested by the king. But this Act of 1607 was conditional on England's acceptance of the terms proposed. No such acceptance was forthcoming and the pro-posals lapsed.

One of the Scottish commissioners was Sir Thomas Craig, an expert on feudal law and sheriff-depute of Edinburgh. He was sufficiently in favour of closer union to write a treatise recommend-ing it. (The treatise, written in Latin, was not published in his lifetime, not indeed till 1909 when the Scottish History Society brought out a text with accompanying translation.)

Some of Craig's arguments were powerful. The kings of England, he wrote, had tried ever since Norman times to unite the two king-doms, either by means of marriage alliances or by conquest since they believed that 'England would never have peace at home nor take her rightful position abroad, so long as a hostile neighbour dwelled so near her borders'. A perfect union was therefore in England's geopolitical interest. But Scotland, long hostile to union, now saw the advantages of a 'peaceful union, infusion or engrafting of the two kingdoms'. The

Border country would no longer be subject to perpetual disorder but 'houses and castles will once more teem with inhabitants; woods, pleasure gardens and vegetable gardens will add to their amenities, and the rich harvests of our rivers and flocks will be gathered in security'. Free trade within the kingdom of Great Britain would be to the benefit of both Scots and English.

Craig's argument was made known to his fellow-commissioners, but failed to persuade his English colleagues. His treatise, being unpublished, could convince nobody. He was ahead of his time. But it is significant that at the beginning of the seventeenth century proposals for an incorporating union found more favour in Scotland than in England.

For thirty years the arrangement of One King, Two Kingdoms worked well enough, the administration of the two countries being kept separate. Then the folly and incompetence of Charles I stirred up opposition in both kingdoms.

In Scotland this was aroused by his attempt to impose religious uniformity by bringing the Scots Kirk into line with the Church of England. Whereas James had been content to establish a moderate episcopacy in Scotland while leaving the framework of Presbyterian Church government and the Presbyterian order of service largely undisturbed, Charles, without consulting either the General Assembly of the Kirk or the usually compliant Scottish Parliament, imposed a Book of Canons that styled the king Head of the Church, and a new service book compiled by his Archbishop of Canterbury, William Laud. Both offended the Scots. Knox's successor as leader of the Reformers, Andrew Melville, had roundly told James VI that the Kirk recognized no Head but Jesus, and James had the good sense to keep his disagreement muted. As for the order of service, the Scots Presbyterians regarded it as popish. Riots broke out in both Edinburgh and Glasgow, and confrontation between king and people became inevitable. In February 1638 the National Covenant was drawn up, binding its signatories to stand in defence of the pure Reformed Religion. The response was indeed truly national; the Covenant was signed by all classes in Lowland Scotland. Though the document professed the signatories' loyalty to the Crown, Charles, not surprisingly, interpreted the Covenant as an act of rebellion. The result was the armed conflict known as the Bishops' Wars of 1639–40.

These wars, and the difficulty of financing them, gave the opposition in England its opportunity. Charles had governed without Parliament for eleven years, years in which opposition had festered, provoked by Laud's Church policy, the imposition of taxes of doubtful legality, and the king's unwillingness to pursue a Protestant foreign policy. There was suspicion of his Catholic wife, Henrietta Maria, of Jesuit influence at Court, and of his failure to support the Protestant cause in the Thirty Years War raging in Germany. He was now compelled to summon Parliament to pay for his Scotch war. Contrary to expectations, the Commons was not disposed to resent the Scots' invasion of the northern counties of England. Instead they made common cause with the Scots rebels, and took the opportunity the Scots had given them to attack the king's ministers and demand redress of their many grievances. Within a few months England was in a revolutionary situation.

In the Civil Wars that followed Scots and English occupied common ground. There were Royalists in Scotland as in England, but Lowland Scotland remained firmly under the control of the men who had signed the Covenant. Their cause was the same as the English Parliament's. Though some historians have advanced economic reasons to account for the Civil War in England, and though these certainly played a part in determining which regions and which social groups decided for king or Parliament, the Marxist explanation of the conflict has not withstood analysis.

Contemporaries, with at least as much reason to claim an understanding of their actions as later historians, identified three causes of the Rebellion: the king's arbitrary government since 1629 which infringed, as men said, the ancient rights and liberties of his subjects; Laud's attempt to impose a High Church ritualistic uniformity on the Church of England and the persecution of dissident Puritans which this entailed; and a foreign policy that seemed pro-Catholic rather than pro-Protestant. The grounds for complaint in Scotland were very similar, though there the question of Church government and of the order of service to be followed in worship was most important.

Accordingly when in the first year of the war the king's armies seemed to have the upper hand, it was clearly in the interest of the English Parliamentarians and the Scots Covenanters to conclude a formal alliance. This was made in 1643, and is known as the Solemn League and Covenant. The Scots undertook to supply an army to assist the Parliament on condition that every subject of both nations should be compelled to assent to this Covenant and that a uniform ecclesiastical constitution be established throughout both kingdoms. There was to be a Church union, even if not a political one: One King, One Church, Two Kingdoms. It was the Scots' intention that this single Church should be Presbyterian, and there is no doubt that they believed they had carried this point, even though the details were left to be decided by an English Assembly of Divines. But the meaning of the Solemn League and Covenant was clear: the oath to be taken provided for the eradication of popery, prelacy and schism, and therefore sought to establish a uniformity every bit as narrow and intolerant of dissent as that which Charles and Laud had tried to impose.

The Scots Covenanters were sure they had got their way. 'The Kirk', in the words of John Buchan, 'had seized the chance to realize its dream of uniformity, but the dream came through the gates of ivory, and was to vanish ere morning.' It vanished because, in the manner of dreams, it was insubstantial. Though Lowland Scotland was uniformly Presbyterian, or very nearly so, there was no such uniformity in England, nor any desire for it, even in the Parliament or its army. The English Puritan opponents of Charles I were themselves divided: some were Presbyterians, others Independents, whom the Scots Covenanters condemned as schismatics, for the Independents rejected the very principle of a national Church, and, while condemning popery and prelacy, also insisted that each godly congregation was distinct, and must be granted liberty of conscience to determine how it should worship. As the Parliamentary general Oliver Cromwell wrote, from his camp at Naseby, on the eve of the battle that destroyed the king's cause beyond hope of military redemption, 'He that ventures his life for the liberty of his country, I wish he trust God for the liberty of his conscience, and you [that is, the Parliament] for the liberty he fights for.' In the year before Naseby the New Model Army had been formed, and its soldiers mostly inclined to Independency. The Presbyterian party might have a majority in what was left of the House of Commons (about a third of MPs had adhered to the king), but they could not control the army they had called into being, and so were unable to enforce the agreement they had made with the Scots Covenanters. That the dream of the Scots was unrealistic is manifest; that they now believed they had been cheated by the English is equally clear.

In truth the Covenanters' dream was not only unrealistic; it was misguided and betrayed their intellectual confusion. Having signed the National Covenant promising to defend their own liberties, and having taken to arms to resist the king's attempt to force the Kirk into uniformity with the Church of England, they were now determined to compel the English to accept their Scots form of Church government – whether they liked it or not. The Presbyterian party in England being too lacking in popular support to make this dream other than an impossibility, the Scots Covenanters now found themselves the object of suspicion and even hatred among those who had been their allies in the war.

The years 1646–51, from the time that Charles surrendered to the Scots army in England to Cromwell's final victory over the Royalists at Worcester, are confused. Charles declined the terms he was offered by the Scots: to put into effect their agreement with his Parliamentary enemies and impose Presbyterianism on England. So, in disgust and abandoning for the time being the attempt to negotiate with the king, the Scots sold him to the English army, and departed north, with the insults and catcalls of the citizens of Newcastle ringing in their ears.

The king, attempting to play one set of enemies off against another, believing that no settlement could be made without him, stumbled towards his trial as 'a tyrant, murderer, and a public and implacable enemy of the Commonwealth of England', and consequent execution. The Scots Covenanters, still determined that the promises enshrined in the Solemn League and Covenant be made good, turned to his son, and invited him to Scotland where, having signed the Covenant himself, he was crowned king at Scone. This Royalist–Presbyterian revival was short-lived. Cromwell defeated the Scots at Dunbar, and again at Worcester after the young Charles II had invaded England hoping that English Royalists would rally to his cause.

Scotland was now controlled, for the first time since the reign of Edward I, by an English army. Cromwell indeed was more completely master of Scotland than Edward had ever been; and there was no resistance. Scotland was incorporated in a British republic. This however did not survive Cromwell's death by eighteen months. In 1660, amid much confusion, the army commander in Scotland, General Monk, marched south, and, after brief negotiations, undertook to restore the monarchy. Charles II returned from exile, welcomed in both his kingdoms.

The Restoration saw a reversion to the pre-Civil War structure: One King, Two Kingdoms. In England Parliament quickly passed an Act of Indemnity and Oblivion, from which only regicides were excluded. In Scotland, the nobility, alarmed by the narrowness and levelling tendencies of the theocracy, resumed for the most part an obsequious royalism. Political revolution had too nearly brought about social revolution. Though Charles II had himself perforce signed the National Covenant in 1650, the time for covenants was past. Even bishops soon returned, against the advice of John Maitland, Earl (later Duke) of Lauderdale, who for almost twenty years was to be the king's minister in Scotland, effectively the viceroy. As for Charles himself, his experiences in 1650–1 had given him a lively distaste for the land of his Stuart ancestors. Presbyterianism, he declared, was no religion for a gentleman, and he never ventured north again. Indeed it was to be more than a century and a half before a reigning monarch would visit Scotland.

Lauderdale himself had been a Covenanter. He was indeed one of the commissioners who had negotiated the Solemn League and Covenant in 1643. He was only twenty-seven then, ignorant of England. With time came greater knowledge; he realized that it was folly to try to impose Presbyterianism on England. Few wanted it, and those few lacked the power to establish that form of Church government.

He was a practical man. Even his enemies, never in short supply, admitted this. Two of them – the Earl of Clarendon, Charles's first chief minister, and Gilbert Burnet, later Bishop of Salisbury – while painting unfavourable portraits of Lauderdale in their histories of their own times, acknowledged his intellectual ability. The king himself said he would 'venture Lauderdale with any man in Europe for prudence and courage'.

He had never been more than a limited rebel. He took up arms originally to defend the liberties of Scotland and its Church against Charles I. He changed sides when it seemed to him that, following the king's defeat, these liberties were in no danger from him, but were threatened by the English army.

So he fought at Worcester for Charles II, and was taken prisoner. He spent the next nine years in confinement. They were years of intellectual development. He read Hobbes's *Leviathan*, cogent argument for the necessity of an absolute power in the state. He corresponded with Hobbes himself. He reflected. He had seen the excesses of the all-powerful Kirk. He had seen the king beheaded, and a republic maintained by armed force. It seemed to him that popular government could be as inimical to law and established custom as an unrestrained king; his deep reading in ancient history and philosophy confirmed this opinion. Between 1641 and 1660 traditional forms of government had been destroyed, but all the attempts to replace them had proved defective, undesirable and unsustainable. Lauderdale concluded that a return to monarchy, supported by a loyal aristocracy, offered the best hope of stability. Any sensible man who had lived through the 1640s and 1650s sought stability.

That however was more easily attainable in England than in Scotland. In England the majority, at least of the propertied class, were in favour of a return to what was essentially the Elizabethan

Settlement without those elements – notably the Prerogative Courts – which had made Charles I's arbitrary rule possible. There was a clear majority of the political class in favour of the Restoration not only of the king but also of the Elizabethan national Church of England, shorn of its Laudian excesses. In Scotland things were different.

Lauderdale himself remained a Presbyterian, but he could not fail to see that the assertion of the liberties of the Kirk, free from state control, which he had formerly supported, had resulted in the denial of all secular authority, which was made subject to that of the Kirk. Logic eventually drove him to accept the need for a moderate episcopacy (which had been James VI's position) because this offered the only means of exercising sufficient control over the Kirk to prevent it from subverting the Crown. As a nobleman, he had been disgusted by the egalitarian tendencies of unchecked Presbyterianism, and learned to fear them. It was not, it now seemed to him, only a matter of James VI's 'No Bishop, No King', but even more alarmingly of 'No Bishop, No King, No Aristocracy'. The Kirk must be controlled if government was to be effective and social revolution avoided. It could not be permitted to disturb the peace and promote civil discord.

Most of Scotland, exhausted by the turmoil of the previous twenty years, accepted Lauderdale's settlement – willingly in the north-east, reluctantly in other quarters. But the extreme Covenanters refused. Acknowledging 'no king but Jesus', they could not admit that the state had the right to order religion. They defended their freedom, though it was not a freedom they would, if in power, have been willing to extend to those who thought differently. In time, by the late 1670s, they were led, or driven, to open rebellion. They became the 'suffering saints' of Presbyterian myth. But the same 'suffering saints' justified not only rebellion but murder. For many Scots in succeeding generations they came to occupy the same sort of place that the IRA does in the imagination of many Irish people: their methods might be deplored, but the cause was just. Robert Louis Stevenson, though by temperament a Jacobite, responded to the memory of the conventicles held in the heather while young boys were posted as sentries to watch for the royal dragoons: 'where about the graves of the martyrs the whaups [curlews] are crying'. The most judicious picture of the persecuted Covenanters is offered by Scott in *Old Mortality*.

Lauderdale had other concerns. One was to seek to resolve the difficulties that Scotland encountered in face of the Acts of the English Parliament which discriminated against its commercial interests. The first Restoration Parliament had been quick to renew Cromwell's policy of Economic Protection. This was directed against the Dutch, the masters of the carrying trade. The Act of Navigation (1660) provided that no goods might be imported into England or English colonies unless they were carried in English ships. A Scottish petition was presented to the English Privy Council requesting exemption from the Act. Lauderdale was appointed to a Commission set up to consider the matter. But the English were adamant. The Commissioners of Customs argued against the exemption, on the ground that the Scots were 'forraigners to this nation, being not under our laws and government'. Lauderdale was unable to win the argument. The Scots Parliament responded by imposing a duty of 60 per cent on English cloth and other manufactures being sold in Scotland. This was to the advantage of neither nation.

Lauderdale was therefore persuaded that only a Parliamentary union between Scotland and England could remove the English suspicion that admitting Scotland to Free Trade would be harmful to their own economic interest. The king was sufficiently in accord to set up, as James VI & I had done, commissions in both his kingdoms to consider the question of Union. Lauderdale, according to Bishop Burnet, pressed the case 'vehemently', but the English were not persuaded. So the matter was again dropped, 'to the wonder rather than the dissatisfaction of both countries', in the words of the lord advocate Sir George Mackenzie.

Lauderdale's career is significant. For almost twenty years he enjoyed near-absolute authority in Scotland. Yet he was unable to resolve the problems created by the structure: One King, Two Kingdoms. He discovered that in this arrangement Scotland was regarded by the English Parliament not as a junior partner, but as a commercial rival and, potentially, a political enemy. He concluded that the arrangement, though not unworkable, worked inevitably to the disadvantage of Scotland. If he couldn't operate it successfully, then nobody could. It would be another quarter of a century before this logic prevailed.

4

Revolution to Union

◥◣━◆━◢◤

FOLLY IS A provoker of revolution. Folly destroyed Charles I in the 1640s. Folly sent his younger son, James VII & II, scuttling from his throne in 1688. A devout Roman Catholic convert, James seemed to the English political establishment determined to subvert the laws of the country and to overthrow or set aside the Elizabethan Church Settlement which had been reimposed at the Restoration of Charles II in 1660. A group of noblemen therefore invited his nephew William of Orange, who was also his son-in-law, and regarded as the Protestant champion, to bring over a Dutch army to 'restore the liberties of England' – by which they meant, to secure the supremacy of their class and their Church. James, deserted by family, politicians and army, lost his nerve and fled to France. This was very convenient. As in 1640 revolution in one kingdom led to revolution in the other. The royal administration in Scotland collapsed.

The replacement of James represented more than a change of monarch. Sovereignty itself was relocated. Though William's wife Mary was James's elder daughter, and arguably his proper successor (assuming you subscribed to the convenient fiction that the son whose birth in 1688 had precipitated the crisis had been introduced to the palace of Whitehall in a warming-pan), this was no normal succession.

In both England and Scotland another convenient fiction was adopted: that James, by his flight, had left the throne vacant and that this amounted to abdication. Consequently William and Mary were appointed joint monarchs by the Parliament in England and by a hastily (and irregularly) summoned Convention in Scotland. The legitimate order had been set aside. Henceforth, in both countries, the Crown was Parliamentary, the monarch owing his title notionally to the will of the people, in reality to the grandees assembled in Parliament. The English Whig philosopher John Locke supplied suitable justification with the theory that a contract existed between king and people, from time immemorial; that in 1688 this contract had been broken; and that the people had accordingly the right, as well as evidently now the power, to appoint a new king. Henceforth, sovereignty would rest with king-in-Parliament (if notionally with the people), and Parliamentary approval of the monarch was necessary. This was further confirmed by subsequent Acts of both Parliaments (in 1701 in England and 1703 in Scotland), which established the succession excluding any Roman Catholic or anyone married to a Catholic.

Legitimacy being no longer the qualification, the emergence of this new contractual monarchy had one important possible consequence. It could no longer be assumed that the same heir or line of succession would be acceptable to both Parliaments. The new view of monarchy might result in the breaking of the Union of the crowns.

There was a second consequence of the Revolution. It was immediate and far-reaching, for it would lead English politicians to reverse their attitude to a more complete union of the two kingdoms. Throughout the seventeenth century England and Scotland, engaged in their internal constitutional and religious disputes, had rarely played more than a peripheral part in European politics. Neither had engaged in the Thirty Years War in Germany, though individual Scots and Englishmen had fought in the Protestant armies. Neither had participated in the various alliances formed to check the ambitions of Louis XIV of France. Indeed both Charles II and his brother James had inclined towards an undemanding dependency on their French cousin.

But William of Orange had, as Stadtholder of the United Provinces of the Netherlands, been Louis' most dogged enemy, defending the liberties of his country and the Protestant cause. For him, the chief attraction of the English and Scottish thrones was the opportunity offered to bring these two kingdoms into the alliance against France. So from 1689 to 1713, with only a brief intermission in 1697–1703, Continental war dominated domestic politics.

The first of these wars is sometimes called the War of the English Succession. James, lodged by his cousin in the Palace of Saint-Germain, had not abandoned hope of his restoration. He had supporters, some firm, others inconstant, in both England and Scotland, also in predominantly Catholic Ireland. Such a restoration was in the French interest, and indeed could scarcely be accomplished without the support of French money and troops. This in turn served to stiffen English and Scots commitment to the war against Louis. James's first attempt, by way of Ireland, was defeated at the Battle of the Boyne, but his supporters, known as Jacobites, did not accept this defeat as irreversible. Jacobite plots and invasion plans were a constant feature of the years that followed, becoming more dangerous after James's death in 1701, since his son (James VIII & III to his supporters, 'the Pretender' to his enemies) was free of the handicap of his father's record as king. Hopes of overturning the Revolution Settlement and restoring the exiled Stuarts would not expire till the crushing of the last Jacobite Rising on Culloden Moor in 1746. Fear of counter-revolution would be a prime motive of those who in 1706–7 negotiated the Treaty of Union between England and Scotland.

There were Jacobites in both countries, but those in Scotland presented a greater threat to the established order. The character of Highland society in Scotland made the raising of an armed force much easier than in England. So English Jacobitism was first conspiratorial, then merely sentimental; Scots Jacobitism military and active.

William, sole monarch since Mary's death in 1694, himself died, childless, in 1702, and was succeeded by James's younger daughter Anne. By then Lauderdale's conclusion that the existing form of Union served neither kingdom well was being reached by politicians either side of the Border. Yet their reasons for arriving at this judgement were very different.

For Scots the 1690s had been a dismal decade, with a succession of poor harvests which brought dearth, even famine. The country's most ambitious venture, the Darien Scheme, devised to open global commercial opportunities to Scotland, had failed, expensively and pitifully. It was the general view in Scotland that the cause of the disaster lay in the failure of the royal government to support the scheme and that this failure was due to the hostility of the City of London and the City's influence at Court. There was something in this, though there were other reasons: poor planning, ignorance of local conditions, ignorance too of the geopolitical circumstances. To accept this however would have required the Scots to admit their own folly and incompetence. This being unpalatable, the English were held to blame, and anti-English feeling ran high, especially in Edinburgh.

Then in 1700 the nearest Protestant heir to the two kingdoms died. This was the young Duke of Gloucester, the Princess Anne's last surviving child. The English Parliament responded with the Act of Settlement which declared that, failing issue of King William, now a widower, and his likely successor Anne, the crown should pass to Sophia, widow of the Elector of Hanover, and her heirs, always provided they were Protestants. This Sophia, now old and detested by Princess Anne, was the granddaughter of James VI & I, and her son George now ruled Hanover.

The Scots Parliament was equally determined to fix the succession on a Protestant, but, in the prevailing climate of anti-English feeling, was not inclined meekly to follow suit. Its Act of Security (1703), while stipulating that Anne's successor must be of the Protestant religion, declared that he (or she) need not be the nominated successor to the throne of England, and hinted that Scotland might choose someone different, if Scottish grievances, chief among them the exclusion of Scots merchants from English colonial trade, were not satisfied.

By this time war with France had again broken out. English politicians were therefore faced with what seemed a very dangerous prospect: the end of the dual monarchy, a Scotland independent of England and possibly hostile, the reopening of a northern frontier which would need to be defended. It was possible too that the Pretender, a pensioner of Louis XIV, might convert to Protestantism, and prove acceptable to the Scots, attached to their ancient line of Stuart kings, if not to the English, hostile as they were to the ambitions of Louis. His great-grandfather, Henry of Navarre, had turned Catholic on the ground that Paris was worth a Mass; the Pretender might think a comparable apostasy the acceptable price for a crown, and England might be faced with a revival of the old Franco-Scottish alliance. This alarming possibility concentrated the minds of English politicians wonderfully. For a hundred years the English had been absolutely indifferent to any proposals for Union, since they saw no advantages in it for England. They were now ready to engage in serious negotiations on the question, not because they liked the idea or loved the Scots, but because the alternative was frightening. If there had been no war with France, they might have thought otherwise.

The situation in Scotland was confused. There were some who saw clear advantages in an 'incorporating' union. It promised economic benefits, though these might not be immediate, and it offered security. Those who thought like this were in their own eyes true patriots and defenders of the Protestant religion. For them too the likely alternative was alarming. They feared that the resumption of full independence would result in a Jacobite rising and civil war within Scotland. Even the prospect of a rising might lead to the English government sending an army north to prevent it. If a rising took place, then again there might be military intervention from the south. In short, they were faced with a choice between a negotiated union and one forcibly imposed by English arms. Scotland could enter a union in partnership or be subjected to one by conquest.

The Jacobites argued against Union. They foresaw that it would make a Stuart restoration less likely. They too were Scottish patriots, but their interpretation of Scotland's interest was different, and their zeal for the Protestant religion, at least in its Presbyterian form, was tepid. Many were Episcopalians, some Roman Catholics or Catholic sympathizers. They belonged to the party excluded from power and office since the Revolution. They feared that Union would make their exclusion permanent. Rejection of Union might help them back to power.

Others were in a middle position. The leader among them was Andrew Fletcher of Saltoun, an East Lothian laird and intellectual, given the sobriquet 'The Patriot'. Once a pupil of Bishop Burnet, he had been involved in Monmouth's rebellion against James in 1685, and had lived in exile as a political refugee subsequently. Fletcher favoured

Union, but not an 'incorporating' one. He may be called a federalist, but in truth his concept of Union amounted to little more than a 'binding' alliance. His experience had convinced him that the dual monarchy worked to Scotland's disadvantage, because the policy of the king, based in London, would always ultimately be determined by English interests, not necessarily compatible with Scotland's. Temperamentally a republican, Fletcher proposed that the Scottish Parliament should set strict 'limitations' on the power of the king, so that the government of Scotland should be located in Edinburgh, and its policy determined there, and not in London. How Fletcher's 'union' would hold if the Scottish Government pursued policies different from those adopted in England was never clear, even to him. There was however no chance of his scheme finding favour; it answered nobody's immediate concerns. So Fletcher became the most severe critic of the draft Treaty that emerged from the discussions of the commissioners appointed by the queen from both her Parliaments. He argued that the Scots being numerically inferior to the English would always be outvoted by English members, and would thus be caught in a trap of their own devising. Understandably he did not foresee the development of the party system which has meant that neither Scots nor English have voted as a national bloc. But his arguments, dormant for almost three centuries, would be revived in the 1980s and 1990s when advocates of devolution or Home Rule argued that Scotland suffered from a 'democratic deficit'; and that a Tory government, supported by only a minority of the Scottish electorate, had no mandate to govern Scotland and force through Scottish policies by means of an English majority in the Commons.

The path to Union was not smooth. There was too lively an animosity, too much distrust. The Scottish Act of Security might have persuaded English ministers of its necessity, but the Scots had yet to be convinced. So a squeeze had to be exerted. The English Parliament now passed an Aliens Act, directed at the Scots. They were offered a choice. They could either proceed to negotiate a Treaty of Union, or accept the Hanoverian succession without any change in the existing relations between the two countries. If however they rejected both

options and persisted in the intention expressed in their Act of
Security, then the provisions of this Aliens Act would come into force.
Every native of Scotland, with only a few exceptions, was to be treated
as an alien in England, and the principal Scottish exports – cattle, linen
and coal – were to be denied entry to the English and Irish markets.
This threatened economic ruin, as one of the chiefs of the so-called
Country Party, the Earl of Roxburghe, immediately realized, shifting
his position accordingly. The Aliens Act was a fine piece of blackmail.

To describe the Union debates, far fiercer in Edinburgh than in
London, is beyond my purpose. Those interested can find very full
accounts elsewhere. It is sufficient now to emphasize that for both
Scots and English the Treaty to which both Parliaments eventually
consented represented a marriage of convenience, not affection. Few
welcomed it whole-heartedly. Yet in one sense it recognized reality.
The truth was that, at least since the Restoration of 1660, Scotland's
independence had been a sham. Fletcher of Saltoun spoke a bitter
truth when he complained that English ministers in London already
determined who should be the queen's ministers in Scotland. Scottish
regiments were already part of a British army. There was no Scottish
navy, and Scotland had no diplomatic representation in Europe.

The lord register-clerk, James Johnstone, summed up the choice
succinctly: 'The true state of the matter was whether Scotland should
be subject to an English ministry without trade, or be subject to an
English parliament with trade.' Subsequent allegations, which possessed a deal of substance, that the Scottish Parliament had been bribed
to vote itself out of existence, served to obscure this harsh reality. But
the men who took the bribes were not blind to it. They knew how
unsatisfactory existing arrangements were. They realized that if they
proceeded according to the provisions of the Act of Security, this reas-
sertion of independence threatened new dangers and could be maintained only if they were prepared to seek a French alliance, which, by
opening the way to the Jacobite party, would threaten the survival of
the Kirk in its Presbyterian form, and would in any case invite an
English invasion. Far from being free and independent, Scotland
might be conquered and reduced to the condition of Ireland.

Accepting the Treaty required a sacrifice of pride, but nevertheless opened the way to peace and prosperity.

Neither followed immediately. The Union in its early years was even more unpopular in Scotland than it had been when in prospect. The Earl of Mar, one of the commissioners who had negotiated the Treaty, was so quickly and thoroughly disillusioned that he led a Jacobite Rising only eight years later. It was to be at least twenty years before the hoped-for economic benefits materialized. In *Rob Roy*, Scott has his Glasgow merchant Bailie Nicol Jarvie defend the Union:

> There's naething sae gude on this side o' time but it might hae been better, and that may be said o' the Union. Nane were keener against it than the Glasgow folk, wi' their rabblings and their risings, and their mobs, as they ca' them now-a-days. But it's an ill wind blaws naebody gude – Let ilka ane roose the ford as they find it – I say, Let Glasgow flourish, whilk is judiciously and elegantly putten around the town's arms, by way of bye-word. Now, since St Mungo catched herrings in the Clyde, what was ever like to gar us flourish like the sugar and tobacco-trade, will anybody tell me that, and grumble at the treaty that opened us a road west-awa' yonder?

The Bailie spoke truth, even if Scott was premature in putting the words in his mouth, for the novel is set around the year 1719, and it was to be near another generation before Glasgow found itself in full flower as a result of the Treaty to which its mob had so vigorously objected.

The Edinburgh mob had been equally violently opposed to Union. Daniel Defoe, in Scotland as the agent of Robert Harley, secretary of state for the Northern Department, reported to his master that he 'heard a Great Noise and looking out saw a Terrible Multitude come up the High Street with a Drum at the head of them shouting and swearing and crying out all Scotland would stand together, No Union, No Union, English Dogs, and the like'.

When the Treaty was signed and the Parliament had departed, the importance of the Scots capital was diminished. Its people were aware of the decline in status and importance. Again Scott, in *The Heart of Midlothian* (set in 1733), has one of his characters, an old woman,

express this feeling: 'When we had a king, and a chancellor, and parliament-men o' our ain, we could aye peeble them wi' stanes when
they werena gude bairns – But naebody's nails can reach the length o'
Lunnon.' Scottish politics had always been intimate. The people
crowded round the gates of Holyroodhouse and swarmed in the
Parliament Close itself; classes mixed higgledy-piggledy in the tower-
ing lands of the High Street. Unpopular ministers might be rabbled
on the way to the Parliament or have their homes besieged. Now
power was remote; it seemed as if London had eaten up Edinburgh.

5

A Marriage of Convenience

THE UNION YOKED the two nations together, but the marriage of convenience neither removed nor abated ignorance and prejudice. Scotland was an unknown land to most Englishmen. The few who ventured north were rarely impressed. They found the country savage, dirty and miserably poor. One returning home in 1704 expressed his relief at crossing the Border:

> I passed to English ground, and hope I may never go to such a country again. I thank God I never saw such another and may conclude with the poet Cleveland:
>
> > Had Cain been Scot, God had ne'er changed his doom,
> > Not made him wander, but confined him home.

Edinburgh amazed visitors from the south. There was no town like it in England, with its tall buildings, some as many as fourteen storeys high on the north side. It was also condemned as unspeakably filthy. In 1705, the English traveller Joseph Taylor found that:

> every street shows the nastiness of the inhabitants; the excrements lie in heaps. The lodgings are as nasty as the streets, and wash't so seldom that the dirt is thick eno' to be pared off with a shovel; every room is well-scented with a close-stool, and the master, mistress, and servants lye all on a flour, like so many swine in a hogsty. This, with the rest of their sluttishness, is no doubt the occasion of the itch which is so common among them.

A human rabbit-warren that could make even a Londoner of that time recoil in fastidious disgust was vile indeed.

Yet Edinburgh was the best of Scotland. The Lowlands, though wretchedly poor and dirty in comparison with the more prosperous parts of England, if no more so and no more backward than the northern English counties through which southerners passed with no less disgust, yet appeared civilized in comparison with the Highlands where even fewer English travellers ventured. Lowland Scots themselves shrank from the Highlands, and had done so for centuries. As far back as 1380 the chronicler John of Fordoun, writing in Aberdeen, had declared that:

> The manners and customs of the Scots vary with the diversity of their speech. For two languages are spoken among them, the Scottish [Gaelic] and the Teutonic [Scots]: the latter of which is the language of those who occupy the seaboard and the plains, while the race of Scottish speech inhabits the Highlands and outlying islands. The people of the coast are of domestic and civilized habits, trusty, patient, and urbane, decent in their attire, affable and peaceful, devout in divine worship, yet always ready to resist a wrong at the hand of their enemies. The Highlanders and peoples of the islands on the other hand are a savage and untamed nation, rude and independent, given to rapine, easy-living, of a docile and warm disposition, comely in person but unsightly in dress, hostile to the English people and language, and, owing to the diversity of speech, even to their own nation, and exceedingly cruel.

They were savages, whom nobody yet thought 'noble'. 'This passage', writes T. C. Smout,

> with its hostility expressed in tones of mingled fear and contempt, is already a mature example of the attitude towards Highland Gaelic society that was to persist in the Lowlands for nearly six centuries. Every medieval writer after Fordoun makes the same division – for John Mair it was the 'wild Scots' and the 'householding Scots', for many of his successors simply 'the Irish' and 'the Scots'.

The English might dismiss all Scots as uncouth, beggarly knaves, but the Highlanders were beyond comprehension. They would remain so, while being occasionally objects of fear, till Highland society was subdued and transformed after the failure of the 1745–6 Jacobite Rising. Then they could become objects of interest.

Yet if few Englishmen had ventured north between the two Unions, the first Union (of the crowns) had opened the way to England for many Scots, needy and demanding immigrants. It was natural that King James should welcome them. He was, as we have seen, eager to bring about a more perfect union of his two kingdoms, and was in any case more at ease with his compatriots. So from the first he was lavish in providing for them. Some 40 per cent of Court appointments went to Scots. One in five of his Privy Council were Scots. Eight Scots noblemen were made Knights of the Garter along with twelve Englishmen. James was soon in love with a handsome young Scot, Robert Ker (or Carr) who caught his eye and took his fancy when he fell from his horse and broke his leg. 'Carr', said an English courtier sourly, 'hath all the favours; the King teacheth him Latin every morning, and I think someone should teach him English too, for as he is a Scottish lad, he hath much need of a better language.' Carr was made Earl of Somerset and lord chamberlain.

He was only the most prominent example of Scots advancing themselves and making their fortunes at the English Court. There was also the king's jeweller and goldsmith George Heriot, known as 'Jinglin' Geordie', and a young Edinburgh merchant Thomas Dalyell, who, starting by importing butter from Orkney to Leith, followed his patron Edward Bruce, Lord Kinloss, to London. Kinloss himself, a Scots lawyer and senator of the College of Justice, who had been James's ambassador to the Court of England, was made Master of the Rolls, the first Scot to infiltrate the English legal establishment; he would have many successors. Dalyell was appointed his deputy, and enjoyed powers of patronage, buying and selling offices and taking a sufficiently good commission on these transactions to enable him when he returned to Scotland to purchase the estate of The Binns on the Firth of Forth.

So many Scots flocked to London in search of fortune that in 1614 James appointed one, William Alexander, poet and tutor to his son Prince Henry, and subsequently Earl of Stirling, to the post of master of requests with the particular responsibility of discriminating between deserving and undeserving Scots seeking positions at Court or in the administration. It was natural that many Englishmen should resent this influx of needy Scots, following what Samuel Johnson would later call 'the fairest prospect a Scotchman ever sees – the high road that leads him to England'.

Englishmen might object, but London and the Court were powerful magnets. Just as the Tudors, being of Welsh origin, had attracted ambitious young men from the Principality, so now the Scots took advantage of their king's accession to the English throne. Benefiting from royal patronage the merchants George Heriot and Sir William Dick established themselves in London and entered into partnership with English houses.

The Civil Wars promoted intercourse between the two nations. The Westminster Assembly of Divines, meeting in 1643 to draw up plans, in accordance with the provisions of the Solemn League and Covenant, for a national Presbyterian Church of England, was attended by six Scots commissioners who participated in its discussions. Though that Church was never established, the Assembly did produce the Westminster Confession of Faith which was accepted by the Kirk as being 'in nothing contrary to the received doctrine', and as necessary 'for the intended uniformity in religion'; it was designed to serve as 'a common Confession of Faith for the three kingdoms', the third being predominantly Roman Catholic Ireland. Soon repudiated in England, the Confession remains the creed of the Scots Kirk. Accordingly that most thoroughly Scotch of institutions, which for three centuries did more to mould and exemplify the national character of Scotland than any other, nevertheless confesses its faith according to a form stamped 'Made in England'.

The Interregnum, when for the first time Scotland and England were governed by Cromwell and the army as one country, did not leave as deep a mark on Scotland as on Ireland. There Cromwell dispossessed many of the native Irish, conquered and Catholic, and granted or sold their lands to his officers. No such transfer occurred in Scotland, but a number, not now to be determined, of the troopers and officers of the New Model Army settled in Scotland when discharged from garrison duty. Scott makes Reuben Butler, the young Church of Scotland minister who serves as the hero of *The Heart of Midlothian*, the grandson of an English trooper. When Dr Johnson visited Inverness on his journey to the Western Isles, he remarked that Cromwell had stationed a garrison there, and that 'the soldiers seem to have incorporated afterwards with the inhabitants, and to have peopled the place with an English race; for the language of the town has long been considered as peculiarly elegant'. It used indeed to be said that the people of Inverness spoke a very pure and correct English, but whether Cromwell's troopers did so seems doubtful. It is more likely that, if this claim was once good, the correctness of their English was due to their being native Gaelic speakers who learned it as a second language.

National differences could be bridged by a common faith. The example of *The Pilgrim's Progress* is to the point. Its author, John Bunyan, was a Puritan, an Independent rather than a Presbyterian, imprisoned in the reign of Charles II for preaching without a licence, for being in fact a political subversive. His book, an allegory of the Christian life and the soul's journey, circulated at first among the uneducated, but became staple reading in God-fearing and devout households. It remained so till the early twentieth century, in Scotland as in England. Probably no book, except the Bible, was more often and more thoroughly read. My own copy belonged to my grandmother, daughter of an Aberdeenshire tenant farmer, in politics a Gladstonian Liberal, in religion a member of the Free Church of Scotland. No book is more often quoted by John Buchan, himself the son of a Free Kirk minister. He even took the name of one of Bunyan's characters, Mr Standfast, as the title of one of his Hannay novels, the book itself being permeated with references to *The Pilgrim's Progress* and quotations from it. Inasmuch as books help to form a culture, while being at the same time its expression, the enduring popularity of Bunyan's testifies to the degree to which Lowland Scots and English shared a common culture.

The ease with which an ambitious Scot could be accepted in

England and prosper there may be illustrated by an account of the career of Gilbert Burnet. Born in Edinburgh in 1643 (but with roots in Aberdeenshire) Burnet was the son of an Episcopalian lawyer and a staunchly Presbyterian mother; she was the sister of Archibald Johnston of Warriston, 'a zealous worker in the vineyard of the Lord', and one of the Scots commissioners who negotiated the Solemn League and Covenant, subsequently executed on a charge of treason at the Restoration. The young Burnet was educated at Marischal College, Aberdeen, selected in preference to Edinburgh, partly for family reasons, but principally because Aberdeen and the north-east were strongholds of Episcopalianism and Royalism. He was ordained an Episcopalian minister and given the living of Saltoun in East Lothian, where he tutored the laird's son, the future 'Patriot' Andrew Fletcher. Visits to London and the Netherlands followed in 1663–4. By his account he sought out 'the best men of all the several forms of religion' and concluded: 'one thing I drank deep in at Amsterdam (which sticks still with me and is not like to leave me) . . . is never to form a prejudice in my mind against any man because of this or that persuasion; for I saw men of all persuasions that were as far as I could perceive so truly religious that I never think the worse of a man for his opinions'. In arriving at this determination, Burnet was ahead of his time.

After two years as Professor of Divinity at Glasgow University, he was introduced to the English Court by his patron Lauderdale. He won the king's favour to such an extent that within a few years he was offered a bishopric, which however for the time being he declined. In the Exclusion Crisis of 1678–81 (the attempt to bar the king's Roman Catholic brother James, Duke of York, from the succession) Burnet favoured the Exclusionists, now known as Whigs. The Exclusion Bill was defeated. James became king four years later, and Burnet prudently withdrew to the safety of the Netherlands. He soon became friendly with the Stadtholder, William of Orange, and his wife Mary Stuart. The Revolution of 1688 restored his fortunes. He returned as William's chaplain and the next year was appointed Bishop of Salisbury. In his middle forties the Edinburgh boy had been admitted to the English establishment, an intimate of the grandees and the king. The years before his death in 1715 were devoted to the writing of the *History of His Own Time*, the only general history of the reigns of the later Stuarts written by a man who had been in a position to observe, and occasionally to influence, the events he narrates.

Burnet traced a path many Scots would follow. The professions – the Church, the law and medicine – the army and navy and the universities of Oxford and Cambridge would serve as the route by which Scots, some of humble birth, advanced from the geographical periphery to the centre of what, within a hundred years of the Treaty of Union, could no longer be accurately termed the English establishment; it had become British. How did this come about?

Burnet's hero, like Macaulay's more than a century later, was William of Orange, the saviour of the liberties of England, Scotland and (Protestant) Ireland. Burnet's may be called the first Whig history; Macaulay recognized him as 'a strong party-man on the right side'.

It is here that Burnet may be seen as having a significance that goes far beyond the manner in which his career shows how comfortably a Scot could establish himself in the upper reaches of English political and ecclesiastical society. If we ask what made the Union of England and Scotland acceptable and effective, the short answer is Whiggism.

The party names, Whig and Tory, originated, as is well known, as insults, terms of opprobrium. A 'tory' was an Irish brigand; a 'whig' or 'whiggamore' a Scots Covenanter and rebel. But the origins were soon forgotten and the labels proudly worn.

They were not political parties as we understand parties today. Historians long ago abandoned the notion that a two-party system existed in the eighteenth century. Instead of coherent parties, nationally organized, there were fluctuating groups, held together by common interests and almost always attached to the fortunes of some great nobleman. But, if Whigs and Tories were not political parties as we understand parties, the words represented certain attitudes of mind, certain prejudices, and even adherence to certain principles.

English Tories were first of all Church of England men. Dr Johnson, a Tory himself, defined the word in his *Dictionary* as 'one who adheres to the ancient constitutions of church and state'. (He defined 'whig' as '1: whey; 2: name of a faction'.) An English Tory disliked Dissenters (as the old Puritans were now called), and often retained a sentimental attachment to Jacobitism. He believed that the interests of England were often subjected to the Hanoverian interest of the German king. He distrusted the City of London and was opposed to an active foreign policy because wars were financed in part by the Land Tax which bore heavily on country gentlemen. He was what would much later be called a Little Englander. He saw small merit in the Union and tended to dislike the Scots, as interlopers and greedy immigrants. Furthermore Scotch religion bore too close a resemblance to English Dissent or Nonconformity. Dr Johnson, imbued with all these prejudices, was the archetypal English Tory intellectual; Squire Western, in Fielding's novel *Tom Jones*, the Tory backwoodsman. (Fielding himself was a Whig.)

Scots Tories, always a minority, were either Episcopalians or Roman Catholics. For the first half of the century they were Jacobites, often active ones. When the cause was dead and there was no longer any chance of a Stuart restoration, they remained sentimental Jacobites, like Johnson in England. They were mostly found in the north-eastern counties, and were weak in Edinburgh, Glasgow and the old Covenanting south-west. They resented and deplored the Union; one of the first acts of Prince Charles Edward when established in Edinburgh in 1745 was to issue a proclamation declaring 'the pretended union of Scotland and England dissolved'.

Toryism was, for most of the eighteenth century, backward looking and impractical. Tories were excluded from office after 1714. Horace Walpole, son of the Whig prime minister, remarked that all the sensible Tories of his acquaintance turned Whig: 'those that remained Tories, remained fools'.

Whiggism was also an attitude of mind, but circumstances made it more than that. Whiggism stood for a Parliamentary monarchy; the king remained head of the Government, but his ministers required the support of the House of Commons. There was no real division between English and Scottish Whigs as between the two 'national'

Tories. There couldn't be, because though English Whiggism had already developed a Whig interpretation of English history even before the Whig name was attached to it, the mature exposition of Whig history was the work of Scots who by their work made it British.

In both countries the Whigs were heirs and defenders of the Revolution of 1688, which they called 'Glorious', and the beneficiaries of the Union and the Hanoverian succession. The Whigs were, mostly, Low Church Anglicans in England and Presbyterians in Scotland. English Dissenters were excluded from public life (by the provisions of the 1673 Test Act), but may be called honorary Whigs, who benefited from the Whig policy of commercial expansion, preferably at the expense of France, and, from the mid-eighteenth century onwards, from what may already be called imperialism. Ultimately Whigs believed in Progress, though few yet articulated this belief. Tories might remain English or Scots, but Whigs were British.

The proto-Whig interpretation of history had its roots in the experience of the sixteenth century. It was, from the first, Protestant history. Because it was that, it originally took a different form in England and Scotland. In Scotland the Reformation was made in opposition to the Crown. The revolt against Rome was justified by James VI's tutor George Buchanan who, in his *History of Scotland* (1582), discovered that the ancient constitution had been popular rather than monarchical; accordingly the Protestant revolt restored what had been, rather than representing a new departure. English historians had an easier task to justify the Reformation. It had been made by Henry VIII and confirmed by Edward VI and Elizabeth: so in the eyes of English historians a national Protestant tradition had been maintained by the English monarchy. A hero for the sixteenth century was the medieval King John, who had resisted, if eventually unsuccessfully, the most powerful of medieval popes, Innocent III. He could therefore be seen as a precursor of Henry VIII, and it is as such that he is presented in Shakespeare's play.

Before long however John had to become a villain. Resistance to the Stuarts made English Protestantism anti-monarchical. They then discovered, as Buchanan had done in Scotland, that their ancient constitution had always been aristocratic and (by unwarrantable extension) popular. So the barons who had extorted Magna Carta from John (now seen as a forerunner of Charles I and his Eleven Years Tyranny) became their heroes. The lord chief justice Sir Edmund Coke found that even the Ancient Britons had enjoyed a Parliamentary constitution. 'More cautious antiquaries', wrote Hugh Trevor-Roper, 'were prepared to settle for the Anglo-Saxons.' So the proto-Whig historians discovered that the English monarchy had always rested on a contract made between king and people – a conclusion the Scots had already arrived at – and that those kings who had broken that contract (Edward II, Richard II and now Charles I and James II) had been dismissed and disposed of. This discovery was very convenient.

This Whig version of history made sense, and very agreeable sense too. It saw English, and subsequently British, history as the story of the advance of liberty, secured in a series of conflicts with an authoritarian Church and Crown. In the years of the Whig Ascendancy, which lasted till the 1760s, it was possible to enjoy its fruits. Curiously the first classic exposition was given by a Frenchman, Paul Rapin de Thoyras, in a *History of England*, written in French and published in Holland in 1723. Yet it was not so curious, for Rapin was a Huguenot, a French Protestant, driven into exile by the policies of Louis XIV. He had fought in the army of William of Orange, and he was concerned to explain, principally to his own compatriots, how it was that England had emerged from its constitutional conflicts, civil wars and a century in which it had played no important part in European politics as the organizer and animator of the Grand Alliance that had checked the power of France and thrown even Louis XIV on the defensive. His answer was that England alone had preserved the old 'free constitution' which had once been enjoyed by all the tribes that had conquered and occupied the Roman Empire, but which had elsewhere been perverted and then suppressed by despotism. England (or the United Kingdom) was proving stronger than France, because it was free and France wasn't. This explanation was very pleasing.

It accorded with the Whigs' own view of experience and actuality. They stood for Parliamentary liberty, the common law, the Protestant religion, religious toleration to all varieties of Protestants, commercial expansion and hostility to France. They had defeated tyrannical monarchs and brought the Crown under their control; they would have said 'back under their control'. A Tory like Dr Johnson might complain that 'the Crown has not power enough'. No Whig could agree. Finally, they remained hostile to Roman Catholicism, and suspicious of it, because in their view it was obscurantist, authoritarian, an enemy to liberty, and in England inclined to encourage sedition, even to the point of treason and rebellion, among its adherents.

The Whig interpretation of history proved in this early form to be unsustainable. Its historical absurdity would be exposed by the Scotch philosopher David Hume in his *History of England*, published in 1761. Hume is often called a Tory, but if he was one, he was a Tory of a new type. He had no more use for Tory ideas of the Divine Right of Kings and paternalist Patriot Kings than for the Ancient Constitution of the Whigs. Indeed he thought this all flummery. The most excellent constitution was not in itself any guarantor of liberty, something which the history of the twentieth century has confirmed, and an opinion which admirers of Stalin's Soviet constitution might have done well to remember. Liberty, as distinct from the licence of anarchy, was the result of social and economic progress and of the softening, or, as he put it, 'sophistication', of manners which was the fruit of that progress. It was social progress, not constitutions, that made for a free state. To Hume it seemed absurd to pretend that medieval barons or seventeenth-century religious enthusiasts (all possessed of a zeal for persecution) understood liberty as men of his own time did. What they called 'liberties' were privileges, or, in the case of the religious zealots, the right or power to impose their will and opinions on all. Hume also recognized that:

> in all governments, there is a perpetual intestine struggle, open or secret, between Authority and Liberty; and neither of them can ever absolutely prevail in the contest . . . The government, which, in common appellation, receives the appellation of free, is that which admits of a partition of power among several members, whose united authority is no less, or is commonly greater than that of any monarch;

but, who, in the usual course of administration, must act by general and equal laws, that are previously known to all the members and to all their subjects. In this sense, it must be owned, that liberty is the perfection of civil society; but still authority must be acknowledged essential to its very existence . . .

Though Hume is known as a Tory, this was not in truth different from Whig doctrine. This is not surprising. Born in 1711, Hume grew to maturity with the Union. He observed that, at a time when Scotland had lost its independence, Scottish society experienced an unaccustomed ease, and Scotland enjoyed an unprecedented intellectual flowering. What was the cause? It could not be the constitution for that was evidently in certain respects defective. Rather, it seemed that, authority being maintained with a light hand, civil society benefited from the consequent liberty of free enquiry, and was able to act on the conclusions to which that enquiry tended. Urbane discussion had supplanted the fierce controversies of bigots.

In both England and Scotland the political passions of the seventeenth century were stilled. Politicians yet argued and intrigued. Pamphleteers – the denizens of Grub Street – still inveighed against the vices and corruption of those who adhered to rival factions. But, in comparison with the previous century, this was mimic war. Defeated or displaced politicians withdrew to the Opposition benches or to their country estates; they no longer needed to fear the scaffold.

For two decades Robert Walpole controlled the Government, eschewed an active foreign policy, dispensed patronage and kept the administration jogging along. He controlled Scotland through managers, chief among them Archibald Campbell, 1st Earl of Islay, brother to the Duke of Argyll, whom in time he succeeded. The Campbells were unusual – a Highland clan whose leaders were Lowland politicians, who had been Covenanters in the 1640s and were Whigs from the time of the Revolution. The terms of Walpole's agreement with Islay were simple: Islay would deliver the votes of the majority of Scotland's forty-five MPs to Walpole (and his successors, the Pelham brothers) in return for being granted liberty in disposing of all Government patronage and control of appointments in Scotland. He built up, like Walpole in

England, a formidable list of clients and dependants, men who owed their career and position to him; in the late 1730s two-thirds of the judges in the Court of Session were Islay's men.

This informal contract gave Scotland political stability, which was in effect freedom from politics. That was what Sir Walter Scott referred to when he said that in the eighteenth century neglect of Scotland had enabled the country 'to win its silent way to riches and prosperity'. At the same time the manner in which Islay distributed patronage – commissions in the army and navy, appointments in the civil service or on government boards – brought obvious benefits to individual families. The Union had opened the resources of a rich state to poor and ambitious Scots. It would do so more abundantly as the century advanced and Britain acquired an empire. When in the last decades of the century, Henry Dundas, from a Midlothian family that belonged to Scotland's *noblesse de la robe*, controlled as the Younger Pitt's right-hand man the patronage of the new Empire in India, Scots prospered there in disproportionate number: wealth was repatriated, new families founded and new country houses built.

Already in 1755, the *Edinburgh Review* (the first of a number of publications to bear that title) could state:

> The communication of trade has awakened industry; the equal admin-istration of laws produced good manners; and the watchful care of the government, seconded by the public spirit of some individuals, has excited, promoted, and encouraged a disposition to every species of improvement in the minds of a people naturally active and intelligent. If countries have their ages in respect to improvement, North Britain may be considered in a state of early youth, guided and supported by the mature state of her kindred country . . .

In other words, Scotland (North Britain) might be the younger brother; but, thanks to the Union, it was catching up fast. In a few years it might even set the tone and lead the way.

Whatever the cultural differences, Scots and English already had sufficient in common to allow some Scots to be accepted as equals in London literary society, in no way strange, foreign or even uncouth. Two such were Dr John Arbuthnott and James Thomson.

Arbuthnott (1667–1735) belonged to a generation that was already middle-aged by the time of the Union, in support of which he published a satirical essay, *A Sermon Preached to the People at the Mercat Cross*. Born in Kincardineshire, and educated at the universities of Aberdeen, Oxford and St Andrews, he settled in London in the reign of William and Mary, and was later appointed physician to Queen Anne – the first in a succession of Scotch doctors to have held that royal appointment. He was elected a Fellow of the Royal Society, and became a close friend of Swift, Gay and Pope. They were all members of the Scriblerus Club, which met in Arbuthnott's rooms in St James's Palace, where he could be on hand to attend the queen's needs. He wrote pamphlets as 'John Bull' arguing for ending the French war, almost as influential as his friend Swift's *Conduct of the Allies*. A moderate Tory, but no Jacobite, he survived his Tory patrons' loss of office in 1714, unmolested. Completely at home in London literary and intellectual circles, his career makes the question whether he should be described as a Scot living in London, as an anglicized Scot or as British seem superfluous. He fitted comfortably into that life because he shared its culture.

The case of James Thomson (1700–48) is even more to the point. Born at Ednam in Roxburghshire, where his father was the parish minister, and therefore a Presbyterian, he was himself intended for the ministry and studied divinity at Edinburgh University. He knew himself however to be a poet, and therefore abandoned his studies and headed for London in search of fortune and reputation. Prudently he provided for his immediate needs by accepting an offer to become tutor to Lord Binning, the son of the Earl of Haddington. So he avoided the misery of Grub Street in which so many of his contemporaries, among them the poet Richard Savage, his friend and Johnson's, found themselves trapped. This offer was made apparently on the recommendation of a fellow-Scot and poet, David Malloch, who was already settled in London and who had changed his name to the less obviously Scottish Mallet. Even in his first months in London, Thomson, as agreeable in manner as he was ambitious, had contrived to meet Arbuthnott, Pope, Gay and indeed the prime minister, Walpole himself.

The next year, 1725, he published the first part of his long poem, *The Seasons*. Its success was immediate, and it became one of the most popular and influential of all the long poems of the century. Thomson was a made man at once. No poem is more central to the Augustan tradition. Johnson was to declare that 'Thomson thinks always as a man of genius.' He remarked also on his originality; he wrote about nature in a wholly new way, and one that was to find many imitators. But the speed with which he won popularity – a popularity that endured throughout the century – makes it clear that he did not write as one emerging from a different or foreign culture. If on the one hand he was influenced by the Scots Humanist poets, notably the Latinist Arthur Johnston (1587–1641), on the other the influences of Spenser and Milton are also evident. Milton, as the great Puritan poet, indeed belonged to Thomson's heritage as a Scotch Presbyterian. *The Seasons* was written in Miltonic blank verse, and his last work, *The Castle of Indolence*, an allegory, in Spenserian stanzas. Thomson was never a deracinated Scot, and his own work would influence that of the Gaelic poets Alexander MacDonald and Ewan MacLachlan. But at the same time he was, or made himself, a British poet, writing incidentally the words of 'Rule, Britannia', first featured in an operatic masque written in conjunction with Malloch. There was no need to deny or disguise his Scottishness. The community existing already between English and Scottish taste made this otiose. Thomson, with his genius for giving expression to the often platitudinous Sublime, is the authentic poetic voice of British Whiggism.

6

Jacobitism

❧

IN THE SUMMER of 2004 a Fife councillor was banned from his local pub for abusing a party of English visitors. He explained that he disliked the English on account of the 1746 Battle of Culloden.

'Every Scot', declared the late-Victorian prime minister Lord Rosebery, 'is a Jacobite at heart.' Despite the evidence offered by this Fife councillor, this has never been more than half true. The other half of our divided self is Covenanting, or, more tamely, Whig. John Buchan saw this division in Rosebery himself: 'behind all his exterior urbanity and humour lay this haunting sense of transience, and while to the world he seemed like some polished eighteenth-century grandee, at heart he was the Calvinist of seventeenth-century Scotland'.

Yet the half-truth is worth pondering; it marks a difference between Scots and English. Of course it wasn't even half true when Jacobitism was a political force, a cause not yet lost. The most that might then have been said was that half the Scots were Jacobites – and a fair number of Englishmen too; but that the other half of Scots looked on the prospect of a Stuart Restoration with the same apprehension as the majority of Englishmen.

While, after his failure to regain his kingdoms by way of Ireland, a hope shattered at the Battle of the Boyne, James VII & II lingered as a pensioner of his cousin Louis XIV in the Palace of Saint-Germain, Jacobitism had little appeal. Few wanted James back as king, though, aware of the uncertainties of the time, there were canny politicians in both London and Edinburgh who thought it prudent to maintain contact with the exiled monarch. Marlborough, once James's protégé, then the man whose defection in 1688 had so unnerved him that he fled, was among them.

Eventually Jacobitism would become the cause only of the 'outs', men excluded from office, even hope of office, in the years of the Whig Ascendancy. It would seem a hopeless cause to sensible men, and would rapidly dwindle to a mere sentimental attachment. But it wasn't that in the early years of the eighteenth century.

In the months before Queen Anne's death in August 1714, a Stuart Restoration seemed possible, despite the Act of the English Parliament which had settled the succession on the Elector of Hanover, and despite the effective confirmation of that Act in the Treaty of Union. The end of the long war with France made the prospect of the return of the Stuart claimant less alarming, even though the predominantly Tory ministry which had negotiated the Treaty of Utrecht the previous year had compelled Louis XIV to repudiate the Pretender and to acknowledge, in effect, that the Parliament of the United Kingdom was entitled to determine who should be king. Yet members of this same Tory ministry, and especially the secretary of state, Henry St John, Viscount Bolingbroke, were engaged in a flirtation with the Pretender, James Edward, and it was rumoured, and widely believed, that he had been brought secretly to London to be ready on hand for the great moment when Anne should die, as it was obvious the poor woman would not be long in doing.

James had indeed written to his half-sister, pressing his claim, and assuring her that, as king, he would rule according to law. He would, he said, 'preserve every man's right, liberty, and property equally with the rights of the Crown', would maintain the Church of England as by law established, and would grant 'such toleration to Protestant Dissenters as Parliament should think fit'. He refused to renounce his own adherence to the Church of Rome, but pointed out, with a degree of optimism, that his constancy and sincerity in this respect ought to be received as proof that he would religiously abide by all promises that he might make. The chance of a restoration was sufficiently real to have both Houses of Parliament debating that summer whether the Protestant Succession was in danger. At this time Jacobitism was every bit as much an English as a Scottish cause.

Nobody has ever been sure just how far Bolingbroke was committed; whether he really intended to try to bring James in as king, or whether he merely toyed with the idea. The temptation was there, certainly. He knew that the Elector of Hanover, who loathed him, would at once dispense with his services if he became George I. But events moved too fast. As he wrote to his friend Swift: 'the Earl of Oxford [his Tory rival Robin Harley] was removed [dismissed from office] on Tuesday; the Queen died on Sunday. What a world is this and how doth Fortune banter us. I have lost all by the death of the Queen, but my spirit.' He had indeed, and was soon fleeing to France to avoid impeachment. He became for a time the Pretender's secretary of state in his mimic government, but the coup, if coup there was, had failed. The Protestant Succession was safe.

This was a great relief, for many Scots and Englishmen alike. Robert Woodrow, a minister of the Church of Scotland and author of a history of 'its sufferings' from the Restoration of 1660 to the Revolution of 1688, spoke for many:

> this month makes a vast change by the Queen's death, and the peaceable succession of King George. The joy is so great and universal that I have seen nothing like it since the Revolution, when I was but young. This is a wonderful dash to the Jacobites; and had the Queen lived a little longer, they think their schemes would have taken effect, and it's not improbable that the Pretender was lately in London and at St James's.

That rumour had reached him in his parish of Eastwood, just outside Glasgow. 'However,' he wrote, quoting the 124th Psalm, 'the Lord hath broken the snare, and we are escaped. I wish we may all observe the Divine hand in it.'

Not everybody was ready to do so. Since the attempt to restore the rightful king by political means had come to nothing, his supporters saw no remedy but force. The moment was propitious. There was discontent in both England and Scotland. The northern counties of England, economically backward, had shared few of the profits of the long war with France. Noblemen and squires had suffered from the Land Tax levied to pay for that war which (they thought) had benefited only Whigs and the City of London. Moreover it was in the north that were to be found old families which had remained Roman Catholic. There was tinder there to be struck.

In Scotland, despite Woodrow's complacency, discontent was still sharper. So far the Union had delivered no economic benefit, and remained deeply unpopular.

There were Jacobites by conviction in both countries, but many, perhaps more, who inclined to the cause did so out of interest. Resentment too played its part in translating Jacobite sympathy into action. In Scotland the Revolution of 1688 had secured the ascendancy of the Presbyterians. Men like Woodrow now belonged to the Establishment while Episcopalian ministers had been driven from their parishes. Nothing comparable had occurred in England, where however the toleration now granted Protestant Dissenters dismayed or angered High Church of England men; in 1709 the Rev. Henry Sacheverell had been impeached and barred from preaching for three years because he had published sermons in which he denounced such toleration and the practice of Occasional Conformity whereby Dissenters made themselves eligible for magistracies and membership of municipal corporations by taking communion, perhaps once a year, according to the rites of the Church of England. There was strong Jacobite feeling in the High Church stronghold, the University of Oxford, and, in Scotland, in the two universities, King's and Marischal, at Aberdeen, for most of the landed families of the north-east were Episcopalians. Among the Highland clans, all the traditional enemies of the Campbells, all those who had suffered from the extension of Campbell power and influence, were naturally likely to favour a Stuart Restoration which must result in the humbling of Clan Campbell.

In both countries there were politicians out of office and disliked and distrusted by the new German king. Among them was John Erskine, Earl of Mar. He had been one of the commissioners who had negotiated the Treaty of Union. Now he reversed his policy and became a Jacobite demanding the abrogation of the Treaty. He raised the standard at Braemar in August 1715 and was soon at the head of the largest army the Jacobites were ever to field.

They could not have had a less competent leader. Mar's judgement was poor, his character feeble. Instead of moving swiftly to seize Edinburgh and thus take control of such machinery of government as remained in post-Union Scotland, he dithered. When eventually he moved south, he found hastily assembled Government troops barring the passage of the Forth at Stirling, the strategic nodal point of Scotland. The battle fought at Sheriffmuir was indecisive. Though the Jacobites outnumbered the Hanoverian army commanded by the Duke of Argyll by three to one, Mar's incompetence and timidity made it, as one Jacobite wrote, 'an affair in which neither side gained much honour, but which was the entire ruin of our party'. The Duke of Argyll had made Scotland safe for Whiggery.

That Jacobite critic was James Keith, brother of the 10th Earl Marischal of Scotland. Keith, only nineteen at the time, came like many Jacobites from an Aberdeenshire family, being born in Inverugie Castle by Peterhead. He would spend his life as an exile, serving with great distinction in the armies of first Russia and then Prussia, becoming indeed Frederick the Great's most trusted marshal. In his memoirs, written late in life, he recorded the dismal course of the Rising of 1715.

> News was brought to us that the same day we fought the Duke of Argyll's army, our troops in England had surrendered. This gave the enemy opportunity to draw down forces from England against us. A second bad effect was the disuniting us amongst ourselves, for several of our party, seeing that the English, which we always looked on as our principal strength, were quelled, began to think of making terms for themselves.

Keith, a man of fine honour, was not one of these. His observation that the Scots Jacobites had looked on the English as 'our principal strength' may surprise those who think of Jacobitism as peculiarly Scots, but what he wrote was very much to the point. It was impossible that the Cause should prevail without English support, and it may be that, if Mar had moved swiftly enough and crossed the Border at the head of an army, that support would have been forthcoming. But it is more probable that Keith, a young man ignorant of England, did not appreciate the difficulty in which English Jacobites, however devoted to the Cause, found themselves.

Seventy years earlier, in the Civil War, it had still been possible for grandees like the Earl of Newcastle and the Marquess of Worcester to bring several thousand troops into the field. These days were gone. Moreover, whereas in 1642 both the Royalist and Parliamentary armies had had to be improvised, attaining a degree of professionalism only in the second or third year of the war, in 1715 the English Jacobites were faced by experienced troops, a regular army, composed of veteran regiments which had fought under Marlborough's command in the long war against France. This itself was a consideration to deter Jacobite sympathizers in England. It was different in Scotland where the clans were still warlike and where even Lowland lairds in the north-east could muster a troop of horse, however doubtful its quality. Yet fear of English Jacobitism was acute, and English rebels were treated with greater severity than Scottish ones.

After the '15 the London Government remained wary of Jacobite disaffection and Jacobite plots. The stability of the new regime could not be taken for granted. Though after the death of Louis XIV the French Government of his nephew the Duke of Orleans, regent for the boy-king Louis XV, was committed to peace with Britain, and in 1718 required the Pretender to leave France for Italy, the Jacobites could still look to Spain for help; this indeed was provided, though on far too small a scale, in 1719, the year of the second Jacobite Rising, quickly subdued. But the next year Francis Atterbury, Bishop of Rochester, was imprisoned in the Tower of London for his alleged connection with an attempt to restore the Stuarts; he had certainly been in correspondence with the Pretender since 1717. Dr Johnson's friend, the poet Richard Savage, had been arrested on a charge of political subversion just after the suppression of the '15. His crime was the possession of 'a treasonable pamphlet', his own doggerel poem entitled 'An Ironical Panagerick on his pretended Majesty George'. For the next year and a half at least he was kept under supervision, subject of Secret Service reports from an agent, Robert Girling, who had been charged with the duty of investigating – and perhaps provoking – subversive talk and activities among young men associated with Gray's Inn.

Of course it was natural, even reasonable, for the Government to charge opponents with Jacobitism, just as in the early years of the Cold War critics of American policy were smeared as Communists. But the Government's willingness to suggest that all critics were treasonable Jacobites didn't mean that there were no Jacobites among its opponents, any more than the McCarthyite Red scare in the USA meant that all branded as Communists were innocent liberals. The Hanoverian Government was wise to be alert to the danger that disaffection would lead men to active participation in Jacobite plots and plans for an invasion. Dr Johnson, whose Toryism brought him very close to Jacobitism, believed that 'if England were fairly polled, the present king would be sent away to-night'. But his common sense led him to add that the people 'would not risk anything to restore the exiled family. They would not give twenty shillings a piece to bring it about.'

That was the point. A peaceful restoration, in the manner of 1660, might be a seductive dream in Oxford, but as a proposition it was quite unrealistic. Restoring the Stuarts meant civil war; and within a few years of the establishment of the Hanoverian dynasty, too many people, in both England and Scotland, had too much to lose, therefore too much to fear.

So by 1745 prospects for the Jacobites were even more gloomy. Long years of internal peace and growing prosperity rendered the English Jacobites still less capable of action, and still more reluctant to hazard their lives and property in so dangerous an enterprise as rebellion. Country squires, like Fielding's Squire Western in *Tom Jones*, set in the year of the Rising, might grumble about 'Hanoverian rats' and Whigs, curse the Land Tax, and drink the health of 'the king over the water'; but they weren't going to bestir themselves on his behalf. Sentimental Jacobitism still flourished in the University of Oxford, but few dons would exchange the comforts of their hall and study for the rigours of the camp. Scott, in *Waverley*, expresses the doubts of English Jacobites when he gives the following reflection to his hero from an old Cavalier family:

whatever were the original rights of the Stuarts, calm reflection told him that since that period [the Revolution of 1688] four monarchs had ruled in peace and glory over Britain, sustaining and exalting the character of the nation abroad and its liberties at home. Reason asked, was it worthwhile to disturb a government so long settled and established, and to plunge a kingdom into the miseries of civil war?

Reason and interest prevailed over such old loyalist sentiment as there might be. Though on his march through England, prince Charles Edward found some recruits in Catholic districts of Lancashire – the Manchester Regiment of 300 men would still be in his army at Culloden six months later – the absence of enthusiasm and the lack of material support from England dismayed the prince's men. They had looked for friends and allies, and found few. Where they didn't encounter only apathy, they sensed hostility; and this was one of the chief reasons why the prince's Council insisted on the retreat from Derby in defiance of his determination to push on and hazard all on an attempt to seize London.

The Jacobites were in a minority in Scotland too. Even the chiefs of traditionally Jacobite clans were dismayed when the prince landed, with only a few men and without the French troops which had been promised. Their first response was to tell him to go home. Alexander MacDonald of Boisdale assured him that 'not a soul would join him'. But Charles replied that he had come home, and shamed them into supporting the Rising. But many clans remained quiet, and Lowland Scotland was hostile.

In Edinburgh, where, according to the philosopher David Hume, news of the approach of the Highland army threw the citizens into a panic, the former lord provost George Drummond and Colin MacLaurin, Professor of Mathematics at the university, organized volunteers to defend the city in support of the royal garrison in the Castle. Among those who responded were a number of students who would be among the luminaries of the Scottish Enlightenment: William Robertson, later Principal of Edinburgh University and historian, Alexander 'Jupiter' Carlyle, future Moderator of the Kirk, William Cleghorn, who would be Professor of Moral Philosophy at the university, John Home, minister of religion and playwright, and the seventeen-year-old Robert Adam, who assisted MacLaurin in repairing the city's dilapidated defences. When it became clear that the city could not be held, the young men retired to a tavern and swore an oath to continue the struggle 'for', in Carlyle's words, 'the security of our country's laws and liberties' – threatened, they were convinced, by a Jacobite success.

The Jacobites occupied Edinburgh. The prince took up residence in the Palace of Holyroodhouse. A herald proclaimed old James Edward, 'James VIII and III', and Charles his regent, and the 'pretended Union' between England and Scotland was declared to be annulled. The formula of One Monarch, Two Kingdoms, which had proved unsatisfactory in the seventeenth century, was therefore revived.

The Hanoverian army commanded by Sir John Cope was scattered at Prestonpans a few miles out of Edinburgh on the East Lothian coast. 'They eskaped like rabets,' the prince informed his father, but he forbade any public celebration of his victory, saying that he was 'far from rejoicing at the death of any of my father's subjects'. After Culloden the Hanoverians would take a different view of such matters, and it was a poor excuse that they had suffered a severe fright. Charles then marched south, assured, he believed, that some 5,000 English Jacobites would flock to his standard.

What followed in Scotland is part of the story of the '45 which is absent from the Jacobite legend. The Scottish Whigs recovered their nerve and rallied. The city of Glasgow, which had, the prince complained, 'showed a little too much Zeal' to his Hanoverian cousins, raised a regiment of militia which joined the army pursuing the retreating Jacobites. The Duke of Argyll secured the Western Highlands. Most significantly Duncan Forbes of Culloden, the Lord President of the Court of Session, Scotland's senior judge, exerted himself to keep those clan chiefs who had not yet joined the prince loyal to the Hanoverians; he also supplied Government troops from his own resources, spending £30,000, which was never repaid. Duncan Forbes is the forgotten hero of the '45: a Scottish patriot, who, as a young law officer, advocate-depute, after the '15, had challenged his own Government's decision to send accused Jacobites to England for trial, which he declared to be in breach of the Treaty of Union. His readiness to defend Scottish interests was as undeniable as his commitment to the Union and the Protestant Succession. A humane and cultured man, friend of James Thomson, Allan Ramsay, Arbuthnott, Pope and Swift, he reproached Cumberland for the barbarity of his conduct after Culloden. Cockburn in his *Memorials* recorded as probable the story that Forbes 'even in the king's presence expressed his decided disapprobation of the violence of the royal army after the battle'.

That battle, in which three of Cumberland's fifteen regular battalions were Scottish, destroyed the Jacobite cause for ever. The hereditary jurisdictions of the chiefs, which gave them power of life and death over their clansmen, and which had made the raising of private armies possible, were abolished, at Forbes's instigation.

Though in time it was the memory of the brutal suppression of the clans and the cruel harrying of the rebels that survived and earned Cumberland the name of 'Butcher', the news of Culloden delighted Lowland Whig Scotland. In Glasgow, where the ministers of the Kirk had preached loyalist sermons even while the Jacobite army was in the city, church bells were rung and bonfires lit when news came of the battle, and Cumberland was granted the freedom of the city. The University of St Andrews delighted to install him as its chancellor. The veteran lawyer, politician, patron of William Adam and numerous artists, John Clerk of Penicuik, almost forty years previously one of the fashioners of the Treaty of Union, thought that the news of Culloden gave 'universal joy'. There were even, he thought, some Jacobites 'who were at least content'. Trade and business could resume. As for the young Alexander Carlyle who, with his friends, had sworn to defend 'the security of our country's laws and liberties', his judgement was 'God forbid that Britain should ever again be in danger of being overrun by such a despicable enemy.'

Jacobitism was both Scots and English, and its enemy Whiggism was also. Yet Jacobite sentiment died away in England almost entirely while it survived in Scotland, to such an extent that Rosebery could say that every Scot is a Jacobite at heart and today the majority of Scots probably think like that Fife councillor that Culloden was a battle in which an English army defeated a Scots one. Why?

One answer is obvious. The Risings started in Scotland and while the '15 is almost forgotten, playing no part in the popular memory or imagination, all the dramatic and romantic and wretched elements of the '45 were Scottish. Scotland saw the beginning and end of the prince's adventure, and, for long, in the Highlands anyway, the '45 was remembered as 'the prince's year'.

This is not surprising. It was the stuff of legend and romance. That a small army of Highlanders and north-east lairds and their people should have come so close to overthrowing the Government of the United Kingdom and sending the Hanoverians scampering back to their German homeland was remarkable enough. Then the disaster of Culloden and the brutalities that followed turned romance into tragedy.

The story did not however end there. The prince left the field of battle pursued by the curses of Lord Elcho – 'run then, you damned cowardly Italian' – and embarked on the five months that do him more credit than any other period in his disordered, disappointed and ultimately futile life. Hunted by the Government redcoats, living rough, always in danger, scratching his skin raw on account of lice, he maintained a resolution and cheerfulness which impressed his companions.

These were many and varied. The most famous among them was Flora MacDonald, who escorted him from the isle of Uist to Skye, with the prince disguised as her Irish maid, Betty Bourke, whom the factor's daughter at Kingsburgh thought 'a very odd, muckle ill-shapen up wife as ever I saw'. When the prince parted from Flora, he said, with the grace which in his good days he could always muster, 'I hope, madam, we shall meet in St James's where I will reward you for all you have done.' But it was the Tower of London, not St James's Palace, that awaited her. As for the prince, the last forty years of his life make a sorry story.

He died insignificantly in the little Palazzo Muti in Rome as a piper played in the courtyard below. That at least was suitable enough, for it is in words and music that Jacobitism survived. Songs such as 'Will ye no' come back again?' and 'Carry the lad that is born to be king, /

Over the sea to Skye' are laments for what is lost and can never return that can still bring tears even to a Whig or Campbell eye. It is easy to dismiss post-'45 Jacobitism as mere sentimentality, and easy also to show just how fragile, partial and uncertain was commitment to the cause even while it was a live one. Yet Jacobite sentiment has never quite died in Scotland; Culloden is a word that sounds painfully in the ear; the sense of something noble and romantic in the enterprise survives. It does so, not only because of the romance which attaches itself to lost causes, but because of the treatment of the Rising in song, poetry and story. Yet this itself could only have been produced by the operation of the narrative on the imagination. If the '45 had been as drab as the '15, there would have been few Jacobite songs and novels.

The greatest of the Jacobite song-writers was Lady Nairne. She was born Carolina Oliphant of Gask in 1766, twenty years after Culloden. So by the time she was grown up, the Rising was forty years distant and Britain was engaged in the great war against Napoleonic France. One might therefore think the last Jacobite campaign remote from her experience. So indeed it was, but she came from a Jacobite family. The Oliphant lairds of Gask had been out in both the '15 and the '45, and had suffered for their loyalty to the Jacobite cause. They were also connections of the Murrays of Atholl, and cousins of Lord George Murray, the prince's general. Carolina married another Murray cousin, Lord Nairne, whose estates had been confiscated and whose title was not indeed restored till 1824. His grandmother had seen her husband, son and four sons-in-law fight in the Jacobite army. All had suffered in fortune. So it is not surprising that, as an imaginative girl, Carolina should have responded to the idea of Jacobitism, or that her songs should be infused with both pride and regret.

In this she resembles Scott, almost her exact contemporary. Jacobitism represented a Scotland that might have been. It was attractive. It was near in time and yet remote – so firmly was the Union now established. The heart was Jacobite, the head Unionist. But it was impossible that Jacobitism could inspire such deep and discordant emotions among Englishmen, even those who, like Dr Johnson, retained an affection for the exiled Stuarts and who were old enough to have lived through the years when a Stuart restoration was within the bounds of political possibility. When that was no longer the case English Jacobitism withered completely. Scottish Jacobitism didn't, because Jacobitism represented an alternative Scotland as it didn't represent an alternative England.

Part Two

Prelude

SCHOOL HISTORIES OF Scotland used to stop in 1707 with the Treaty of Union, or in 1746 with the final defeat of the Jacobites. Some histories intended for adult readers did so also. It is easy to see why. As long as history dealt chiefly with war, politics, diplomacy and constitutional developments, there was no separable distinct Scottish history after these dates. There was only British history. Of course there was no such distinct English history either, but, simply because the Parliament of the United Kingdom seemed, and indeed was, the continuation of the Parliament of England, while the Parliament of Scotland had been dissolved, it was easy, natural, and not even mistaken, to regard the history of the United Kingdom after 1707 as merely the next stage in the history of England. That was certainly how English politicians of the eighteenth century saw it. Again, London remained the capital city, while Edinburgh lost its old importance.

Ecclesiastical history was indeed an exception to the rule that Scottish history was now subsumed in British. But even here the Treaty of Union seemed to have drawn a line. There would be no more attempts to force Anglicanism on the Scots, or Presbyterianism on the English. The questions which had agitated the seventeenth century were settled. It was of course possible to write a narrative history covering the disputes within the Church of Scotland, and the various secessions from the established Kirk, but these were, more and more, of limited or specialized interest.

Social, economic and cultural histories of Scotland remained possible; local histories abounded. Eventually, in the second half of the twentieth century, political histories of modern Scotland would be attempted.

None of this alters the fact that narrative history of the sort that deals with relations between states was British after 1707. Even the Jacobite Risings are properly to be seen as British civil wars.

The first part of this book has followed the traditional narrative pattern, tracing, if briefly, the relations between sovereign states, as Scotland and England remained even after 1603. I have tried to show how the unsatisfactory nature of the regal Union established in that year drove both Scots and English, unwillingly, to accept what appeared to be the necessity of a Parliamentary or incorporating union.

The second part of the book examines the consequences of that Union, and the experience of being British. It does so by dwelling on a number of significant figures and themes. Others might have been chosen instead. Those I have selected display a literary bias, for which however I feel no need to apologize. I have written about those aspects of the subject which most interested me.

Though there is no longer a clear narrative, the chapters are nevertheless so arranged as to tell a story, or rather several stories within one overarching story; read in order, they do, I trust, reveal something of the complexity of the emotions aroused by that triangle of forces represented by the words: English, Scottish, British.

I

Celticism

⸺ ⸙ ⸺

THE ENGLISH POET William Collins, whom Johnson described as a lover of 'fairies, genii, giants, and monsters', wrote an elegiac ode on James Thomson's death. One line read: 'In yonder grave a Druid lies.'

This was absurd. Thomson, that plump, comfortable Lowland Scot, who spent the last decade of his life in the pleasant rural retreat of Richmond, could scarcely have been less like a Druid; impossible to imagine him in an oak-grove conducting, as the Druids were then believed to have conducted, human sacrifices. But the Celts were becoming fashionable, and so Collins thought it appropriate to call the placid son of a Roxburghshire manse a Druid, or priest–bard of the pre-Roman Britons.

The word 'Celt' was itself recent. It was originally Greek, applied to tribes inhabiting the Balkans. The Romans took it over, naming the Gauls, either side of the Alps, Celts. In time the Celts or Gauls south of the mountains became Italians and called themselves Romans. Two of the greatest Latin poets, Catullus and Virgil, came from the Celtic north of Italy. Catullus is said to have brought into the Latin language two or three strange or foreign words, possibly Celtic in origin.

Then, in the later centuries of the Roman Empire, the Celts disappear; or rather the word disappears. The people of course remain, however changed by intermarriage. The word is not found in any of the languages now conventionally called Celtic: Welsh, Breton, Irish Gaelic, Scots Gaelic, Cornish, Manx. Their self-descriptive term is some variety of Gael or Gaul. The only people on record as having been in their own tongue Celtae were the Gauls of central France. So Caesar says anyway in his account of his Gallic Wars.

Then in 1703 a French abbot, Paul-Yves Pezron (1639–1706), wrote a book entitled *L'Antiquité de la Nation & de la Langue des Celtes*. An English version was produced three years later by David Jones, described in the *Dictionary of National Biography* as 'historical writer and translator'. His title was different: *The Antiquities of Nations; More particularly of the Celtae or Gauls, taken to be Originally the same People as our Ancient Britains*. So the Celts were introduced to England.

There had of course long been what we may agree now to call a Celtic strain in history, mythology and literature. The story of Arthur, popularized by the twelfth-century Welsh monk Geoffrey of Monmouth, given definitive shape by Malory in the fifteenth century, had been called since the thirteenth century the 'Matter of Britain'. Milton as a young man intended to make Arthur the subject of his long-imagined epic – before being diverted to Eden. But, though the historical Arthur, assuming he existed, may have been a Romanized Briton, and so, to us today, a Celt, nobody at the time when Jones published his translation of Pezron's book had ever thought of calling him that, just as nobody till then had thought of styling the inhabitants of pre-Roman Britain, north or south, Celts.

But the Celt suited the mood of the early eighteenth century. He caught on. Collins himself wrote another ode, 'On the Popular Superstitions of the Highlands of Scotland', of which indeed he knew next to nothing, but the idea of which had impressed him greatly:

> At ev'ry pause, before thy mind possest,
> Old RUNIC bards shall seem to rise around,
> With uncouth lyres, in many-coloured vest,
> Their matted hairs with boughs fantastic crown'd.

The polite Augustan literary world, weary of refinement, was acquiring a taste for the picturesque. Thomson himself, though no Runic bard, had pointed the way. It took various forms: an idealization of rural peace and felicity, faintly echoing Horace and Propertius; the strangeness of Gothick; admiration for the untamed and unspoiled nature of peoples who might be deemed 'natural', uncorrupted by urbanism or commerce, thus giving the poet opportunity to exercise any talent for the 'Sublime' that he might possess.

Thomas Gray (1716–71), though a Londoner (and an Etonian) who passed almost all his adult life in the easy comforts of a Cambridge college, was seized with a taste for the picturesque and the Sublime, exemplified in his poem *The Bard* and in his enthusiasm for Welsh and Norse literature.

Johnson found *The Bard* absurd, offering 'the puerilities of obsolete mythology'. 'I do not see', he wrote, 'that The Bard promotes any truth, moral or political.' But Johnson, though his authority was recognized, if often resented, was out of tune with changing taste. He might declare that 'the man who is tired of London is tired of life', and might have written, in imitation of Juvenal, a great urban satire, *London*; but his fellow-poets preferred the picturesque, writing either in pastoral nostalgic vein – is there a more characteristically Augustan adjective than 'sylvan'? – or striving, sometimes ridiculously, to attain the Sublime. Ironically perhaps, given Johnson's often expressed dislike of the Scots, the finest urban poetry since Pope was being written in Edinburgh, by young ill-fated Robert Fergusson:

> Near some Lamp-post, wi' dowy Face,
> Wi' heavy Ein, and sour Grimace,
> Stands she that Beauty lang had kend,
> Whoredom her Trade, and Vice her End.

Neither picturesque nor sublime, but simply good, Fergusson, the finest Scots poet between Dunbar and Burns, is immensely satisfying. But he died young, only twenty-four, in the mad-house, probably of alcoholism and suffering *Delirium tremens*; and his work was unknown in England, and too soon and for too long forgotten in Scotland, though not by Burns, who admired it and learned from it. Johnson too, one thinks, had he known Fergusson's verse, would have appreciated its combination of elegance and controlled vigour.

It was however a very different sort of Scot whose poetry captivated the age – though Johnson again was from the first a dissenter. This was James Macpherson, author of *Ossian*.

Macpherson was a Highlander and therefore a Gaelic-speaker, born in Kingussie in 1736, and educated at Marischal College, Aberdeen.

There he studied under Thomas Blackwell, author of *An Enquiry into the Life and Writings of Homer*. The nature of poetry in any age, Blackwell argued, was related to the social environment in which the poet lived; and the most sublime epic poetry, that of Homer, was the product of a society emerging from barbarism and advancing towards civilization. This argument chimed with that advanced by the Neapolitan philosopher Giovanni Battista Vico in his *Scienza Nuova* (1725), though it's unlikely that Blackwell had read that, and would be developed by the philosophic historians of the Scottish Enlightenment, notably Adam Ferguson in his *Essay on Civil Society*. It interested the young Macpherson, who had poetic ambitions and whose Gaelic heritage offered to his imagination a picture of just such a society as Blackwell described. At the age of twenty-two he published a long poem called *The Highlander*, which drew on Gaelic legends and attracted some attention.

The following year, on a visit to Moffat in Dumfriesshire, he met the poet and playwright John Home, author of the verse tragedy *Douglas*, which had had a great success on its first production in Edinburgh. 'Whaur's your Wullie Shakespeare noo?' cried one patriotic enthusiast, somewhat over-elated. The conversation turned to Gaelic poetry, of which Home, being a Lowlander, was ignorant. Macpherson said he was in possession of some original examples, and was persuaded to make translations. These impressed Home, who showed them first to his friend Hugh Blair, later Professor of Rhetoric and Belles-Lettres in Edinburgh, and then to other friends in London. All were admiring, excited and enthusiastic. Macpherson, naturally gratified, then suggested that these were but fragments of an epic, perhaps some 9,000 lines long. He had heard it, or bits of it, from an old man in Lochaber, but it would be desirable to find the manuscript. He was at once commissioned to do so.

Travelling with a cousin, the Gaelic poet, Ewan Macpherson, he made a tour of the Western Highlands and Islands. In Benbecula he was given some Gaelic manuscripts (which he never returned) by MacDonald of Clanranald. Elsewhere he collected ballads recited to him. Then he went back to Edinburgh and set to work, collating,

translating, adapting and inventing. In the autumn of 1760 he published the result of his labours: *Fingal*, an epic, created by Ossian, a
third-century bard, himself the son of Fingal, the Scottish counter-
part of the legendary Irish hero Finn.

The work was an immediate, an astonishing, success. It appealed to
that taste for the Sublime and beautiful, and was in keeping with the
cult of the Noble Savage, which Rousseau had made the starting-
point of *Le Contrat Social*. In short, it was just what the times required.
The poem was hailed, especially in Edinburgh, as the equal of Homer
and superior, being more 'natural', to Virgil. But its success was truly
international, and was to endure for at least half a century. Goethe
found Ossian comparable to Shakespeare. Napoleon delighted in
Cesarotti's Italian version and never travelled without it, finding solace
in Ossian even on his voyage to captivity on St Helena. He had the
imperial apartments in Paris and Rome decorated with huge murals
representing Ossianic scenes: in the Tuileries the bard himself could
be seen welcoming the ghosts of the emperor's soldiers as they passed
over to the Elysian Fields.

However, doubts as to the authenticity of the poem had been
expressed very soon after its first publication, especially in London.
The motive of some sceptics was political. Macpherson, seeking a
patron who would help raise him from poverty and insignificance, had
dedicated his book to the prime minister, the Earl of Bute, an introduction having been secured by John Home, Bute's private secretary.
Bute, a Scotsman, a Court favourite and inexperienced politician, was
unpopular, his preferment deeply resented by the Whig politicians
who had been displaced from the monopoly of office they had long
enjoyed, and to which they believed themselves entitled. Bute's ele-
vation had therefore provoked outbursts of hostility towards Scotland
and the Scots.

> Into our places, states and beds they creep;
> They've sense to get what we want sense to keep,

wrote Charles Churchill. His friend John Wilkes – rake, journalist,
politician and demagogue – expressed the most violent Scotophobia

in his newspaper, *The North Briton*. His language was so extreme that in Paris he was challenged to a duel by a young Scot, John Forbes, son of an Aberdeenshire Jacobite exile, and in Edinburgh apprentice boys burned his effigy. In reality Wilkes had no sincere animus against Scots; he was essentially an opportunist. Educated at Leiden University, he had been on friendly terms with the numerous Scotch students there; Boswell too was a friend and drinking companion. In attacking the Scots he was playing a populist card.

There were of course other, non-political, and more serious reasons for the doubts soon expressed about the authenticity of Macpherson's 'Ossian'. Johnson was a sceptic from the first: if the poems were authentic, let Macpherson produce the original manuscripts which he claimed to have translated, and let these be examined by some competent authority acquainted with the Gaelic (or Erse, as Johnson called it) language. Some Scots were sceptical too. David Hume arrived independently at the same opinion as Johnson. Though first impressed, he told Dr Blair that Macpherson must either produce the manuscripts as evidence or be condemned as an impostor.

Macpherson couldn't do this. Though he had drawn on Gaelic sources, and did possess some Gaelic manuscripts, these bore no resemblance to his poems. Indeed, when, after much blustering, he allowed Johnson's friend William Shaw to see his papers, Shaw reported that the manuscript shown him contained only lists of Irish genealogies, and an account of Montrose's wars, which had unfortunately taken place at least 1,300 years after Ossian was supposed to have composed *Fingal*. Macpherson's response was to abuse his critic. This manuscript is incidentally one of the minor mysteries of the story. It seems extraordinary that Macpherson should have produced it if it was as Shaw averred. One can only conclude that though Macpherson could speak some Gaelic, and understand the spoken language (though even here he may have had to rely on the interpreting skills of his cousin, the poet Ewan Macpherson), he couldn't read it. Nevertheless, unabashed by the criticism, he published a second long poem, *Temora, an Ancient Epic in Eight Books*. This was less successful; he had exhausted his vogue, and it was indeed the end of his literary career.

That career had served its purpose. He had secured the patronage and preferment he sought. He first obtained a post as secretary to the Governor of the Floridas, and was next appointed Minister Plenipotentiary of His Highness the Nabob of the Carnatic to the Court of St James's. This was worth £12,000 a year. He purchased a rotten borough in Cornwall (where there was no shortage of them) and took his seat in the Commons. He became active and influential in the affairs of the East India Company, and profited accordingly. He bought an estate in his native Banffshire, commissioned Robert Adam to build him a house there, and compelled the neighbouring lairds to acknowledge his bastard children as their social equals. When he died in 1796 he was buried, at his own expense, in Westminster Abbey: a fit conclusion to a successful life. Macpherson was, in short, an admirable, if unattractive, example of what J. M. Barrie was to call one of the 'more impressive sights in the world – a Scotsman on the make', in his case forcing his way into the British Establishment; but he was also a man who helped to awaken the interest of the British public in the Scottish Highlands and who contributed to the formation of the Idea of the Celt.

His epic's inauthenticity had eventually to be generally recognized. In 1805, Walter Scott, writing in the *Edinburgh Review*, admitted that the case against Macpherson was irrefutable. 'Nevertheless,' he added, 'our national vanity may be flattered by the fact that a remote and almost barbarous corner of Scotland produced a bard who gave a new tone to poetry throughout Europe.'

Yet even that wasn't the end of the story. Modern Gaelic scholars have found more that is authentic in Macpherson's Ossian than earlier critics allowed. They have identified some fifteen ballads that went to the making of the poem. Moreover, knowing far more than Johnson did about oral cultures, we find it less improbable than he supposed it to be that long passages of verse should be committed to memory, and so transmitted from generation to generation. Macpherson's difficulties arose in part from this: that he acquired some of his material in oral form, and then, instead of admitting that he had stitched this together with lines of his own, pretended to have taken the whole poem from ancient manuscripts. Doubtless if he had told the truth his work would have made a smaller sensation. For his contemporaries its charm lay partly at least in its alleged authenticity. Consequently Macpherson first received credit for a discovery he had not made, and was then denied recognition of his ingenuity and originality.

Nevertheless, though Macpherson's own reputation sank, his 'Ossian' survived. A hundred years later that very English poet Matthew Arnold – peculiarly English in his readiness to criticize whatever he found inadequate, misguided, ignorant and brutish in the contemporary culture of his own people – delivered a series of lectures at Oxford on 'The Study of Celtic Literature' – a task he undertook with an assurance that was not diminished on account of his ignorance of the languages by then styled Celtic. This did not matter for he found the Celtic strain as surely in works written in English as in those he could read only in translation. 'Its chord of penetrating passion and melancholy, again, its Titanism as we see it in Byron – what other European poetry possesses it like the English, and where do we get it from?' he asked; and answered:

> The Celts . . . The Celts are the prime authors of this vein of piercing regret and passion, this Titanism in poetry. A famous book, Macpherson's 'Ossian', carried in the last century this vein like a flood of lava through Europe . . . Make the part of what is forged, modern, tawdry, spurious, in the book, as large as you please . . . But there will still be left . . . a residue with the very soul of the Celtic genius in it. Choose any one of the better passages in Macpherson's 'Ossian' and you can see even at this time of day what an apparition of newness and power such a strain must have been to the eighteenth century:
>
> > I have seen the walls of Balclutha, but they were desolate . . . The fox looked out from the windows, the rank grass of the wall waved round her head. Raise the song of mourning, O bards, over the land of strangers. They have but fallen before us, for one day we must fall. Why dost thou build the hall, son of the winged days? Thou lookest from thy towers to-day; yet a few years, and the blast of the desert comes; it howls in thy empty court, and whistles round thy half-worn shield. Let the blast of the desert come! we shall be renowned in our day.

'All Europe', Arnold says, 'felt the power of that melancholy, but no nation of Europe so caught in its poetry the passionate penetrating accent of the Celtic genius, its strain of Titanism, as the English.'

To justify this assertion he quotes Byron (who was by his own account 'born half a Scot and bred a whole one'); and then finds 'this Celtic passion of revolt so warm-breathing, puissant and sincere' in the work of 'a yet greater poet . . . in the Satan of Milton':

> What though the field be lost?
> All is not lost; the unconquerable will,
> And study of revenge, immortal hate,
> And courage never to submit or yield,
> And what else is not to be overcome.

'There, surely,' Arnold suggests, 'speaks a genius to whose composition the Celtic genius was not wholly a stranger!'

Well, perhaps, though all this is merely on the level of assertion, scarcely demonstrated, even if we recall, as Arnold in these lectures does not, that early intention of Milton's to make the British (that is, Celtic) hero Arthur the subject of his long-pondered epic.

So the Celts, long ago defeated, nevertheless triumphed. By the twentieth century, the Scots, Irish and Welsh were all popularly established as Celtic nations, a conclusion which would have surprised and disgusted many nineteenth-century Lowland Scots, among them especially those scholars who had tried to establish that the first language of the Picts, about which we all remain ignorant, was Gothic, a primitive German. It might, a couple of centuries earlier, have disgusted William Dunbar himself; his contempt for his Gaelic-speaking poetic rivals, and for their language, was complete. Not so now: we are Celts, and the 'garb of old Gaul', the kilt, is our national dress. When a professional rugby union league comprising teams from Scotland, Ireland and Wales was formed, it was, inevitably, designated the Celtic League.

It is easy to see why even Lowland Scots have acquiesced in this Celtic identity. First, it is not a wholly false one. Whatever other ancestors we may have – and these will certainly be various – we are also descended from the people who inhabited Scotland before Romans, Saxons or Angles, and Normans came; and also of course from the people, whoever they were precisely, who lived here for several thousand years after the last Ice Age, before the Celts themselves arrived.

The second reason for our adoption of a Celtic identity is equally understandable. To be Celtic differentiates us, to our mind, from the English, the Saxons, the Sassenach – though, oddly enough, this last word, which is Gaelic, was for centuries applied by the inhabitants of the Scottish Highlands to the people of the Scottish Lowlands. The more homogeneous British society has become, the more life in one part of the kingdom has come to resemble, and in many respects be scarcely distinguishable from, life elsewhere, the more important and agreeable it is to mark out differences. So Scotland is Celtic and England Saxon, a conclusion which also pleases those Scots who would like to see the Treaty of Union repealed, and Scotland resume political independence. If we are not the same people, if there are real ethnic differences, then there is less reason for us to be yoked together in political Union.

Thirdly, it is gratifying to be a Celt. The Celts are thought to be more colourful, more interesting, more sensitive, more poetic, generally more gifted, than the stodgy Saxons. Celts are more eloquent, which is a matter of pride, even though, as Alistair Moffat remarks in his book *Arthur and the Lost Kingdoms*, their eloquence 'was a function of illiteracy. This involved the training of memory in a way that book-readers cannot now imagine. Important speech had to be formed in a manner that could be easily recollected. The devices of metre, rhyme, alliteration, symbolic lists were all harnessed to the construction of an enormous house of Celtic memory.' This is true, though the same could have been said of Anglo-Saxon (Old English) and of Old Norse. *Beowulf* and the Norse sagas were recited or chanted in halls many years before they were written down. Such superiority in eloquence as Celts may claim probably, if there is really such superiority, derives only from the fact that Gaelic societies, in Scotland, Wales and Ireland, remained generally illiterate longer than those in the English-speaking parts of these islands.

Fourthly, the history of the twentieth century dimmed the enthusiasm evident in the <u>Victorian</u> era for identification with Germany, for <u>Teutonism</u> as embraced by Thomas Carlyle, as well as by English historians such as Freeman and Stubbs, and by empire-builders like Cecil Rhodes. (The scholarships to Oxford University which Rhodes endowed were open to students from Germany and the USA as well as to students from countries within the British Empire – but to no other foreigners.) The two German wars changed things. The term 'the English-speaking Peoples' supplanted talk of the 'Anglo-Saxon race'. That would have to do, the English, unlike the Scots, not having an alternative Celtic identity to fall back on.

Or perhaps they do. There is a strange new development: the Angles, Saxons and Jutes are being called into question. Nobody of course denies the reality of the Heptarchy, or of the three later kingdoms of Northumbria, Mercia and Wessex. They existed and they were Anglo-Saxon kingdoms with an aristocracy that spoke the Teutonic tongue that used to be called Anglo-Saxon and is now more usually known as Old English, the language in which *The Anglo-Saxon Chronicle* was written. Clearly too Alfred and all these Ethelberts and Ethelreds, Edgars, Egberts and Edwards knew themselves to be Angles or Saxons. When in the eighth century the Northumbrian monk Bede wrote his *Ecclesiastical History of the English People*, he declared that the island of Britain was populated by four nations, and that five languages were spoken. The nations were the English, the British, the Irish and the Picts. By the Irish he meant the Scots; just who he thought the British were is less clear: the Welsh certainly, the people of Strathclyde and southern Scotland probably; and Britons living under Saxon rule possibly. Each group had its own language, and the fifth language was Latin, spoken and written by churchmen. Bede's own work was in Latin.

Later came the Danes who, after the Treaty of Wedmore made with the Saxon king Alfred in 878, were granted what we should now call sovereignty over all England north and east of the old Roman road, Watling Street; and this area was known as the Danelaw.

None of this is disputed. Old histories used to speak of the Britons being either killed or driven into Wales and what was then known as West Wales – that is, Cornwall. For centuries the English were happy to accept this, and to think of themselves as Saxons. By the seventeenth century the Saxons had come to be regarded as a good thing. Opponents of the Stuart kings traced back the inherited liberties of England to Saxon times, and spoke of Saxon resistance to the imposition of 'the Norman yoke' after 1066. Hereward the Wake, resisting the Normans from his stronghold in the Fens, was resurrected as an English hero, even folk-hero, and was made the subject of a novel by Charles Kingsley. The nineteenth-century English were for the most part happy and proud to be Saxons. That was certainly how they appeared to Scots venturing south. The geologist and journalist Hugh Miller, writing his *First Impressions of England* in 1847, remarked on the 'unthinking, unsuspicious, blue-eyed, fair-complexioned Saxons'. Pope Gregory the Great's quip about the boy-slaves he saw in the market in Rome, 'non Angli sed Angeli', featured in every school history-book, though in the imagination it might be subtly transformed: the English were both Anglian and angelic, God himself being a Protestant Englishman.

What is now being questioned is not of course the fact of a Saxon conquest of England. That would defeat the most determined revisionist, the evidence for such a conquest being incontrovertible; England is after all Angle-land. It is the scale of immigration that is being debated. Francis Pryor, trained as a prehistorian and therefore peculiarly inclined to put most credence in archaeological evidence, declares in his *Britain AD* that:

> it is probably fair to say that serious scholars who believe in large-scale Anglo-Saxon mass migration are now in a minority. Most people, myself included, accept that there was a certain amount of movement in and out of Britain . . . We might well discover one day that certain Anglo-Saxon cemeteries in, say, East Yorkshire, contain the bodies of immigrant populations. I do not believe, however, that such discoveries will invalidate the consensus that the changes attributed to the arrival of Anglo-Saxons were usually caused by people changing their minds, rather than their place of residence.

I suspect Pryor is exaggerating when he speaks of a consensus, this being in any case something rare among historians. But it is probably fair to say that few now believe in the mass expulsion of the Britons by invading Saxons, and it is certainly possible that the Saxons, for a couple of centuries anyway, stood in much the same relation to the Britons they found there as the Normans did to the Saxons after 1066.

This would mean that the English today are as much a Celtic people, or have as much Celtic blood in them, as the inhabitants of the Scottish Lowlands.

There are of course good reasons for rejecting the theory and adhering to the traditional view. The first is that this view is indeed traditional; it is what people have believed for centuries, and that is something which should not be discounted. Moreover the foundation of that belief rests in the centuries we speak of as post-Roman and Anglo-Saxon. The sixth-century British or Welsh monk Gildas had no doubts about the reality of the Saxon invasions and conquests; they are the theme of his book, *De Excidio et Conquestu Britanniae*. Nor, a couple of centuries later, did Bede, himself an Angle living in the Anglian kingdom of Northumbria. It's not unreasonable to suppose that Gildas and Bede knew what they were writing about.

A second reason for accepting that Anglo-Saxon immigration was on a considerable scale is linguistic. Anglo-Saxon or Old English supplanted the Celtic tongue over almost all that is now England. This is actually rather remarkable. Nothing comparable happened in France, Italy or Spain, countries which also experienced invasion by Gothic or Germanic peoples from beyond the old bounds of the Roman Empire. Gothic, Lombard and Frankish kingdoms were established, but the language of these old provinces of the Empire remained Latin-based (Latin itself having supplanted Celtic). Yet even those who deny that there was large-scale Teutonic immigration into England accept the reality of language change. To my mind this is evidence of settlement on a considerable scale. The incomers may not have displaced the natives, but they were sufficiently numerous to impose their language on them.

The history of Normandy offers an example to the contrary. In 911 that province was ceded to a Viking force, Northmen who became Normans. They were probably in origin Danes, speaking a variety of the Norse tongue. Yet the Normans who conquered England a century and a half later were French-speakers. Established in England as a ruling class, they continued to speak French (Norman-French) for at least 200 years. Yet, linguistically, the conquered defeated their conquerors. It was the English language that prevailed, though enriched by the admission of thousands of French words.

The point is that in both Normandy and England – and even more so in the Norman kingdom of Sicily – the Normans were so outnumbered by their subject people that it was the language of the subjects which survived. Apply this test to the Saxon settlements in post-Roman Britain, and it is reasonable to conclude that they were sufficiently numerous for their language to triumph.

Some, Pryor among them, question this too. He writes:

archaeologists of the 'culture-historical' school regard such things as culture, religion, and language as being fundamental to the identity of the groups they study. Being perceived as indicators of identity, they are traditionally viewed as unchanging. Language and religion, for example, were believed to remain fundamentally the same. If one or both of them changed, it was likely that a new group of people had taken over. But the real world is not as simple as that. In parts of Britain, such as southern Ireland or Cornwall, for example, the 'native' British languages were replaced by English in a very short time, mainly during the eighteenth and nineteenth centuries, while in northern Wales most Welsh-speakers are actually bilingual in Welsh and English. In these instances the people remained the same but the language changed. Religion too can change with great rapidity, as Henry VIII so clearly showed.

This is a fair point, the adoption of Christianity over the greater part of the Roman Empire making it still more forcibly. People can lose their language. The gradual and inexorable retreat of Gaelic in Scotland is a good example. This, like the replacement of Irish Gaelic and Cornish by English, has been accelerated in an age of literacy, print-culture, state-sponsored schooling for all and mass communications. In such circumstances a dominant language, that of the ruling group or the state, will suppress, even obliterate, the language of a subject minority. But in other circumstances, as the example of the Normans suggests, the ruling group must be sufficiently numerous if its language is to win the linguistic battle. One may therefore conclude that, since Anglo-Saxon prevailed, and became the tongue of almost all that is now England, and of the eastern Borders, the Lothians and the north-east of Scotland, it succeeded in doing so because its native speakers were there in sufficiently large numbers for their political dominance to be reflected in linguistic change.

Therefore it would seem probable that the old view remains largely correct. The English are of Anglo-Saxon stock, as are the Scots of the eastern Lowlands and eastern seaboard, though with a larger admixture of British–Celtic inheritance than used to be thought, that admixture being still larger in the case of Lowland Scots.

What does however have to be revised is the old idea of an absolute distinction between Celt and Saxon. The notion that Scotland, Wales and Ireland are 'Celtic' nations, racially different from Saxon England, is at best an agreeable fiction. There are Celtic (retaining that convenient word) and pre-Celtic elements in all four countries, and Anglo-Saxon ones too. Moreover, to these must be added the strains introduced by the immigrant groups that have come and settled here throughout history, arriving sometimes as armed invaders, even as conquerors (Vikings, Normans), sometimes as craftsmen and traders (Flemings, Germans, Italians), sometimes as refugees (French Huguenots, Jews, East African Asians), sometimes as economic migrants (Lithuanians, West Indians, Africans, Pakistanis, Bangladeshis, Indians) – all together making for that mixture we call, having no other word, the British.

Simon James, in *The Atlantic Celts: Ancient People or Modern Invention?*, concludes that the modern sense – invention or reinvention – of a Celtic identity is primarily a means of establishing a difference from the English. It is a form of propagandist history. This certainly fits comfortably with eighteenth-century Scottish enthusiasm for Macpherson's 'Ossian'. The Union with England being, after the final defeat of Jacobitism, firmly established, even those Scots who welcomed the new political stability and the opportunities given for economic expansion feared the loss of a sense of self, and were alert to the danger of being absorbed into what might be essentially an English state. Becoming Celts was a way of remaining distinct while simultaneously belonging to the greater whole.

The argument will continue, partly because there is no way in which it can be brought to a sure conclusion. Readers may, for instance, have spotted a discrepancy in the historical examples I have offered; it relates to the history of Gaul, where, as I said, the language, despite barbarian invasions and the establishment of Frankish and Burgundian kingdoms, remains 'Latin-based'. So indeed it does. Modern French is correctly described as a Romance language. But of course the Gauls whom Caesar subdued were not Latin-speakers. Their language, or languages, were some form of Celtic. It took several centuries of incorporation in the Empire for Latin to establish itself there, and for the Celtic tongues all but to disappear, except from Brittany, which is a special and controversial case. Yet nobody pretends that this was the consequence of large-scale immigration from Rome or Italy. The Gauls, or at least the Gallic elite, chose to become Romans; they did so in response, not only to Roman rule, but to the influence of what, one assumes, they recognized as a superior culture – certainly a literate one. The Gauls themselves did not disappear when they became Romanized. This is recognized today. The French speak happily of 'our ancestors, the Gauls' (among them the only people known to have called themselves 'Celts' in their own tongue); the comic-book hero Astérix, defying the Romans, is a popular expression of France's Gallic–Celtic heritage, the British Arthur returning in burlesque form; and one of the emblems of France, worn on the jerseys of the national football and rugby teams, is 'le coq Gaulois'. Moreover 'esprit gaulois' means broad Gallic humour and 'contes gaulois' are spicy or risqué stories.

This French history certainly suggests that languages may change while the people remain the same, adopting the tongue and manners of their conquerors. So that may have happened in England with respect to the Anglo-Saxons and the native population of Britons. Of course the two cases are not identical. The Romans were literate as the conquered Gauls were not; in post-Roman Britain the position was reversed. There it was the incomers who were illiterate, while the upper class of Romanized Britons could read and write. There were other ways too in which Roman civilization might have been deemed higher than that of the conquered Gauls, whereas, again in Britain, the opposite was the case. So if a comparatively small number of Anglo-Saxon invaders imposed their language, as well as their rule, on the people they subdued, this would have been a rare example of a less developed culture triumphing over a more developed one – rare but not impossible.

That possibility was explored by Alfred Duggan, one of the best historical novelists of the twentieth century. His book, *The Conscience of the King*, tells in the first person the story of Cedric, founder of the royal line of Wessex and ancestor of Alfred the Great. Duggan's Cedric is actually a Romano-Briton who as a result of family quarrels and a threat to his life flees the country, attaches himself to a Saxon war-band, becomes its leader, and eventually establishes himself as a king in part of what would be Wessex (the land of the West Saxons). Duggan makes this credible. There is one very illuminating moment – illuminating because it catches a moment of cultural transition. Just before his flight, the narrator is sitting in the garden of his family villa reading. The author is, as I recall, Ovid, poet of urban sophistication. Then Cedric remarks, in a throwaway line, that he thinks this was the last time he ever read a book: the civilized Romano-Briton is about to become a barbarian Saxon. It is very convincing; and there may indeed have been such cases.

It is therefore possible, and quite reasonable to suppose, that the greater part of the population of Anglo-Saxon England remained British – therefore, if you like, Celtic. If so, the English may think themselves, should they choose, every bit as Celtic as the French, and not much less Celtic than the Scots, Irish and Welsh – always assuming that there is reason to apply the word 'Celtic' to them.

Which brings us back to Arthur and the epic that Milton did not write.

>What remains?
>This: that when Rome fell, like a writhen oak
>That age had sapped and cankered at the root,
>Resistant, from her topmost bough there broke
>The miracle of one unwithering shoot
>Which was the spirit of Britain – that certain men,
>Uncouth, untutored, of our island brood
>Loved freedom better than their lives; and when
>The tempest crashed about them, rose and stood
>And charged into the storm's black heart . . .

These lines, pseudo-Miltonic in places, pseudo-Tennysonian elsewhere, come from a long poem, *The Island*, published in 1944. The author was Francis Brett Young, better known as a popular novelist. Young was very English, a novelist of the tranquil and rural midlands, especially Worcestershire; he was a friend of the prime minister Stanley Baldwin (Kipling's cousin). Baldwin enjoyed his novels and recommended them publicly. *The Island* is very much a product of the Hitler war, an outpouring of proud patriotism. The lines I have quoted, old-fashioned in style as they are, rise to a height that other sections of the poem seldom attain; the hero, representative of the 'spirit of Britain', is of course Arthur, the Once and Future King, and, whoever or whatever Arthur may have been, one thing is certain: he was not English.

The significance is obvious, the Churchillian echoes resonant. Of Arthur's men Young writes, 'they were so few'. So they are linked both to the Battle of Britain pilots and to Henry V's 'happy few' at Agincourt. Arthur now lies, surrounded by his knights in a dream-like sleep, awaiting the call to rise and return to save Britain in peril. Or perhaps he has already done so.

This Arthur is a figure of legend, and most of the Arthurian cycle is the creation of poets and romancers. Yet this creation itself arises, we believe, from folk-memories.

More than 2,000 places in Britain claim some association with Arthur. They range from Cornwall to the Highland Line in Scotland. Many of these associations are doubtless quite recent, invented or discovered in response to the popularity of the legend. But there is a sub-stratum of fact.

The fullest literary evidence of Arthur's existence is offered by Nennius, a Welshman, who wrote his *History of the Britons* in Latin in the early ninth century, which is admittedly some 300 years after Arthur's presumed or probable dates. But Nennius is convincing because he is so matter of fact. More and more Saxons, he says, had been settling in Britain and their kings controlled more of the country. 'It was during this period that the war-leader Arthur, together with the kings of Britain, was fighting against them.' He then lists twelve battles in which Arthur was victorious. Describing the eighth of these, he emphasizes that Arthur was a Christian, unlike the enemy: 'He bore the image of the Holy Virgin Mary on his shoulders: on that day the pagans turned in flight, and were slaughtered in great numbers, through the Grace of our Lord Jesus Christ and his Holy Mother, the Virgin Mary.' The last of these battles is Mount Badon, which had been mentioned 200 years earlier by the Welsh monk Gildas (born in Strathclyde). Gildas however does not mention Arthur as even one of the commanders. According to a later Welsh historian, Gerald, this omission was because Arthur had killed Gildas's brother: 'when he heard of his brother's death, or so the Britons say, he threw into the sea a number of outstanding books he had written about Arthur's achievements'.

But Arthur is named in a poem almost contemporary with him and Gildas. It is called *The Gododdin*, which was the name of a tribe whom the Romans had called the Votadini, and who lived in south-east Scotland. It is believed to have been composed in Dun Eidyn (Edinburgh) by a bard Aneirin, around the year 600. One stanza is written in praise of a warrior called Gwawrddur. We are told of his mighty deeds and of how 'he would feed black ravens on the wall / of a fortress; though he were not Arthur / Among the strong ones in battle / In the van, an alder-palisade was Gwawrddur'. The suggestion is clear: Gwawrddur was a great warrior, but less than Arthur.

Some three centuries after Nennius, William of Malmesbury, monk and librarian at the Abbey from which he takes his name, has two stories about Arthur, whom he calls 'a man more worthy to be extolled in true histories than to be dreamed of in fallacious fables'. William may have drawn from the tenth-century *Annals of Wales*, where the story is told of 'the battle in the west in which the famous Arthur king of the British and his betrayer Mordred fell by wounds inflicted by each other'. Whether he did or not, these annals were known to Geoffrey of Monmouth, author of the *History of the Kings of Britain*, the highly imaginative work from which the Arthurian legend takes off, to be elaborated in verse romances made in France and Britain, until it received what was for so long its definitive form in Malory's *Morte d'Arthur* – the Matter of Britain.

Most of the sources are Welsh, and most of the sites traditionally associated with Arthur are in the south-west of England. It was, for instance, at Glastonbury, at Easter 1278, that, according to the Abbey's historian, Adam of Domerham, Edward I 'at twilight, had the tomb of the famous King Arthur opened. There, in two caskets, with their images and arms depicted on them, were found separately the bones of the said king, of wondrous size, and those of Queen Guinevere, of matchless beauty.'

Edward was the first king of England since 1066 to have been given a Saxon, rather than Norman, name; he was also the conqueror of Wales and would-be conqueror of Scotland, the king who tried to make one kingdom of the island of Britain. His enthusiasm for Arthur is understandable; he presented himself as heir to the three kingdoms and three peoples: England, Wales, Scotland: the Normans, English and British.

Arthur is the British myth that survives. The land may be invaded and conquered, the people dispersed or subdued. But Arthur remains. Whether the historical Arthur hailed from Wales, Cornwall, Somerset, Cumbria or the Scottish Borders – the case for all these places of origin having been made – scarcely matters. That the Arthurian cycle was elaborated far beyond any historical reality is irrelevant. Arthur is Britain. Moreover, the Arthur of the imagination, the Arthur of Camelot and the Round Table and the Grail legends, never utterly parts company from the dark original, from the true

Matter of Britain when 'certain men / Uncouth, untutored, of our island brood / Loved freedom better than their lives'.

Why? Alistair Moffat, who argues in *Arthur and the Lost Kingdoms* for an Arthur originating in the Scottish Borders, insists that 'the answer to this conundrum is a simple one. We are not Saxons, for the most part, or Vikings either and Normans hardly at all. We are the children of a defeated Celtic culture. And we live a sort of myth history, something from that ancient time between remembering and forgetting . . .'

If there is anything in this, then differences between Scots and English are less than is supposed, and of more recent formation. Arthur is our enduring myth, and Ossian, even in Macpherson's concoction, appealed because the poem struck chords in the folk memory.

2

Boswell and Johnson

THE GREAT MEN of the Scottish Enlightenment – Hume, Smith, Ferguson, Reid, for example – were intellectuals in the true sense of the word. They employed the powers of the mind to examine the physical world and human society, the nature of experience, the basis of knowledge and belief. They did so with such vigour and intelligence that the world is even now in their debt, and their influence is still to be detected in our thoughts and acts.

James Boswell was an intellectual of a different and more modern sort. He delighted in ideas, but rarely thought them through. He played with them and flitted from one enthusiasm to another. Whereas such as Hume and Smith commanded the respect even of those who disagreed with them, Boswell in life and death more often invited contempt. Macaulay went so far as to declare: 'if he had not been such a great fool, he would never have been a great writer', a characteristically antithetical judgement. Knowing more than Macaulay could of Boswell's writings – his *Journals* and private papers were not published till the twentieth century – we may conclude that the historian was carried away by his love of dramatic contrast. He saw the greatness of Boswell's *Life of Johnson* – 'Eclipse first and the rest nowhere', as he said – and he saw the foolishness of Boswell; and yoked them memorably together. But there was more to Boswell than he allowed.

Boswell was born in 1740 into an Ayrshire landed family. He could trace his descent back to one of the early Stewart kings, and thence to Robert the Bruce, and was proud of this – inordinately proud indeed, for his case was not so uncommon. His father, like many Lowland lairds, practised the Law and became a Senator of the

College of Justice, with the honorary title of Lord Auchinleck, this being the family estate. A stern Presbyterian and Whig – 'a Roman father' in his son's opinion – he found the young James an embarrassment and a sore trial.

He could scarcely be blamed or reproached. The young man had an extraordinary appetite for life, for all possible varieties of experience, and no sense of direction. He suffered from melancholia, which we would now call depression, and hypochondria, but he was also high-spirited and intensely sociable. He was a proudly patriotic Scot, who was irked by Scottish life. He felt now superior, now inferior, in his Scottish nationality. Edinburgh constrained him; London delighted him. It presented him with opportunity and, more importantly, freedom from responsibility. He was, or felt himself to be, more fully himself in London than in Edinburgh. His genius was liberated in the metropolis.

His nature was paradoxical. Byron's judgement on Burns might, in part, be applied to him (and indeed to Byron himself): 'tenderness, roughness, – delicacy, coarseness, – sentiment, sensuality – soaring and grovelling, dirt and deity – all mixed up in that one compound of inspired clay'. Boswell was a loving husband who was continually unfaithful, an idealist who wallowed in the gutter. He deeply resented his father's control, rebelling against it; yet adopted a succession of alternative fathers to whose judgement he deferred, and to whom he eagerly enslaved himself. Lord Auchinleck viewed his son's carrying-on with contempt: 'Jamie's gaen clean gyte. He's done wi' Paoli [the Corsican nationalist leader] and whase tail dae you think he has pinned himself to now, man? A dominie, an auld dominie, wha keepit a schule and ca'ed it an academy.'

The 'auld', and failed, 'dominie' was Samuel Johnson, thirty-one years older than young Boswell. Johnson was not to everyone's taste, a rough rude bear of a man – though in truth his manners were no more coarse than those of some of Lord Auchinleck's colleagues on the Scottish bench. The effeminate Horace Walpole, who had never known want or hardship, being well provided with government sinecures thanks to his father, the prime minister Sir Robert, found him 'an odious and mean character . . . His manners were sordid, super-cilious and brutal . . . arrogant, self-sufficient, and overbearing by nature'. Johnson was indeed an intellectual bully, impatient of oppo-sition, fearsome and crushing in argument. But Boswell was deter-mined to meet him. He was famous, and Boswell collected celebrities. There was more to it than that, however. At home in Scotland he had read Johnson's essays in *The Rambler* 'with delight and instruction, and had the highest reverence for their author, which had grown up in my fancy into a kind of mysterious veneration'. He was a disciple in search of a master.

They first met in 1763 when Johnson was fifty-four and Boswell twenty-three. For Johnson the grim years of struggle and poverty, of the 'night-walks' with the talented unstable poet Richard Savage, of hack-journalism and debt, were now behind him. He had completed his great work, *The Dictionary of the English Language*. The previous year he had been granted a state pension of £300 *per annum* in recog-nition of his achievement as lexicographer, poet, man of letters. His odd unhappy marriage had been ended by his wife's death.

Boswell was nervous. Scots were unpopular in London. The young king, George III, had made his tutor and 'dearest friend' the Earl of Bute prime minister, to the fury, as we have seen, of the Whigs, deprived of what they considered their prescriptive right to the monopoly of office. Scotsmen accordingly thronged London hoping for jobs and positions from their compatriot – the first Scot to have headed the Government of the United Kingdom. It was less than twenty years since the Jacobite Rising. Scots were still tainted with the mark of rebellion. Englishmen regarded Scotland as a poor country, though in reality it was becoming rich faster than England, and so Scots in London suffered the fate that is common to immigrant groups; they were both resented and envied.

Johnson was known to share this prejudice. He had had too many Scots rivals in his Grub Street days. Expression of this dislike might now embarrass him, for he owed his pension to Bute's regard. But he still disliked the clannishness of the Scots, their eagerness to boost one another, which he compared unfavourably with the behaviour of the

Irish who were, he joked, an honest people since they always spoke ill of each other. Told that Scotland was a fine country with many 'noble prospects', he snapped, 'the noblest prospect which a Scotchman ever sees is the high road that leads him to England'.

The meeting in Tom Davies's bookshop in Russell Street, off Covent Garden, began badly for Boswell. Introduced to the Great Man as 'a gentleman from Scotland', he sought for a palliative, and found a lame excuse: 'I do indeed come from Scotland, but I cannot help it.' 'That, sir, is what a very great number of your countrymen cannot help.' Despite this awkward beginning, the record of which we owe, characteristically, to Boswell himself, the acquaintance soon flourished. A month later, when Boswell called for a second time on Johnson in his lodgings in Inner Temple Lane, he was told, 'Come to me as often as you can, I shall be glad to see you.' It was not long before Boswell could boast, 'I am now on a very good footing with Mr Johnson.'

The fact was that Boswell, for all his faults and foolishness, had charm, that least definable but most disarming of qualities. Moreover Johnson liked young people and enjoyed their company because 'in the first place I don't like to think of myself as growing old. In the next place, young acquaintances must last longer.'

There was yet another basis for the friendship that was developing. They were more alike than might have been supposed. Both were neurotic, unstable, depressive. Johnson hated to be alone. He depended much on agreeable company to alleviate boredom and lift the 'black dog' from his shoulders. Boswell provided this. In exchange Johnson gave him good advice, offered acceptable criticism and boosted his self-esteem, more fragile than casual acquaintances exposed to his boasting might have guessed. Johnson's criticism was acceptable because Boswell felt assured of the great man's affection. He was a father with whom he could be at ease.

Though one thinks, naturally enough, of Johnson and Boswell as a pair, inseparable as Holmes and Watson, and so may imagine that they were constantly in each other's company, in fact in the twenty-one years between that first meeting and Johnson's death, there were several in which they maintained contact only by letters; while for the greater part of every year Boswell's work as an advocate in the Scottish courts confined him to Edinburgh, and he could spare only a few weeks for a London jaunt. Their tour of the north of Scotland and the Western Isles, lasting from 14 August to 22 November 1773, was by far the longest time they spent uninterruptedly together, and in which Boswell had Johnson under daily observation. For him it was a special treat, if at times an anxious one. On the one hand he delighted in showing his great friend off to his fellow-Scots, and was conscious that this raised his own consequence. On the other he was anxious lest Johnson make a bad impression, as he was quite capable of doing. So, for example,

> Mr Keith breakfasted with us. Dr Johnson expatiated rather too strongly upon the benefits derived to Scotland from the Union, and the bad state of our people before it. I am entertained with his copious exaggeration upon that subject; but I am uneasy when people are by, who do not know him as well as I do, and may be apt to think him narrow-minded. I therefore diverted the subject.

Likewise, in displaying his native land to Johnson, he experienced the same mixture of pride and anxiety, lest he think ill of what he saw.

Johnson loved travelling, but for much of his life had been unable to afford to do so – unlike Boswell, who had already visited the Netherlands, France, Corsica, Switzerland and Italy. Apart from a couple of short visits to France (after the Highland jaunt) Johnson's Scottish tour was his only considerable expedition, and by far the most demanding he ever undertook. It carried him for the first time in his life north of the English midlands where he had been born and which he frequently returned to.

Why the Hebrides? Johnson opens his account of their journey with the bald statement: 'I had desired to visit the Hebrides, or Western Isles of Scotland, so long that I can scarcely remember how the wish was originally excited.' Boswell is more specific. He tells us that they had first talked of making such a journey some time as far back as the year of their first meeting. Johnson had told him then how his bookseller father 'had put Martin's Account in his hands when he was very young, and that he was much pleased by it'. That book with the title *A Description of the Western Isles of Scotland*, by M. Martin, Gent., was first published in 1703. Few Englishmen, and few Lowland Scots, had followed Martin, and Boswell remarks that Martin's work 'had impressed us with a notion that we might there contemplate a system of life almost totally different from what we had been accustomed to see; and to find simplicity and wildness, and all the circumstance of remote time and place, so near to our native island, was an object within the reach of reasonable curiosity'.

There are two points of interest here. First, Boswell assumes – and assumes that this will not surprise the reader – that he and Johnson will approach this 'system of life', and respond to it, in the same way. It will be as 'totally different' from the experience of the Lowland Scot as of the Englishman. The Hebrides are undeniably part of the old kingdom of Scotland, and thus in a sense belong to Boswell as they do not to Johnson; nevertheless they stand apart from 'our native island' – that is, the island shared by Johnson and Boswell. The 'reasonable curiosity' of which he writes is common to both Scot and Englishman. Boswell expects to find the Hebrides as foreign as Johnson undoubtedly will. He has more in common with his travelling companion than with those whom they will meet – and not just because the two are friends.

Second, there is this matter of 'simplicity and wildness'. This might be thought more likely to appeal to Boswell, the proto-Romantic, admirer of Rousseau, than to Johnson, who believed that 'the full tide of existence was to be found at Charing Cross' and thought that the man who was tired of London was tired of life. Johnson, resolutely, even severely, Classical, despised Rousseau, and thought the cult of the Noble Savage absurd and contemptible. Nevertheless he felt the attraction of venturing beyond the pale of civilization as he understood it. The Highlands and Western Isles were *terra incognita* to almost all Englishmen and, as Johnson realized, to Lowland Scots also. 'To the southern inhabitants of Scotland', he wrote, 'the state of the mountains of this island is equally known with that of Borneo and Sumatra.' They were remote. They were wild. Travelling was at best uncomfortable, would often be arduous. It was an adventure and one which

Johnson, the old Grub Street hand, knew might make the subject of a profitable book.

He was then going as a reporter. The inhabitants were, in their mode of life, their social organization and their language, practically foreigners. How strange to find so different a society within King George's dominions! It was certainly worthy of investigation. Moreover, it was not yet thirty years since the Jacobite army, drawing its most conspicuous elements from Gaelic-speaking Scotland, had invaded England and thrown London into panic and confusion. Johnson could remember this well, and his own sympathies, like those of his dead friend Savage, inclined him to feel at least a sentimental attachment to the Stuarts. He was a Tory of the most old-fashioned sort, and John Buchan in *Midwinter* imagines him, not improbably, as being at one moment on the point of committing himself to the prince's cause.

So it was of peculiar interest to him that for part of their journey they should follow the route which the prince had taken after Culloden, and it was more than interesting, it was moving, to meet on Skye Flora MacDonald, who had played so notable a part in enabling Charles to escape his pursuers. She had, Johnson writes, 'a name that will be mentioned in history, and, if courage and fidelity be virtues, mentioned with honour'. For Boswell, 'to see Dr Samuel Johnson, the great champion of the English Tories, salute Miss Flora MacDonald in the isle of Sky [*sic*] was a striking sight; for, though somewhat congenial in their notions, it was very improbable they should meet here'. This was indeed a coup on which Boswell might congratulate himself. To cap it all, Johnson slept in the very bed which the prince had occupied, though, he told Boswell, 'I have had no ambitious thoughts in it.'

Johnson had still another motive for undertaking the journey. He had, as already remarked, been one of the most sceptical concerning the authenticity of Macpherson's 'Ossian'. Indeed he had been so outspoken that Macpherson had threatened him with violence. 'The poems of Ossian', Johnson roundly declared, 'never existed in any other form than that which we have seen.' He found Scottish credulity with regard to 'Ossian' understandable, and risible. 'A Scotchman must be a very sturdy moralist who does not love Scotland better than truth.' But it was pointless for Lowland Scots to argue for the poem's authenticity; they had no means of knowing: 'for of the past and present state of the whole Earse nation, the Lowlanders are at least as ignorant as ourselves'. Johnson now hoped, by questioning people in the Highlands and Hebrides, to settle the matter once and for all. He did so to his own abundant satisfaction. 'The Earse never was a written language; there is not in the world an Earse manuscript.'

Johnson had travelled north in a spirit of enquiry, however fixed many of his opinions were. No Romantic to dilate over Noble Savages, he was nevertheless a conservative, with a reverence for whatever was long established and settled. He was therefore disturbed by what he learned on his travels. That 'system of life almost totally different from what we had been accustomed to see' was being subjected to rapid and disruptive change. The pacification of the Highlands had seen the clan chiefs deprived of their hereditary jurisdiction, and therefore of their patriarchal role. So Johnson remarked:

> The chiefs, divested of their prerogatives, necessarily turned their thoughts to the improvement of their revenues, and expect more rent, as they have less homage. The tenant, who is far from perceiving that his condition is made better in the same proportion, as that of his landlord is made worse, does not immediately see why his industry is to be taxed more heavily than before. He refuses to pay the demand, and is ejected; the ground is then let to a stranger, who perhaps brings a larger stock, but who, taking the land at its full value, treats with the Laird upon equal terms, and considers him not as a Chief, but as a trafficker in land. Thus the estate perhaps is improved, but the clan is broken.

In short, the Highlands and Islands had begun to move from an economic system which was regulated by a sense of mutual obligation to one in which the relation between landlord and tenant was expressed in financial terms. Modernization substituted what Carlyle was to call the cash nexus for ties of service, loyalty and protection. Johnson, with only a few weeks in the Highlands, grasped what was happening. He regretted it; but one may note that in the first sentence of the paragraph quoted he recognized that it was necessity which led the chiefs to turn their thoughts 'to the improvement of their revenues'.

It was not surprising that he should have grasped the situation so quickly. The same thing was happening, had been happening over a longer period, in England and Lowland Scotland, nowhere more intensively than in his native midlands. There the Enclosure movement was proceeding apace, and the peasantry being transformed into day-labourers who owned nothing, or driven from the land into the swelling cities. His friend Goldsmith had described, and deplored, the consequences in his poem *The Deserted Village*:

> Ill fares the Land, to hasting Ills a Prey,
> Where Wealth accumulates, and Men decay.

The famous couplet might be economically illiterate in the eyes of disciples of Adam Smith, but it was fair comment on what was being experienced in the Highlands.

Though the Clearances, which have left such a bitter folk-memory in the Highlands and Western Isles, belong properly to the next generation, emigration, encouraged or voluntary, was already under way. Boswell recorded 'a dance which, I suppose, the emigration from Sky has occasioned. They call it "America".' He noted that:

> last year when a ship sailed from Portree for America, the people on shore were almost distracted when they saw their relations go off; they lay on the ground, tumbled, and tore the grass with their teeth. This year there was not a tear shed. The people on shore seemed to think they would soon follow. This indifference is a mortal sign for the country.

Flora MacDonald and her husband Allan MacDonald of Kingsburgh would themselves leave for the American colonies within a few months of playing host to Johnson and Boswell. Their stay would be short and unhappy, for Allan, like many once Jacobite Scots, took the Loyalist side in the War of American Independence, and was driven off his land when that independence was secured.

Johnson's considered judgement on the application of Government policy and market economics to the Highlands was severe:

To hinder insurrection, by driving away the people, and to govern peaceably, by having no subjects, is an expedient that argues no great profundity of politicks. To soften the obdurate, to convince the mistaken, to mollify the resentful, are worthy of a statesman, but it affords a legislator little self-applause to consider that where there was formerly an insurrection, there is now a wilderness.

In writing that paragraph, so expressive of the bitterness with which many Scots have come to view the degradation of the Highlands as a result of the failure of the '45, Johnson certainly had in mind the epigram which Tacitus put in the mouth of the Caledonian prince Calgacus, directed at the Romans: 'they make a desert, and call it peace'. Scots critical of the policies of the Hanoverian Government, and of the expulsion of the people to make way for sheep-runs, and then the deer-forests that made the Highlands a playground for the rich, absentee landlords, will be surprised only to find these sentiments expressed by an English High Tory.

Not unexpectedly Johnson had been critical of much that he met with in the course of his journey north. In St Andrews, for instance, he observed that 'the kindness of the professors did not contribute to abate the uneasy remembrance of a university declining, a college alienated, and a church profaned and hastening to the ground'. The visit there provoked the thought that 'it is surely not without just reproach, that a nation, of which the commerce is hourly extending, and the wealth encreasing, denies any participation of its prosperity to its literary societies; and while its merchants or its nobles are raising palaces, suffers its universities to moulder into dust'.

This was a decidedly partial judgement, for St Andrews was exceptional, the only one of Scotland's five universities to be in such a condition. Yet Johnson was critical of the standard of university education in general.

The students, for the most part, go thither boys, and depart before they are men; they carry with them little fundamental knowledge, and therefore the superstructure cannot be lofty. The grammar schools are not well supplied, for the character of a school-master being there less honourable than in England, is seldom accepted by men who are capable to adorn it, and where the school has been deficient, the college can effect little.

This last sentiment was perhaps less appropriate to his time than to ours. He continued:

Men bred in the universities of Scotland cannot be expected to be often decorated with the splendours of ornamental erudition, but they obtain a mediocrity of knowledge, between learning and ignorance, not inadequate to the purposes of common life, which is, I believe, very widely diffused among them, and which countenanced in general by a national combination so invidious, that their friends cannot defend it, and actuated in particulars by a spirit of enterprise, so vigorous, that their enemies are constrained to praise it, enables them to find, or to make their way to employment, riches, and distinction.

At first sight this long sentence, obscure at certain points – what is meant, for instance, by the phrase 'a national combination so invidious'? – seems to fly in the face of the common opinion that the Scottish universities were then flourishing, while Oxford and Cambridge languished in sluggish indolence, Gibbon describing his fourteen months at Oxford as 'the most idle and unprofitable of my life'. Historians support that common opinion. Linda Colley writes: 'ambitious Scots also benefited from having more and better universities as training grounds. In the century after 1750, for example, Oxford and Cambridge produced only 500 medical doctors. Scotland educated 10,000.'

Yet the two positions, Johnson's and common opinion's, are not irreconcilable. They were arguing from different premises, from different views of the proper function of a university. Colley's use of the word 'training-grounds' is significant. For Johnson, the university was properly devoted to an ideal of pure scholarship – 'the splendours of ornamental erudition' that had no necessary practical application. The Scottish universities were geared to producing active and broadly educated citizens. George Jardine, who began teaching logic at Glasgow University the year after Boswell and Johnson's Tour, expressed its aims in his *Outlines of Philosophical Education, illustrated by the Method of teaching the Logic Class at the University of Glasgow*. The aim was to develop in the students a moral sense and the faculty of independent judgement; they would have been educated in history, philosophy, literature and science, so that 'all the faculties of the mind are exerted, and powers unused before are awakened into life and activity'. Scottish university education produced scholars, certainly, but it was in its aims eminently social: the young mind was to be 'awakened into life and activity'. The generalist course of study fitted men for careers outside the university. Even Johnson recognized that men bred in these universities were equipped to 'make their way to employment, riches, and distinction'.

Without abating his ingrained sense of English superiority, he observed, with some satisfaction, that 'the conversation of the Scots grows every day less unpleasing to the English. Their peculiarities wear fast away; their dialect is likely to become in half a century provincial and rustick, even to themselves. The great, the learned, the ambitious and the vain, all cultivate the English phrase, and the English pronounciation.'

There were exceptions, including some of the Senators of the College of Justice, notably Lord Braxfield, but the observation was generally just. David Hume himself spent much effort and 'took pains in the Study of the English Language', and was careful to eradicate Scotticisms from his prose, though, he joked, 'as to my Tongue, I regard it as totally desperate and irreclaimable'. The Select Society in Edinburgh published a set of guidelines to correct what it described as Scots' 'imperfect knowledge of the English tongue'. Acknowledging that many educated Scots could write it 'with some tolerable purity', they added that not enough attention was paid to speech, mastering which was 'more important and more universally useful' than writing correctly. This may seem poor-spirited and even contemptible to Scots cultural nationalists today, but of course the same, or a comparable, determination to rid oneself of provincial habits of speech and aspire to a metropolitan correctness was evident even then in other European countries, France certainly, and has been common practice since.

Those who bristle at Johnson's use of the word 'dialect' might do well to reflect that Burns himself, on the title-page of the Kilmarnock edition of his works, announced them as 'Poems: Chiefly in the Scottish dialect'. The prose of his letters is for the most part in vigorous and 'correct' English, which he had thoroughly mastered.

It is fair to add however that few in London thought that Johnson's own spoken English was without blemish. Boswell himself remarks on his hero's retention of his midlands accent, removed even then from polite or correct pronunciation. His fellow-townsman and former pupil, the great actor David Garrick, used to imitate him, squeezing a lemon and crying 'Who's for poonch?'

3

Scott

⌐⌐⌐

ONE OF THE best modern books about Scott is A. N. Wilson's *The Laird of Abbotsford*. Described by its author as 'a work of pure self-indulgence, the product of reading or re-reading the Waverley novels during a period of illness', its excellence lies partly in its combination of enthusiasm with discrimination, partly in the way in which he tells or reminds us how Scott's influence was pervasive throughout the nineteenth century.

'The Victorians', Wilson writes,

canonized him. Indeed, he was scarcely cool in his grave, before his fellow-citizens had planned the vast Gothic memorial in Princes Street, which would dwarf an average-sized cathedral spire. The encrustations of his cult expanded and grew. We approach him through it, like Armada gold thick with barnacles: something over a thousand paintings inspired by his work and well over fifty operas, not to mention the Gothic residences, all partaking a little of the quality of Abbotsford, which sprawl in unending lines through Great Malvern, Leamington Spa and north Oxford . . .

Scott's fantasies became the reality of the succeeding generation. The stag at eve not merely drank his fill in thousands of limp suede-bound editions, but sprouted antlers over the furniture at Osborne. The moonlight which Scott never actually saw shining down on Melrose Abbey casts its eery glow on the nineteenth-century Gothic monasteries of Llanthony and Mount St Bernard. Every well-educated Victorian and Edwardian schoolboy learnt inner cleanliness not only through organized games and syrup of figs, but through imbibing Scott's *Tales of the Crusaders*. And even today, the pibroch sounds and the tartan is worn not just by Highlandmen, but in dining-rooms from Balmoral to Minneapolis . . .

Wilson's tone is light and affectionate, his examples humorous. But the sense is sound. Scott's fame was phenomenal, and unprecedented, in Scotland naturally, but also in England, throughout Europe, and in America where Mark Twain, only half joking, held him responsible for the War between the States because Southern gentlemen patterned themselves on the heroes of his tales of chivalry.

Scott's poetry and novels not only formed the taste of the generations that followed. They altered the relationship between England and Scotland, and in doing so contributed to the sense of an encompassing British patriotism. They did so by giving Scots a better and stronger understanding of their own past, in a manner which enabled them to go beyond that past and accept the reality of the United Kingdom, and by revealing both Scotland and Anglo-Scottish relations in a new light to the English. It was not just that he made Scotland seem interesting and romantic, even more completely than 'Ossian' had already done, though this was important. It was also that there was no truckling, no sense of inferiority, in his writings. He put Scotland on a level of equality with England. He was not the first Scottish poet or novelist to be popular in England: Thomson and Smollett had preceded him. But they had done so by eliding their Scotch peculiarities. Scott insisted on his, and made them matter to his English readers. Sydney Smith remarked, thanking Scott's publisher Archibald Constable for sending him *The Bride of Lammermoor*, that when he started reading one of 'W. Scott's novels', everything else was set aside till he had finished it.

Nobody could have been more thoroughly Scotch than Scott. Born in Edinburgh where his Presbyterian father was a lawyer – a Writer to the Signet – he came on both sides of his family from Borders stock. His great-grandfather, Walter Scott, known as 'Beardie', was himself great-grandson of another Walter Scott, commonly called 'Auld Wat of Harden'. 'I am', he wrote, 'therefore lineally descended from that ancient chieftain whose name I have made to ring in many a ditty, and from his fair dame, the Flower of Yarrow – no bad genealogy for a Border minstrel.' Beardie was a Jacobite, who narrowly escaped hanging. His son Robert 'turned Whig . . . and fairly abjured his father's politics and his learned poverty'. He became tenant of the farm of Sandyknowe, by Smailholm Tower, where the young Walter spent part of his childhood. The boy early acquired:

> a very strong prejudice in favour of the Stuart family, which I had orig-
> inally imbibed from the songs and tales of the Jacobites. This latter
> political propensity was deeply confirmed by the stories told in my
> hearing of the cruelties exercised in the executions at Carlisle and in
> the Highlands after the battle of Culloden. One or two of our more
> distant relations had fallen on that occasion and I remember detesting
> the name of Cumberland with more than infant hatred.

This attachment to the exiled Stuarts never quite died. In some respects Scott remained a sentimental Jacobite all his life. Yet, as his Jacobite novels – *Waverley*, *Rob Roy* and *Redgauntlet* – show, he came to accept that the Jacobites and those who supported them had been bypassed by the course of history. Scott was too intelligent to believe in historical inevitability. Yet, as one versed in the philosophical historical thinking of the Scottish Enlightenment, he accepted the idea of moral and social progress, and recognized that the Jacobite cause belonged to a society that was passing away.

Scott was never anti-English, however jealously he sought to maintain whatever was characteristically Scottish. One memory of his first visit to England – a year spent in Bath in the hope that he might there be cured of his lameness, the result of infantile paralysis – was his introduction to Shakespeare. This became a lifelong addiction; he quotes Shakespeare more often than any other writer. The heroes of *Waverley* and *Rob Roy* are both young Englishmen, a device which allows him to portray Scotland and the Jacobites from an unexpected angle. Darsie Latimer, the hero and part-narrator of *Redgauntlet*, is half English, belonging to a family with estates either side of the Border. Edward Waverley and Francis Osbaldistone are admittedly poor things, mere sticks, a deficiency which nevertheless serves Scott's purpose. They are observers, acted upon, rather than actors them-selves. Darsie is more spirited, yet also immature, fanciful, given to misunderstanding at first everything that happens to him. Scott could undoubtedly have created more interesting heroes had he chosen. So why didn't he? An examination of Waverley may serve to answer this question, and show the intelligence of his approach.

Waverley is a public novel. That is, it deals with events which occur in real historical time. Scott is concerned to explore and determine the significance of a historical episode that had for him a deep emo-tional significance. He sometimes thought that if he had been a young man at the time of the '45 he would have been 'out', as the word went, with the prince, and perhaps hanged for his pains. No one was ever better equipped to write the Jacobite novel that told the moving dra-matic story from the moment the prince raised his standard to the closing tragedy of Culloden and the heroic escape through the heather. But this is not what Scott did.

The novel begins in England. Young Edward Waverley is the scion of an old Cavalier–Tory family. In his youth, in his uncle's library, he indulges himself in the reading of old romances, but his uncle, Sir Everard, is a prudent timid man: a sentimentalist who is also a realist. He can't bring himself, in conversation with his nephew, to style the Elector of Hanover king; nevertheless it is in King George's army that he buys Waverley his commission. He regrets, even despises, the Whig supremacy, but doesn't question that it is here to stay. So the first impression the reader gets of the Jacobite cause is that it is dead, some-thing worthy perhaps of mouth-honour, in secret, but nothing to do with the real world.

Edward Waverley comes north to take up his commission. A little later he visits, with a letter of introduction, the old Jacobite Baron Bradwardine in his castle of Tully-Veolan:

> The houses seemed miserable in the extreme, especially to an eye
> accustomed to the smiling neatness of English cottages . . . The whole
> scene was depressing; for it argued, at the first glance, at least a stagna-
> tion of industry, and perhaps of intellect. Even curiosity, the busiest

passion of the idle, seemed of a listless cast in the village of Tully-Veolan; the curs alone showed any part of activity.

This is a dismal picture. No doubt it is historically accurate. Scots villages of the time were indeed wretched places. But it also serves as an image of the degradation of Jacobitism. And when we meet the laird of Tully-Veolan, Baron Bradwardine himself, the futility of the cause seems still more apparent. The Baron is an out-and-out loyalist, but also a pedantic scholar with a high sense of honour and no understanding of practicalities. But he is not only that. He is also, as A. O. J. Cockshut (*The Achievement of Sir Walter Scott*) remarked, one who cares 'not only for the records and quarterings of his own lineage, but for Livy and Virgil, in fact for the fundamental European culture, which underlies and outlasts all differences between English and Scot, Highland and Lowland, Jacobite and Hanoverian'. The Baron may be a comic figure, but he is also admirable. When, near the end of the novel, after the cause is lost, he laments, 'To be sure we may say with Virgilius Maro, *Fuimus Troes*' and that 'we poor Jacobites are now like the conies in Holy Scripture . . . a feeble people, that make our abode among the rocks', Scott expects, I think, the attentive reader to remember that the Trojans, driven from their burning city in flight, became the Romans; so, in like manner, the defeated Jacobites would become truly British. Indeed we have seen that happen: Allan MacDonald, husband of Flora, remaining a British loyalist in the American War of Independence.

A contrast to Bradwardine is offered by the Highland chief Fergus McIvor. Again the unwary reader is in for a surprise. We may expect the Highland chief to be a figure of romance, devoted body and soul to the Jacobite cause. Certainly he is brave and resourceful, and ultimately he does indeed die a victim, or martyr to the cause to which he has attached himself. But long before this moment arrives we have learned that he is a calculating Jacobite, and might indeed never have chosen that side but for the urging and influence of his high-minded sister, Flora. He is a Jacobite also because he is by temperament a gambler. If the prince wins he will be a great man. Even so, Fergus is jealous of those who join the Jacobite army on its march south, considering them 'in the light of new claimants upon the favours of the future monarch, who, he concluded, must therefore subtract for their gratification so much of the bounty which ought to be shared among his Highland followers'.

So Waverley learns, and the reader, especially perhaps the English reader, learns, that men may be Jacobites just as they may be Whigs and Hanoverians: that is, for personal advantage. In making this point Scott divests his Scots Jacobites not only of their romance, but of their strangeness to his English readers. Jacobites are not merely adherents of a lost (and romantic) cause; they may also be men with the same ambitions as those on the other side.

One of Scott's great qualities is his inclusiveness, his ability to see that society is made up of men and women animated by different ideas and principles, who nevertheless resemble each other. There is a moment in chapter 47, just before the Battle of Prestonpans, when the two armies are enveloped in a mist; no longer to be distinguished, one from the other, by differences of dress and equipment, they are as one – merely men, Jacobite and Hanoverian and, by imaginative extension, Englishmen and Scots. Waverley by the end of the novel has come to realize this.

In Scott's fiction, victory is never absolute. Succeeding generations are heirs to both parties in a conflict. In *The Tale of Old Mortality* Scott portrayed the extreme Covenanters, with whom he had no political sympathy, with the same understanding he brought to Claverhouse and his Cavalier dragoons. The Scotland of his time was the product of that quarrel unresolved in its own generation. To understand Scotland, he let his English readers know, you had to feel its stern Calvinism as strongly as its romantic and picturesque qualities. The land of the mountain and the glen was also the country of four-hour sermons.

The novels set in Scotland between the second half of the seventeenth century and his own time are Scott's greatest work. They made Scotland matter to contemporaries. No one could read them and think it an insignificant country. Following on his narrative poems, especially *The Lady of the Lake*, which without much exaggeration may be said to have created the Scottish tourist industry, they gave the Scots a better sense of their own past, and brought to the English an awareness of this land to the north which their ancestors had despised, but which now seemed simultaneously exotic and familiar, demanding and inviting, strangely wonderful. The cult of Scottishness so strong in nineteenth-century England derived from the Waverley novels.

It survived into the twentieth century. George Orwell encountered it at the preparatory school in Sussex which he called St Cyprian's in the essay, *Such, Such Were the Joys*. He encountered it in a debased form, and, disliking his memories of the school, described it sourly:

> The school was pervaded by a curious cult of Scotland, which brought out the fundamental contradiction in our standard of values. Flip [the headmaster's wife] claimed Scottish ancestry, and she favoured the Scottish boys, encouraging them to wear kilts in their ancestral tartan instead of the school uniform, and even christened her youngest child by a Gaelic name. Ostensibly we were supposed to admire the Scots because they were 'grim' and 'dour' ('stern' was perhaps the key word), and irresistible on the field of battle. In the big schoolroom there was a steel engraving of the charge of the Scots Greys at Waterloo, all looking as though they enjoyed every moment of it. Our picture of Scotland was made up of burns, braes, kilts, sporrans, claymores, bag-pipes and the like, all somehow mixed up with the invigorating effects of porridge, Protestantism and a cold climate.

So far, very clearly, all this may be said to stem from the enthusiasm for Scotland created by the Waverley novels. But Orwell, characteristically, continues: 'But underlying this was something quite different. The real reason for the cult of Scotland was that only very rich people could spend their summers there . . .' This is an Orwellian note that would have surprised the many no more than comfortably off people who also ventured north from England in the summer, and would soon be taking bus-tours to the Highlands. 'And the pretended belief in Scottish superiority', Orwell adds,

> was a cover for the bad conscience of the occupying English, who had pushed the Highland peasants off their farms to make way for the deer forests, and then compensated by turning them into servants. Flip's face

always beamed with innocent snobbishness when she spoke of Scotland. Occasionally she even attempted a trace of Scottish accent. Scotland was a private paradise which a few initiates could talk about and make outsiders feel small.

Many modern Scottish nationalists would find themselves in agreement with Orwell's bitter and contemptuous condemnation of this 'cult of Scottishness', relishing especially his use of the expression 'the occupying English'; and, inasmuch as Scott may be held to have been responsible for the cult, condemning him too. Yet, while the snobbishness is undeniable and the cult itself may be held up to ridicule, as indeed it was to be mocked in the Highland novels of Compton Mackenzie, it was surely better that the aristocrats and new-rich industrialists who bought Scottish estates, or leased grouse-moors and deer-forests, should have felt and expressed a love for Scotland and an admiration of what they supposed to be characteristic Scottish qualities than that they shouldn't. The picture of Scotland presented to Orwell at his prep school may have been partial and inadequate, but it wasn't entirely false. It was after all one that many Scots – and especially exiled Scots – themselves delighted in. If little English boys of Orwell's generation were encouraged to regard Scotland with admiration, even in many ways to see it as superior, well, that was better than the contempt which seventeenth-century and even eighteenth-century Englishmen had generally felt for their northern neighbour. It was better than the way they viewed the Irish and the Welsh. Finally, if they granted Scots a certain moral superiority, that was just what, by the nineteenth century, Scots were very ready to claim for themselves. The fact is that the English cult of Scotland helped to make the Union of the two peoples work in a manner agreeable to both.

This has taken us some way from Scott. Yet the distance travelled is not so great, for, without Scott's poems and novels, it is very unlikely that this cult of Scottishness would have developed. More than any other single person, he invented the Idea of Scotland, an idea that pleased both Scots and English.

He did more than that, however. He also invented, or at least refurbished, an Idea of England. He did this in his most popular novel, *Ivanhoe*. It merits examination of a sort it hasn't often received.

Ivanhoe is a strange book. On the one hand it is absurd; absurd as history and absurd as a novel. Any novel in which a chief character is dead in one chapter and brought to life again later simply to help move the plot along is unquestionably absurd. Yet Ivanhoe is also entrancing and compelling. Many Scott enthusiasts are embarrassed by it. It evidently lacks that moral seriousness which is a mark of great fiction, and which is to be found in the Scotch novels. It is not realistic as, for example, *The Heart of Midlothian*, *Old Mortality* and *Redgauntlet* are realistic. It is not even historically accurate as that late-medieval novel *Quentin Durward* is. And yet . . .

John Buchan, who adored it and was also, I suspect, at times anyway, somewhat ashamed of his adoration, defended it thus:

> a pageant so far-flung and glittering that, in spite of its artificiality, it captivates the fancy. There are no less than one hundred and fifty-three characters at some time or another on the stage. With generous profusion he piles excitement on excitement, weaving, like his favourite Ariosto, many different narratives into one pattern, and managing it all with such skill that there are no gaps in the web. It is a success – though on a far greater scale – of the same type as Byron's metrical romances. Improbabilities, impossibilities, coincidences are accepted because the reader's mind is beguiled out of scepticism. The scene is so novel, the figures so vivid that we bow to the convention and forbear to doubt.

This certainly conveys some of the magic which *Ivanhoe* may still have for readers. It goes some way to explaining why Goethe hailed it as 'a wholly new art', and why, of all Scott's novels, it has been most often adapted for the stage and most often filmed. It suggests why it was his most popular novel in his own lifetime, and why it was favoured holiday reading for Victorian children. Yet it doesn't touch on its most curious, and perhaps most important, feature. A. N. Wilson comes close to doing so when he writes: 'it is almost as impossible to judge it by purely literary standards as it is to judge Pugin's Houses of Parliament – which Lord Clark has called a "Waverley novel in stone" – by purely architectural standards. Both, in a way, are not merely works of art, but brilliant pieces of myth-making.'

Indeed yes; but what was the myth Scott was making? It was the myth of 'Merrie England', of the making of England, and this was an extraordinary thing for a Scotch novelist to attempt, and, even more remarkable, to bring off. He opened up to his readers what had been a closed or forgotten world: medieval England.

Some folk-memory of it had survived, notably in the ballads of Robin Hood, himself a character in the novel. But, inasmuch as the Middle Ages were known, they were despised, as a time of uncouth manners, and an age sunk in superstition. Shakespeare, admittedly, in his history plays, had covered a wide tract of late-medieval England. But even he ventured only once, in *King John*, further back than the late four-teenth century. In any case, there is little that is authentically medieval in these plays – less indeed than in *Ivanhoe*. Shakespeare's Plantagenets, Lancastrians and Yorkists are Tudor politicians, thinly disguised.

In the introduction to the Magnum edition of the Waverley novels, written in 1830, Scott declined 'to enumerate so many reasons why the author of the Scottish novels, as they were then exclusively termed, should be desirous to make an experiment on a subject purely English'. He went on, however, to explain his purpose.

The period of the narrative adopted was the reign of Richard I, not only as abounding with characters whose very names were sure to attract general attention [this offering him a sound commercial reason for his choice of time and setting] but as affording a striking contrast betwixt the Saxons by whom the soil was cultivated, and the Normans who still reigned in it as conquerors, reluctant to mix with the van-quished or acknowledge themselves as of the same stock. The idea of this contrast was taken from the ingenious and unfortunate Logan's tragedy of *Runnamede*, in which, about the same period of history, the author had seen the Saxon and Norman barons opposed to each other on different sides of the stage. He does not recollect that there was any attempt to contrast the two races in their habits and sentiments; and indeed it was obvious that history was violated by introducing the Saxons still existing as a high-minded and martial race of nobles.

They did however survive as a people, and some of the ancient Saxon families possessed wealth and power, although they were exceptions to the humble condition of the race in general. It seemed to the author that the existence of these two races in the same country, the vanquished distinguished by their plain, homely, blunt manners, and by the free spirit infused by their ancient institutions and laws; the victors, by the high spirit of military fame, personal adventure, and whatever could distinguish them as the flower of chivalry, might, intermixed with other characters belonging to the same time and country, interest the reader by the contrast, if the author should not fail on his part.

So, just as in the Scotch novels, Scott pointed the contrast between Jacobite and Hanoverian, Tory and Whig, Cavalier and Covenanter, and brought his readers to the realization that the Scotland they inhabited had been made by both parties in these quarrels, and could not be understood fairly if the contribution of either to the Scotland of their, and indeed his, own time was denied, so he hoped now to show a comparable process at work in the making of England.

It is worth looking also, if we are to understand Scott's purpose fully, at the Dedicatory Epistle which served as a preface to the original edition of the novel. Scott loved to frame his fiction in such a way as to pretend to a spurious authenticity, and this dedicatory epistle, explaining the provenance of the work, is ascribed to an imaginary character, an Englishman, Laurence Templeton of Toppingwold, near Egremont, Cumberland.

Templeton expresses first his surprise:

that no attempt has been made to excite an interest for the traditions and manners of Old England, similar to that which has been obtained [by Scott himself] in behalf of those of our poorer and less celebrated neighbours. The Kendal green, though its date is more ancient, ought surely to be as dear to our feelings as the variegated tartans of the north. The name of Robin Hood, if duly conjured with, should raise a spirit as soon as that of Rob Roy, and the patriots of England deserve no less their renown in our modern circles, than the Bruces and Wallaces of Caledonia. If the scenery of the south be less romantic and sublime than that of the northern mountains, it must be allowed to possess in the same proportion superior softness and beauty; and upon the whole we feel ourselves entitled to exclaim with the patriotic Syrian – 'Are not Pharpar and Abana, rivers of Damascus, better than all the rivers of England?'

So just as the Scotch novels had raised, even been written, to inform and promote a northern patriotism, so now *Ivanhoe* might do as much for England. That a Scot, even in the guise of a Cumbrian squire, should set out to attempt this was, and is, surely remarkable.

Still in the persona of Laurence Templeton, Scott then suggested that the task being undertaken in *Ivanhoe* was more demanding than that which the author of *Waverley* had performed. He had had the advantage by reason of 'the very recent existence of that state of society in which his scene was to be laid. Many now alive well remembered persons who had not only seen the celebrated Roy McGregor, but had feasted and even fought with him.' The dramatic events of the Scottish novels were situated in recent, and verifiable, history. In contrast, in England 'civilization has been so long complete, that our ideas of our ancestors are only to be gleaned from musty records and chronicles'. In other words, the formation of the English nation, which is one of the themes of *Ivanhoe*, had happened so long ago that English men and women had lost all sense of how it came about. An Englishman,

> when placed in his own snug parlour and surrounded by all the comforts of an Englishman's fireside, is not half so much disposed to believe that his ancestors led a very different life from himself; that the shattered tower, which now forms a vista from his window, once held a baron who would have hung him up at his own front door without any form of trial; that the hinds, by whom his little pet-farm is managed, a few centuries ago would have been his slaves; and that the complete influence of feudal tyranny once extended over the neighbouring village, where the attorney is now a man of more importance than the lord of the manor.

Now *Ivanhoe* may be in certain respects ridiculous, certainly fantastic, not what we recognize as a serious novel at all. That sentence probably requires qualification, our understanding of what may be considered a serious novel being more liberal than was the case when realism or naturalism was the dominant mode. But this is not a question to be answered here, my purpose not being literary criticism. There can however be no doubt that it achieved this stated purpose: to give English men and women a sense of their own past, to restore to them the idea of medieval England. Admittedly Scott's Merrie England is one that no medieval historian would recognize today, certainly would not endorse. But that too is beside the point. What Scott was providing was an English myth, and, in offering this, he was wholly successful.

Novels influence taste and opinions if they are blown by the prevailing wind. Fifty years earlier, *Ivanhoe*, if it could conceivably have been written then, would have flopped, have been regarded as no more than a curiosity, as influential perhaps as Beckford's Arabian tale, *Vathek*. But it coincided with the awareness of how the Industrial Revolution, which Scott himself viewed with sceptical dismay, was changing not only the landscape but the relations existing between men, especially between capital and labour. This altered relationship was not yet understood. It would be another quarter of a century before Carlyle would analyse and denounce it. But it was felt. It was there as an undercurrent. *Ivanhoe* appealed to those made uneasy by its disturbing tremor.

Scott's medieval England is a land of much cruelty, violence, injustice and superstition. Nevertheless it is a coherent community, one in which Robin of Locksley (Robin Hood) can tell the disguised Richard Coeur-de-lion that it is his duty to be 'as well a good Englishman as a good knight'. In a time of rapid and discordant change, the onrushing of a commercial and manufacturing age in which relations between men were expressed by the cash nexus, *Ivanhoe* offered not only an escapist fantasy, though it offered that very agreeably too; it suggested an alternative vision of how things had been, and how relations between men might be again. Scott called in the Old World to redress the balance of the New.

He appealed to very intelligent and very serious men. Henry

Liddon, in his *Life of Pusey*, the guiding spirit of the Tractarian Movement in the Church of England, wrote:

> Of the new interest in the Middle Ages, the pioneer in this century was Sir Walter Scott; his indirect relation to the Oxford Movement was often dwelt upon by Pusey in private conversation. That relation consisted not only in the high moral tone which characterized Scott's writings and which marked them so sharply off from the contemporary writers of modern fiction, but also and especially in the interest which he aroused on behalf of ages and persons who had been buried out of sight to an extent that to our generation would appear incredible.

Scott's medieval novels, by exciting the imagination of men like Pusey and his ally in the Oxford Movement, John Henry Newman, contributed to the revival of the Catholic spirit in the Church of England. Not only the dominant Gothic style in Victorian church architecture stems from this revival, but also the High Church ritualistic Anglo-Catholic strain in the Church of England. Some of the leading figures in the Oxford Movement, notably Newman himself, were led by the logic of their arguments into the Church of Rome. Scott's granddaughter and her husband Sir John Hope-Scott were among those who 'poped' and indeed built a Roman Catholic chapel at Abbotsford, where Newman frequently said Mass. Scott, who once wrote that he thought 'popery such a mean and depriving superstition', might have disapproved (though on one occasion he told his friend Byron that he wouldn't be surprised if Byron didn't end in the Church of Rome, and spoke this prophecy without disapproval). Be that as it may, Scott's medieval novels contributed to the realization that England and Scotland had been Roman Catholic countries longer than they had been Protestant ones, and to the understanding that their Roman Catholic past was an ineradicable part of their historical tradition.

Ivanhoe is about the making of England, about the fusion of the two nations, Saxon and Norman, into one English nation. It taught a lesson, doubtless unconsciously, relevant to Scott's time and to the succeeding decades. Disraeli, incidentally as a young man one of

Scott's innumerable visitors at Abbotsford, wrote in *Sybil* of England being:

> two nations; between whom there is no intercourse and no sympathy; who are as ignorant of each other's habits, thoughts and feelings, as if they were dwellers in different zones, or inhabitants of different planets; who are formed by a different breeding, are fed by a different food, are ordered by different manners, and are not governed by the same laws.

He might have been speaking of Scott's Saxons and Normans. In fact his two nations were the Rich and the Poor. But the message was the same as Scott's: they must become One Nation if the country was to be at ease.

There is another possible reading of *Ivanhoe*. It is ingenious, if also far-fetched. It is a British reading rather than a purely English one. The two nations are not only Saxons and Normans who must come together to be English, but also Scots and English who must blend into one British nation. There is nothing of course in the text to support this suggestion. Yet it makes some sense, following the pattern of the Scottish novels themselves which trace the course of the formation of modern Scotland through the collision of opposing forces, ways of life and ideology to produce a synthesis. The suggestion is also supported by the Hungarian Marxist critic Georg Lukacs's reading of Scott's work. Lukacs sees Scott's worldview as being that of the real logic of English history, which he calls the 'English compromise'. So Scott exposes the falsity of extremist positions, both left and right (to use an anachronism) and brings the moderates, the men of sense on both sides, together. Typically he chooses as the 'eye' of his novels a figure who can see both the virtues and the vices of warring parties, and who becomes the representative, for the reader, of good sense, moderation, humanity, compromise. The crisis points of Anglo-British history are resolved, Lukacs suggests, by the emergence of just such consciously unheroic middle-way figures. Compromise is effected to accommodate change while warding off any revolutionary breach with the past. By Scott's time, he argues, this same logic requires that Scottish nationality be subsumed in Britishness.

The argument is ingenious, halfway persuasive. It has however to be tested against what Scott actually thought, said and wrote. This requires an examination of his attitude to the Union, and that was neither wholly clear nor wholly consistent.

Indeed it was so far from clear that Scott has suffered attack as a Tory Unionist from some Nationalists and been hailed as a defender of Scottish interests who was never wholly reconciled to the Union by others. Edwin Muir called him (and Burns) 'sham bards of a sham nation'. Hugh MacDiarmid held him to be 'the source of the paralysing ideology of defeatism in Scotland, the spread of which is responsible at once for the acceptance of the Union and the low standard of nineteenth-century Scots literature'. On the other hand P. H. Scott, recognizing that 'Scott was in fact living in the middle of the only period since the Union when Home Rule was not a conceivable policy', yet insists that Scott 'did regard himself', when he wrote *The Letters from Malachi Malagrowther on the Proposed Change of Currency*, as 'struggling for the cause of Scottish Independence'.

As against this, the English historian Hugh Trevor-Roper stated bluntly: Scott 'believed passionately in the Union with England. He was a British patriot.' His son-in-law and biographer J. G. Lockhart wrote that if any 'anti-English faction, civil or religious' had sprung up in his lifetime, Scott would have opposed it fiercely.

Others have sought evidence of his views from his novels. In *Rob Roy*, for instance, the gardener Andrew Fairservice declared:

> that it was an unco change to hae Scotland's laws made in England [where by the way Fairservice had spent most of his life] and that, for his share, he wadna for a' the herring-barrels in Glasgow, and a' the tobacco-casks to boot, hae gien up the riding o' the Scots Parliament, or sent awa' our crown, and our sword, and our sceptre, to be keepit by the pock-puddings in the Tower o' Lunnon. What wad Sir William Wallace, or auld Davie Lindsay, hae said to the Union, or them that made it.

Andrew Fairservice's opinion chimes nicely with that expressed by Mrs Howden in *The Heart of Midlothian*: 'I dinna ken muckle about the law, but I ken, when we had a king, and a chancellor, and parliament-men o' our ain, we could aye peeble them wi' stanes when they werena gude bairns – But naebody's nails can reach the length o' Lunnon.'

The other side of the argument is put by Bailie Nicol Jarvie, to whom in fact Fairservice was replying:

Whisht, sir! Whisht! it's ill-scrapit tongues like yours that make mischief atween neighbourhoods and nations. There's naething sae gude on this side o' time but it might hae been better, and that may be said o' the Union. Nane were keener against it than the Glasgow folk, wi' their rabblings and their risings, and their mobs, as they ca' them now-a-days. But it's an ill wind blaws naebody gude – Let ilka ane roose the ford as they find it – I say, Let Glasgow flourish, whilk is judiciously and elegantly putten around the town's arms, by way of bye-word. Now, since St Mungo catched herrings in the Clyde, what was ever like to gar us flourish like the sugar and tobacco-trade, will anybody tell me that, and grumble at the treaty that opened us a road west-awa' yonder?

All the speakers are equally eloquent. All make their argument forcefully. But none of their speeches tells us what Scott himself thought, and the different points of view shouldn't be taken as evidence that he himself was confused. A novelist's opinions are not to be identified with those expressed by his characters. He makes them say what it seems right that they should say in the situation in which they find themselves. Few things irritate novelists more than the assumption that they are of the same opinion as their characters. It may be significant that Bailie Nicol Jarvie is the only character in the Waverley novels to speak out strongly in favour of the Union, but in the novels set in the early eighteenth century when the Union might be considered an issue, as it wasn't in Scott's own lifetime, few of the characters actually have occasion to remark on it. Those who do are either Jacobites or, like Andrew Fairservice, ones whose judgement we are not invited to respect.

Scott himself, in a letter written in 1825 to the Irish novelist Maria Edgeworth, called the Union 'an event which, had I lived in that day, I would have resigned my life to have prevented, but, which, being done before my day, I am sensible was a wise scheme'.

This can't be taken as an expression of whole-hearted approval. Nor is it condemnation. It reveals that Scott's view was ambivalent. It also reveals a degree of self-knowledge. His sentiments were hostile to the Union; his reason assented to it. Indeed his stance on the question was much like his position with regard to Jacobitism. He was convinced he would have been 'out' with the prince, and he felt the same melancholy as Redgauntlet expressed when he sighed, 'Then the cause is lost for ever,' but the argument of *Waverley* is undeniable: that the defeat of the '45 was for the best.

The circumstances in which the Union had come about might be shameful and deplorable, but the result was something he could not wish undone. It led, as he wrote in the *Tales of a Grandfather*, to 'a happy change from discord to friendship – from war to peace and from poverty and distress [in the old pre-Union Scotland] to national prosperity [in the Scotland of his own time]'.

Yet, while he accepted that 'the last shades of national difference [between England and Scotland] may almost be said to have disappeared' – a judgement in which he was certainly mistaken – he also was quick and jealous in the defence of whatever remained peculiarly Scottish. His indignant and pained outburst when Francis Jeffrey and the reforming Whigs had proposed changes in the administration of justice, to bring this more in line with English practice, has been often quoted, yet is worth quoting again, as expressing a sort of national feeling which even the most Unionist of Scots have recurrently exhibited: 'No, no – 'tis no laughing matter; little by little, whatever your wishes may be, you will destroy and undermine, until nothing of what makes Scotland Scotland shall remain.'

Whereas, ever since the Union, Englishmen have found no difficulty in equating the United Kingdom with England, Britishness with Englishness, seeing no difference, no contradiction, between them, Scots have been in another case; and Scott, *maxime Scotticus* as he was, displays this duality. He was a British patriot, unquestioningly in the wars against Revolutionary and Napoleonic France. But he was also a Scottish patriot ready to speak out whenever it seemed to him that some essential Scottishness was threatened. He was in no sense anti-English and was happy to regard England as 'our sister and ally'. He was steeped in English history and culture, which, it is clear from his critical work and his habit of ready quotation, he regarded as his culture also; and yet he was, in Lockhart's words, 'ever sensitively jealous as to the interference of English statesmen with the internal affairs of his native kingdom . . . Whenever Scotland could be considered as standing [apart] on any question from the rest of the Empire, he was not only apt, but eager to embrace the opportunity of again rehoisting, as it were, the old signal of national independence.'

This duality may be illustrated by an account of the visit of George IV to Edinburgh in 1822. None of his Hanoverian predecessors had thought to visit Scotland; they hadn't indeed ever visited the north of England. Indeed no reigning monarch had set foot in Scotland since Charles II was crowned king at Scone in 1651. Scott became the stage-manager of a venture which might very easily have turned into an embarrassing failure. George IV, extravagant, selfish, hugely fat, was an immensely unpopular monarch. The Duke of Wellington described him and his brothers as 'the damnedest millstones about the neck of any Government that might be imagined'. Consequently, in the words of Sir John Plumb, 'from 1812 to 1837 the Royal Family was held in almost universal contempt'. London in particular loathed the king. His attempt to divorce his appalling wife, Caroline of Brunswick, on grounds of adultery and scandalous behaviour had made her the heroine of the city mob. But George had his virtues and one of them was imagination. In 1821 he had visited first Dublin and then his ancestral kingdom of Hanover. The following year he proposed to come to Scotland. As Plumb wrote:

> He paraded Edinburgh in the kilt, resplendent in the Royal Stuart tartan and flesh-coloured tights, and yet managed to keep his dignity. The Scots loved it. Quaintly enough George IV had struck the future note of the monarchy . . . be-kilted, be-sporraned, be-tartaned, riding up Princes Street . . . to the roaring cheers of the loyal Scots, he was showing the way that the monarchy would have to go if it were to survive into an industrial and democratic society.

Scott immersed himself in this pageant enthusiastically. He had several reasons for doing so. In the first place of course it appealed to his sense of theatre, to the romantic side of his nature. Born too late to attend Bonnie Prince Charlie at the Palace of Holyroodhouse, he was able to create for a fortnight an imitation of the old Scottish royal Court.

But there were serious political purposes behind the charade. The end of the war with Napoleon had led to years of acute economic distress. Unemployment was high, rioting common, radicalism and republicanism preached in both Scotland and England. Associations were formed – called 'union societies' – demanding universal suffrage and annual Parliaments. In the west of Scotland, in Ayrshire, Lanarkshire and Stirlingshire, according to T. M. Devine, 'they were transformed from discussion clubs into insurrectionary cells bent on achieving the overthrow of government by physical force'. The result was the so-called Radical War of 1820. It was soon suppressed and three of the dissidents' leaders were hanged for the crime of armed insurrection.

There were nationalist aspects of this Radical War. References to Wallace and Bruce were frequent. The banner carried by the Strathaven Union Society bore the legend 'Scotland Free or a Desart'. Nevertheless it was a class movement, rather than a nationalist one. Scottish radicals were in close touch with their fellow-proletarians in the north of England. The proclamation issued, on 1 April 1820, by a body styling itself 'the Committee of Organization for forming a Provisional Government' took the form of an 'Address to the Inhabitants of Great Britain and Ireland'. The text called for the restoration of Liberties now lost, formerly guaranteed in Magna Carta and the Bill of Rights. The strategy itself provided for a joint uprising in the west of Scotland and the north of England. There was little interest in the proclamation in other parts of either Scotland or England. Indeed, inasmuch as the Radicals' language 'showed a fusion of Scottish and English symbols of freedom' (as Devine put it), it may be said to have been rather an affirmation of the Union than, even in Scotland, an expression of nationalism. And indeed the Labour movement as it developed, first in trade-union activity, and then with its own political party, in the course of the nineteenth century, was firmly British.

The Radical War alarmed the Government, but was easily suppressed, partly because government spies had penetrated the movement, so that troops were to hand to counter it. But the mood of rebellious uncertainty it represented was another reason for Scott to engage so eagerly in the promotion and organization of the king's visit. It would show Scotland loyal; it would encourage loyalty in the country.

He conceived it also as a means of binding up some of Scotland's historic wounds, as an act of reconciliation between Highland and Lowland, Jacobite and Whig. (During the visit he persuaded the king to agree to the restoration of the Jacobite peerages to those families deprived of that honour after the '45.) In this act of reconciliation, it may be said that the king's visit served as a real-life equivalent of *Waverley*. It drew a line under the past, while at the same time indicating that both parties in these old disputes were now as one, jointly contributing to the present and future. Scotland could sing Jacobite songs while hailing the Hanoverian monarch. The descendants of Highlanders who had occupied Edinburgh in the '45 and sought to expel George II, now thronged the city in a display of loyalty to his great-grandson.

Some of Scott's contemporaries, his own friends among them, were highly critical of this 'Celtification of Scotland'. Even Lockhart, usually loth to criticize his father-in-law, thought it absurd, a 'hallucination'; the real traditions of Scotland – by which he meant the Lowlands – were being identified with a people who had 'always constituted a small and always unimportant part of the Scottish population'. Historically Lockhart was right: the association of all Scotland with tartanry and the clans was utterly bogus. It was equally ridiculous, and also distasteful, that this celebration of Highlandism should coincide with the disintegration of traditional Highland society, that disintegration being hurried along by some of the chiefs, such as Aeneas MacDonnell of Glengarry, who made such a fine show in the royal pageantry devised by Scott. It was grotesque that Sir Ewan McGregor should reply to the king's toast to 'the clans and their chieftains' with one to 'the Chief of Chiefs – the King'.

But Scott was wiser than his critics. He sensed, if he did not articulate, the need for a form of national identity – a new form – which would satisfy his fellow-countrymen by presenting them with an image of Scotland of which they could feel proud and which would be distinctly different from anything to be found south of the Border. At the same time it was to be an image which would impress the English, compelling them to accept that the political Union was a partnership between two nations with different traditions, which were nevertheless joined harmoniously together. At the time of the debates on the Treaty in 1706–7, there had been opposition to the idea of an 'incorporating union'. That opposition had failed, been defeated. The Scottish political state was indeed incorporated into the new British entity, which in all its political manifestations was in truth essentially English. But, though the great figures of the eighteenth-century Enlightenment had sought to eradicate or correct their Scots accent, the assimilation was never complete.

Culturally, the Union was not a fully incorporating one. It was, after all, almost eighty years after that Union that Scotland's national bard had emerged in Robert Burns. True, as Scott himself realized and as the influence of his work on England made evident, there was a deal of cultural community. Nevertheless differences survived. At moments admittedly Scott feared that the total loss of Scottish identity by absorption in England might come about; in the Preface to his *Tales of a Grandfather*, he wrote that 'the last shades of national difference may almost be said to have disappeared'. Yet, with all his affection for England and his high regard for the English, he did not wish this to happen, while at the same time he had no desire to break the political Union which was to him an established fact. He knew, from his reading of history and from his observation of events in France after 1789, how fragile the established order can prove to be, and how damaging and disruptive any attack on it. As an instinctive conservative he could not but do all in his power to support it. It is this understanding that lies behind his promotion of a new form of

Scottish identity compatible with the Union, and capable of winning the respect and admiration of the English.

Those Scots who have come to deplore 'tartanry' and the 'bogus image of Scotland it has promoted', who dismiss it as a 'Scotch myth' and blame Scott for its dissemination, should consider what was then the alternative: anglicization and the erosion and eventual disappearance of all differences between the two peoples.

In his endeavour to prevent this, he was successful. The idea of North Britain was killed stone-dead, even while the Union itself was strengthened. Of course he could not have met with this success if he had been swimming against a strong current. Even before Scott enchanted English readers with his long poems and his novels, Ossian, as we have seen, had already made Scotland appear interesting, different, romantic. Then, the contribution of Scots soldiers, and especially of the Highland regiments, to the wars against Napoleon had won the admiration of the English while also confirming Scottish commitment to the idea of the United Kingdom. The Scots were no longer seen as potential rebels. Whereas, during the war against revolutionary France, the Irish had seen England's danger as Ireland's opportunity, sought French aid and staged a rising in 1798, the Scots had proved themselves truly British. Scotland was a partner in the incorporating Union, taking a full part in the expansion and administration of the Empire in India and manning Nelson's navy and Wellington's army.

Scots were prominent in almost every area of British life. Though Scotland had retained its own legal system, many ambitious Scots distinguished themselves at the English bar – poor Boswell had been an exception in failing there. They had given England lord chief justices and Britain lord chancellors. The Younger Pitt learned his economic and fiscal theories from Adam Smith, and the *Edinburgh Review* laid down the laws of taste in matters literary and cultural. Scottish universities attracted young Englishmen eager to study the sciences which Oxford and Cambridge still disdained. James Watt, with his English partner Matthew Boulton, developed the steam engines that powered an industrial revolution and would soon by their application to rail and ship transform men's ideas of time and distance.

In a sense Walter Scott was pushing at an open door. Old enmities and suspicions were already dying when he began to write. Scotland and the Scots had earned the respect of the English. His narrative poems and the long sequence of the Waverley novels turned that respect into affection.

4

Aspects of the Nineteenth Century

᠅

NATIONS ARE MADE by history, geography, ambition, chance. Some, like Prussia, are forged in war. That had been Scotland's experience in the time of Wallace and Bruce. War helps form a nation's consciousness of itself as a thing apart, distinct from the enemy, the other. War offers the occasion for the emergence of a representative myth. As Scotland looked back to the medieval wars of independence, France to Joan of Arc, so England's sense of itself grew out of Crécy and Poitiers, Agincourt and the 'happy few . . . [the] band of brothers', and the defeat of the Spanish Armada.

Now, at the turn of the nineteenth century, the wars against Revolutionary France and Napoleon stimulated a novel British patriotism, the idea of the British nation incorporating and transcending its historical parts. No doubt the wars of the eighteenth century had gone some way to creating this, but they had been limited wars which indeed the British state had fought often by proxy. The war against Napoleon was different.

Many in both Scotland and England had at first felt sympathy, even enthusiasm, for the Revolution in France and its proclamation of the Rights of Man. The Whig leader, Charles James Fox, hailed the Fall of the Bastille in 1789 with the words, 'How much the greatest event . . . in the history of the world! And how much the best.' It was a blow for liberty. Besides, the French monarchy had been England's – or Britain's – most persistent and dangerous enemy. The idea of liberty resulting from the overthrow of the established order delighted many but alarmed the bastions of order in Britain. Societies of the Friends of the People were formed in both England and Scotland. They were soon infiltrated by Government agents, and suppressed. Restrictive laws were passed. In Scotland Sedition Trials, ordered by Henry Dundas, the first presided over by the veteran judge Lord Braxfield, came down hard on the idealists as disturbers of the realm. The Establishment, either side of the old Border, stood firm, shoulder to shoulder. Braxfield (a hundred years later to be the model for Stevenson's Weir of Hermiston) replied to the assertion of one of the accused that Jesus Christ had himself been a reformer, with the pithy dismissal, 'Muckle he made o' that. He was hangit.'

In Ireland the Protestant-led United Irishmen sought French help as they fought to regain independence. 'England's danger is Ireland's opportunity' – a line that confirmed the distrust of the Irish in the minds of both Scots and Englishmen. The Irish Rebellion in 1798 was crushed. The Government looked for a new answer to the recurrent Irish Question. They found it in the model provided by the Treaty of Union between England and Scotland. Ireland must likewise be brought, as it were, into the body of the kirk by an incorporating union. But not all the lessons of 1707 were learned. That had left Scotland with its native institutions still functioning autonomously. The Presbyterian Church had been confirmed, in security and perpetuity, as the national Church of Scotland. But Ireland was predominantly Roman Catholic and the failure in 1801 to restore civil and political rights to Irish Catholics impaired the Union from the start. Scotland had been tenderly treated and so become British. The mass of the Irish were neglected, oppressed; so Ireland was never to be converted into West Britain. This failure was matter for comment and adverse criticism in the pages of the Whig *Edinburgh Review*.

Sympathy for the Revolution withered when the excesses of the Revolutionaries became evident. Fear of France revived as the Revolutionary armies swept across Europe. That fear was sharpened when Napoleon established first the Consulate, then the Empire. France, the hereditary enemy, was stronger, more ambitious and more dangerous than ever. Napoleon had some British admirers, among the Opposition Whigs and intellectuals like Hazlitt and Byron. But, though his career dazzled, few questioned the necessity of fighting him.

In 1804–5 fear of a French invasion was very real. Napoleon's army was camped on the Channel coast. Throughout Britain volunteers drilled. Beacons were prepared to be lit when the French landed. But in the autumn of 1805 Napoleon turned east, as Hitler was to do after the Battle of Britain. The camp of the Army of the Invasion of Britain was broken up even before Nelson's victory at Trafalgar in October secured British mastery of the seas for the duration of the war, and made the blockade of the Continent possible. While Napoleon fought and defeated Austrians, Prussians and Russians, Wellington conducted a long, patient, ultimately successful campaign against the French in the Spanish Peninsula, until at last, as Napoleon's Continental Empire crumbled, he was able to cross the Pyrenees into France itself. The historian of the Peninsular War would be Sir William Napier, one of his generals, a Scot and a descendant of Napier of Merchiston, the inventor of logarithms; the Napiers would be among the foremost of imperial soldiers. Finally, in 1815, came Waterloo; the enduring image of that battle is Lady Butler's highly imaginative painting of the charge of the Royal Scots Greys, recalled by Orwell in his essay about his schooldays.

Though at Trafalgar Nelson's famous signal had begun with the words 'England expects . . .', no one could doubt that the war against Napoleon had been a British enterprise. Highland regiments – the Black Watch, the Gordon Highlanders and the Cameron Highlanders – were to the fore in victories from Alexandria (1801) to Waterloo. They took pride of place, and dazzled the French, when the Allied armies marched into Paris. As Devine explains, 'The heroic deeds of the Highland regiments revived the old soldierly tradition within the Union and signalled that instead of falling to the status of an English province, the Scots had fully contributed in blood to the imperial cause. They therefore merited treatment as equals and partners.' This equality existed in the eyes of both English and Scots. Memories of the Scots as 'Jacobite rebels' dimmed, or were transformed in such a way as, paradoxically, to establish the Scots as naturally loyal to what they saw as the traditional order – which was now British and Hanoverian. The regent, the future George IV, contributed to this reconciliation of divergent traditions by commissioning the great sculptor Canova to carve a memorial to the exiled Stuarts for St Peter's in Rome. Now that there were no Stuart claimants to disturb the peace, the kings who never reigned were there accorded their royal titles: James III, Charles III and Henry IX. (Only the most prickly Scot might object that James should have been VIII & III, and that no King Henry had ever ruled Scotland.)

There was another consequence of the Napoleonic Wars contributing to the creation of a British national identity. For twenty years the Continent was closed. The Grand Tour undertaken by so many noblemen, gentlemen, scholars and artists in the eighteenth century became impossible. The young Byron was unusually adventurous in heading for Greece and Albania, but he had to travel by way of Portugal, Gibraltar and Malta. Less enterprising young men contented themselves with journeys within Britain. Scott's long poem, *The Lady of the Lake*, made the Trossachs a popular destination. In *Pride and Prejudice* Jane Austen had Elizabeth Bennett's uncle and aunt, the Gardiners, speak of their Scottish tour. Improved transport rendered such excursions less demanding than in earlier times. The years between 1750 and 1830 were the Coaching Age, made possible by the construction of new roads. In Scotland alone some 3,000 miles of turnpike (or toll) roads were built. Scots in their turn discovered the delights of the English Lake District and west country. It was no longer only the nobility and adventurers who travelled.

Though denied access to the Continent the British did not become isolationist. On the contrary the war years were a period of imperial expansion. More territory in India was annexed by the army of the East India Company and the regular British regiments seconded to it. West Indian islands, formerly French or Spanish, were seized. Though the struggle against Napoleon engaged the nation, and though armies were maintained in western Europe intermittently throughout the years of struggle, Britain was preparing to turn its back on the Continent. The political classes became less European, their sense of British identity strengthened.

In the century which followed Waterloo there was to be no British military engagement in western Europe. It was the century of Empire, in which the United Kingdom pursued its global interests, now recognized as its destiny; and in consequence stood semi-detached from the Continent.

In Europe it was the Age of Nationalism. Germany and Italy, for centuries divided into numerous polities, emerged from war and revolution as nation-states. In central and eastern Europe, long-submerged nationalities acquired self-consciousness. The Ottoman Empire entered on a slow process of disintegration. The multinational Habsburg Empire found it expedient to grant recognition to subject-peoples, Czechs, Slavs, even Poles. The United Kingdom was not quite immune from the infection. Irish discontent eventually found expression in a resurgent nationalism, demanding, at the least, a measure of Home Rule.

But Scotland was largely unaffected. There was little demand for any degree of self-government. Indeed there was not even a distinct Scottish administration till 1880, and then the duties laid on the revived office of Secretary of State for Scotland were of the utmost modesty. The occasional squeak of working-class radical protest took on a nationalist accent; but for the most part Scottish radicals did not differ in their demands from English radicals: they sought the extension of the franchise, the legalization of trade unions, better working conditions, better pay. They may have felt Scottish but they acted in pursuit of a class interest, the same throughout the United Kingdom. As for the Scottish elite, its members were happy to be fully associated in the Government and administration of the United Kingdom and the Empire, in which they felt themselves to be equal partners and which offered noble prospects and glittering careers to their sons.

Scotland was British, its politics British politics, its economy part of a British imperial economy. Scottish progressives, Whigs and Liberals, were keen to elide such differences between Scotland and England as survived. It had been the practice since the Union to leave the management of Scottish affairs to a Scot, Islay and Dundas being the most conspicuous examples. As long as they kept Scotland quiet and delivered the votes of Scots MPs to the Government, they satisfied the demands of their English masters. Scott, as we have seen, extolled this benign neglect in *The Letters of Malachi Malagrowther*. But the Scots Whigs thought otherwise. Henry Cockburn, friend of Francis Jeffrey and contributor to the *Edinburgh Review*, which itself sought to lay down laws of taste and judgement to the whole United Kingdom, was delighted when in 1827 the prime minister, George Canning, though a Tory, empowered the home secretary (an Englishman) to assume management of Scottish affairs. That, said Cockburn, would be very properly the end of 'the horrid system of being ruled by a nasty jobbing Scot'. Likewise Cockburn, a Scots lawyer, was eager to assimilate Scots law to English. On Parliamentary reform he thought that 'the nearer we can propose to make ourselves to England the better. The sole object was to bring Scotland within the action of the constitution.'

This was Cockburn's intellectual judgement. The more Scotland resembled England the better. Assimilation was the desirable object. Yet Cockburn, like so many Scots, was a divided man. His sentiments diverged from his opinions, were sharply at odds with them. On the one hand he might write, equably: 'The feelings and habits which had prevailed at the Union, and which had left so many picturesque peculiarities on the Scottish character, could not survive the enlarged intercourse with England and the world.' Yet, on the other hand, he regretted their passing. The eighteenth century had been:

> the last purely Scotch age. Most of what had gone before had been turbulent and political. The eighteenth was the final Scotch century. We whose youth tasted the close of that century and who lived far into the Southern influence, felt proud of a purely Edinburgh society which raised the reputation of our discrowned capital and graced the deathbed of our national manners.

His melancholy is attractive. It is sentimental, not necessarily for that reason insincere. The mood was widely shared. It could find no political expression; the Scots not being a subject-nation like the Irish, there was no need of nationalism. Yet something specifically Scotch must be clung on to, for self-respect if for no other reason. So an apolitical Scottish patriotism flourished.

It was in part the legacy of Scott, who had kindled in his readers that strong sense of Scottish history, fostering the conviction that we were no mean people. So, in this most British of centuries, the cult of Wallace, and to a lesser extent Bruce, found new expression. In 1810, the Earl of Buchan, an Erskine, the eccentric founder of the Society of Antiquaries of Scotland, erected a massive statue of Wallace, in red sandstone, on the bank of the Tweed just above Dryburgh Abbey. Then the Wallace monument was built by public subscription to stand on Abbey Craig outside Stirling. Dominating the Forth valley, it overlooks the field of his victory in 1297. Other statues celebrating Wallace's defiance of Edward I were set up in Aberdeen and Edinburgh, where he guards the castle gate with Bruce.

There was sense in this as well as sentimentality. The significance of the Wallace cult was expressed early in the twentieth century in a child's history of Scotland, H. E. Marshall's *Scotland's Story*, a companion volume to *Our Island Story* and *Our Empire Story*, all books on which middle-class Scots of my generation were reared. Marshall wrote:

> The hatred between England and Scotland has long ago died out. The two countries are now united into one kingdom, under one King. And everyone knows that it is best for Scotland and best for England that it should be so. Wallace in his life did his very best to prevent that union. Yet both Englishmen and Scotsmen will ever remember him as a hero, for they know that, in preventing Edward from conquering Scotland, he did a great work for the empire to which we belong. If Scotland had been joined to England in the days of Edward, it would have been as a conquered country, and the union could never have been true and friendly. When hundreds of years later the two countries did join, it was not because one conquered the other, but because each of the two free nations, living side by side, wished it. Thus the union became firm and unbreakable, and all Britons may honour the name of Wallace for the part he had in making it so.

Over-simplified as the argument may be, it expresses what by the nineteenth century had become a truism: that the wars of Wallace and Bruce had ultimately made the Union what it was – a partnership. So much was this the accepted view, among the English as well as the Scots, that the English writer of manly stories for boys, G. A. Henty, gave one of his novels the title *In Freedom's Cause*, a stirring tale of the wars of Wallace and Bruce written from the Scots' point of view. It was my favourite book when I was eight.

Sentimental Jacobitism flourished likewise, in all social classes. Jacobite songs continued to be made and sung. Jacobite novels abounded. Jacobitism, in its time abhorred by Lowland Presbyterian Scotland, had become a harmless expression of Scottishness, marking off our difference from England without in any way threatening to endanger the Union.

The cult of Mary Queen of Scots served a like function. It was natural enough that the most romantic figure in Scottish history should appeal to the Romantic Age, again to the English also. Queen Victoria herself subscribed to the cult of Mary, who was after all her ancestress. So did Swinburne, though the poet belonged to a Northumberland family that had warred with the Scots across the Border for centuries. In Scotland the cult of Mary was tempered by Presbyterian historians whose hero was John Knox, and who followed George Buchanan in depicting her as a dangerous Roman Catholic reactionary. But even the Rev. John Cunningham, in his *Ecclesiastical History of Scotland*, while accusing Mary of plotting with 'the greatest bigot and bloodiest persecutor of the time', Philip II of Spain, couldn't altogether deny her sympathy. Certainly her appeal to popular sentiment was strong. My grandmother, born in 1875, and reared in the Free Kirk, told me as a child that she could never forgive Elizabeth of England for 'her cruelty to poor Mary' – Queen Victoria's sentiments exactly.

That unquestioning attachment to the Union could sit comfortably in the Victorian Age alongside a powerful Scottish sentiment is a matter requiring explanation. The most obvious, if unflattering, explanation is that the expression of this Scottish sentiment served as compensation for the surrender of sovereignty in 1707. By insisting on the survival of a distinct Scottish identity within the United Kingdom, the Victorian Scot was able to hide from reality. A modern nationalist might compare nineteenth-century Scots unfavourably with the Irish. Instead of resenting and opposing the English dominance of the Union, as the Irish did, the Scot fawned upon his English superiors, and strove to impress them. Being subconsciously ashamed of such behaviour, he played up his Scottishness, and displayed a vigorous patriotism in all those areas which could have no influence upon contemporary politics.

There is another simpler, and perhaps more probable, explanation, which at least has the merit of requiring no *ex post facto* psychological theorizing. There was very little anti-English feeling in nineteenth-century Scotland. Therefore it was quite easy for people to be comfortable with the dual identity, Scottish and British.

England then impinged very lightly on Scotland, and there was, comparatively speaking, so little awareness of England, of English attitudes and characteristics, that Scots were rarely made conscious of being the smaller and therefore less powerful partner in the Union.

One of Stevenson's early essays, *The Foreigner at Home*, published first in the *Cornhill*, the literary periodical of which Thackeray had been the first editor, examines the relations between the two peoples. The English, he remarked, were usually ignorant of Scotland.

> I once travelled with a man of plausible manners and good intelligence – a University man, as the phrase goes – a man, besides, who had taken his degree in life and knew a thing or two about the age we live in. We were deep in talk, whirling between Peterborough and London; among other things he began to describe some piece of legal injustice he had recently encountered, and I observed in my innocence that things were not so in Scotland. 'I beg your pardon,' he said, 'this is a matter of law.' He had never heard of Scots Law; nor did he choose to be informed. The law was the same for the whole country, he told me roundly; every child knew that. At last, to settle matters, I explained to him that I was a member of a Scottish legal body, and had stood the brunt of an examination in the very law in question. Thereupon he looked me for a moment full in the face and dropped the conversation.

Stevenson admits that this display of ignorance of differences existing between England and Scotland was 'a monstrous instance', but adds that 'it does not stand alone in the experience of Scots'. There are Scots lawyers who could even today affirm that they have had comparable experiences. Indeed the Labour Government's announcement in the late summer of 2003 of its intention to transfer the judicial functions of the House of Lords to a new Supreme Court serves as another example, for it appeared to have been devised without reference to its significance or import for Scots law, though it was to be effected by a Scotsman, Lord Falconer, who happened to be an English lawyer.

'England and Scotland', Stevenson continues, 'differ indeed in law, in history, in religion, in education, and in the very look of nature and men's faces, not only widely, but also trenchantly . . . A Scotchman may tramp the better part of Europe and the United States and never again receive so vivid an impression of foreign travel and strange lands and manners as on his first excursion into England.' Actually Stevenson's experience of Europe when he wrote this essay was limited to the Netherlands and France, and a childhood visit to Italy. Moreover there were many Scots of his generation who, reared in Glasgow and visiting Manchester or Liverpool, would have found far more that was familiar than strange.

Stevenson however was writing from his own experience, and comparing Edinburgh and the Lothians with London and the south of England, especially East Anglia, where he had spent some time as a guest of his friends Sidney Colvin and Frances Sitwell.

> It is not alone in scenery and architecture that we count England foreign. The constitution of society, the very pillars of the Empire, surprise and even pain us. The dull, neglected peasant, sunk in matter, insolent, gross, and servile, makes a startling contrast with our own long-legged, long-headed, thoughtful, Bible-quoting ploughman. A week or two in such a place as Suffolk leaves a Scotchman gasping. It seems incredible that within the boundaries of his own island a class should have been thus forgotten.

Though Scots ploughmen now drive tractors and are no longer very likely to quote the Bible, something of this contrast may survive to the present day. And there is another: no Scot can spend time in the southern English countryside, which one Italianized Scot, Norman Douglas, used to say was 'like living in a salad', without feeling that this is a place where nothing of historical significance has happened for centuries; there is no memory of battles and war, little evidence of houses built for defence or to withstand a siege. It is a land at peace.

Stevenson then compared 'the atmosphere in which Scotch and English youth begin to look about them, come to themselves in life, and gather up those first apprehensions which are the material of future thought and, to a great extent, the rule of future conduct'. Though foreigners might remark on the gloom of the English Sunday, Stevenson thought otherwise.

> Sabbath observance makes a series of grim, and perhaps serviceable, pauses in the tenor of Scotch boyhood – days of great stillness and solitude for the rebellious mind, when in the dearth of books and play, and in the intervals of studying the Shorter Catechism, the intellect and senses prey upon and test each other. The typical English Sunday, with the huge midday dinner and the plethoric afternoon, leads perhaps to different results.

And what are these? Why, 'about the very cradle of the Scot there goes a hum of metaphysical divinity; and the whole of the two divergent systems is summed up, not merely speciously, in the first two questions of the rival catechisms, the English tritely enquiring, "What is your name?", the Scottish striking at the very roots of life with, "What is the chief end of man?" and answering nobly, if obscurely, "to glorify God and to enjoy Him for ever". The fact of such a question being asked opens to us Scotch a great field of speculation; and the fact that it is asked of all of us, from the peer to the ploughboy, binds us more nearly together. No Englishman of Byron's age, character and history would have had patience for long theological discussions on the way to fight for Greece; but the daft Gordon blood and the Aberdonian schooldays kept their influence to the end.' Fair enough perhaps; but, as Stevenson admits, 'The Shorter Catechism, which I took as being so typical of Scotland was yet composed in the city of Westminster.'

He then contrasts the experience of university in the two countries.

The English lad goes to Oxford or Cambridge; there, in an ideal world of gardens, to lead a semi-scenic life, costumed, disciplined and drilled by proctors. Nor is this to be regarded merely as a stage of education; it is a piece of privilege besides, and a step that separates him still further from the bulk of his compatriots. At an earlier age the Scottish lad begins his greatly different experience of crowded class-rooms, of a gaunt quadrangle, of a bell hourly booming over the traffic of the city to recall him from the public-house where he has been lunching, or the streets where he has been wandering fancy-free. His college life has little of restraint, and nothing of necessary gentility. He will find no quiet clique of the exclusive, studious and cultured; no rotten borough of the arts. All classes rub shoulders on the greasy benches . . .

Now this is a conventional, if elegantly expressed, picture of the differences between universities in Scotland and England. It is also an absurdly partial one. There was some exaggeration in the suggestion that, at his own university of Edinburgh, 'all classes rubbed shoulders on the greasy benches'. Though there were a few students there who would 'at the session's end . . . [each] resume the labours of the field beside his peasant family', such were in a very small minority, and it is unlikely that Stevenson ever rubbed shoulders with the sons of urban manual workers. In Scotland, as in England, only a very small number of boys attended university; the total roll of the four Scottish universities in his time scarcely exceeded 10,000. Then, though Oxford and Cambridge might be the only universities in England with which a Scot was acquainted, there were now others: Durham, London, Manchester, Leeds for example. Moreover, university colleges, at first following courses and sitting examinations devised by London University, were being established in most of the cities and large towns of the English provinces; it would not be long before these became universities in their own right. The social mix in these new 'redbrick' universities would be at least as diverse as in the Scottish ones. So, for example, D. H. Lawrence, son of a coal-miner, would attend the University College, Nottingham, and Lawrence was only a generation younger than Stevenson himself. But Stevenson, like many Scots, was at least as ignorant of England as the majority perhaps of Englishmen were of Scotland. He knew less of Joseph Chamberlain's Birmingham than he did of Paris.

Stevenson was however puzzled to find an explanation for the Scottishness of Scotland and for the difference between England and Scotland. He couldn't define this. After all, 'the division of races is more sharply marked within the borders of Scotland itself than between the countries. Galloway and Buchan, Lothian and Lochaber, are like foreign parts; yet you may choose a man from any of them, and, ten to one, he shall prove to have the headmark of a Scot.' Through history, Highlanders and Lowlanders had been at odds. 'Even the English, it is recorded, did not loathe the Highlander and Highland costume as they were loathed by the remainder of the Scotch. Yet the Highlander felt himself to be a Scot' – and was recognized as such by the Lowlander.

'Is it', he asked, 'common education, common morals, a common language or a common faith, that join men into nations? There were practically none of these in the case we are considering.' Despite their absence,

> in spite of the difference of blood and language, the Lowlander feels himself the sentimental country man of the Highlander. When they meet abroad, they fall upon each other's necks in spirit; even at home there is a kind of clannish intimacy in their talk. But from his compatriot in the south the Lowlander stands consciously apart. He has had a different training; he obeys different laws; he makes his will in other terms, is otherwise divorced and married; his eyes are not at home in an English landscape or with English houses; his ear continues to remark the English speech; and even though his tongue acquire the Southern knack, he will still have a strong Scotch accent of the mind.

A Scotch accent of the mind? An English accent of the mind? These notions may be worth investigating. How, for instance, do they stand among those who have moved from one country to the other: Scots who have settled in England and their descendants, English, fewer perhaps in number, who have come north to Scotland, and whose children are reared there? Do Scots become English and English Scots?

5

Two Historians

'THEY TOLD ME', said the narrator of Somerset Maugham's novel *Cakes and Ale*, 'Carlyle was a great writer and I was ashamed that I found the *French Revolution* and *Sartor Resartus* unreadable. Can anyone read them now?' 'Oh well,' is the reply, 'Carlyle was a pretentious windbag.' So much for the Great Men of earlier generations.

'No one now', wrote the historian G. M. Young, 'would place Macaulay either as a writer or a thinker above or even on a level with Burke.' 'Macaulay's convictions', Hugh Trevor-Roper declared, 'caused him to make dogmatic judgements in fields where he was unqualified to speak and would never stoop to learn. To the modern reader, the dogmatism of his comments, in such fields, can be even more offensive than their ignorance or insensitivity.'

Yet, to mid-Victorians, Carlyle and Macaulay were indisputably among the great men – and the great minds – of the time. Their influence was unquestionable.

Carlyle was a Scot who removed to London to become the 'sage of Chelsea'. Macaulay's father was a Highland-born Scot. The historian, born in Leicestershire, called himself an Englishman. Yet one observer of his Parliamentary performances wrote: 'His voice is one of the most monotonous and least agreeable of those which usually belong to our countrymen north of the Tweed.'

Macaulay was a man of the Whig Establishment, confident in the virtue and superiority of his own time, country and class. Carlyle was a pious rebel. Neither was an orthodox believing and practising Christian.

Carlyle, born 1795, the elder by five years, rebelled against the theological certainties of the seventeenth century, the intellectual scepticism of the eighteenth and the materialism of the nineteenth. He looked for heroes and despised democracy. Yet no one did more to draw the attention of the reading public to the dangerous and unhappy condition of England in the Hungry Forties; Macaulay in contrast made a speech to which his editor gave the title 'Loveliness and Intelligence of Leeds'. If it was Disraeli who remarked that England was composed of Two Nations, the rich and the poor, it was Carlyle who put the thought in his head. George Eliot called him the greatest intellectual influence of the age, and said there was scarcely an important book or 'superior mind' that did not bear the stamp of his influence. That influence was felt far more strongly in England than in Scotland, though no one could have been more thoroughly and unmistakably Scotch than Carlyle.

His life was one of chronic dissatisfaction, not only on account of the dyspepsia and insomnia from which he suffered. His refusal to be satisfied with what was presented to him began early. Arriving at the University of Edinburgh in 1809, aged only fourteen, having walked there from Ecclefechan in Dumfriesshire, his family being too poor to make another mode of travel possible, he soon found it not greatly to his taste. 'The young vacant mind was furnished with much talk about the Progress of the Species, Dark Ages, Prejudice and the like . . . We boasted ourselves a Rational University; in the highest degree hostile to Mysticism.' And with what result, as it seemed to him? 'All were quickly enough blown into a state of windy argumentativeness; whereby the better sort had soon to end in sick, impotent Scepticism; the worser sort explode in finished Self-conceit.' The Enlightenment, at its fag-end, was expiring in what seemed to the earnest seeker after Truth, already deep in Goethe and the German Romantics, to be either complacency or frivolity.

Later, as a hack journalist, Carlyle had cause to be grateful to Francis Jeffrey and his *Edinburgh Review*. Yet he never became one of its stars, as Macaulay did. It was nevertheless thanks to Jeffrey's encouragement and patronage that he found himself 'in a sort, fairly launched upon Literature'. 'Jeffrey's acquaintanceship seemed, and was for a time, an immense acquisition to me; and everyone regarded it as my highest good fortune.' Yet gratitude, which Carlyle was certainly capable of feeling, couldn't still his critical sense. He soon discovered an insufficiency in his patron. 'Here is a man', he concluded, 'whom they have kneaded into an Edinburgh Reviewer, and clothed the soul of in Whig formulas' – a judgement applicable to Macaulay too. Carlyle shook his head, gloomily, over the waste. A success as the world judged success, poor Jeffrey was 'not deep enough, pious or reverent enough, to have been great in Literature'; or, the unspoken thought may be, in Life.

Carlyle, like many another lad o' pairts, had come to Edinburgh intended for the ministry, but his childhood faith was soon in disarray. 'Did God Almighty come down and make wheelbarrows in a shop?' he asked his devout and much loved mother. For some years, he dwelled in the Slough of Despond, perplexed, brooding, a traveller lost in the mirk. In this he was far from alone. If the world was, as new conceptions of geological and biological time were making clear, in a state of perpetual flux, what was there of solidity to cling to? Tennyson, a friend of Carlyle's, addressed the same problem:

> The hills are shadows and they flow
>> From form to form, and nothing stands:
>> They melt like mist, the solid lands,
> Like clouds they shape themselves and go.

The certainties of centuries were dissolving.

Carlyle resisted the temptation of despair – a temptation Macaulay could never have felt. It was too early for Nihilism, of which in any case Carlyle, with his need to believe, was temperamentally incapable. Yet at the same time he was sceptical of ideas of Progress, attractive to less philosophic minds. But what was there to keep hold of?

Carlyle's answer is to be found in his *Reminiscences*, by some way the most attractive and agreeable of his books; many might say the only agreeable one among them. These were written mostly after the death of his wife, Jane Welsh, in 1866. But the earliest, his memoir of his father James Carlyle, dates from the 1830s, before Carlyle was in the full flower of his fame. It is a piece fundamental to our understanding of him and of the rural Scotch society in which he was reared.

'Annandale', he remembered, 'had long been a lawless "Border" country; the people had ceased from foray-riding' – ceased indeed soon after the Union of the Crowns when the Border was pacified. Nevertheless, they had not shaken off 'its effects; the "gallant man" of these districts was still a wild, natural, almost animal man'. One can detect a note of sympathy for the type, as if Carlyle wished it was his. His grandfather, Thomas like himself, had been of this sort: 'his stroke was ever as ready as his word, and both were sharp enough. Not by nature or inclination industrious' – unlike his grandson, who toiled at his task and complained as he toiled – 'he preferred to hunt hares with lurchers in the company of his kinsman, Adam Carlyle of Bridekirk, a swashbuckler of those days'. The Carlyles might be poor, but they could, in the old Scots fashion, call the laird cousin. Carlyle would retain a strong sense of this 'natural man' and a nostalgia for the unreflective rural society to which he belonged, one in which men acted by instinct.

James Carlyle, his father, was however deeply serious, formed for industry, piety, duty. 'From the time when he connected himself with the Religious – became a Burgher (strict, but not strictest, species of Protestant Dissenter) may be dated his spiritual majority; his earthly life was now enlightened and overcanopied by a heavenly; he became a Man.'

Carlyle was the first child of his father's second marriage, to Margaret Aitken, 'a woman to me of the fairest descent, that of the pious, the just, and the wise'. The character of his parents determined his upbringing. 'Frugality and assiduity, a certain grave composure, an earnestness (not without its constraint, then felt as oppressive a little, yet which now yields its fruit) were the order of our household. We were all practically taught that *work* (temporal or spiritual) was the only thing we had to do; and incited always to do it *well*.' Carlyle never departed from this conviction: that work, well performed, was what justified and gave meaning to existence. This was a message for his times, when Britain was coming to boast itself 'the workshop of the world'.

As for politics, James Carlyle took, his son tells us, a lively interest in great events: the American War, the Revolution in France, the rise and fall of Napoleon. But, 'for the rest, he never meddled with Politics; he was not there to govern, but to be governed; could still *live*, and therefore did not *revolt*'. Carlyle's contempt for Parliamentary politics was to become complete. There seem to have been only two Parliamentarians of his time whom he held in any regard: Cobden who campaigned for the repeal of the Corn Laws that kept the price of bread unnecessarily high, and Peel who put through that measure, breaking his own party in doing so. In the 1840s Carlyle saw something of his longed-for hero in Peel, the Harrow- and Cambridge-educated son of a Lancashire mill-owner, precisely because Peel was more interested in measures than in speeches, in getting things done than in playing the Parliamentary game. Peel was a supremely practical man, a supremely competent one too. After his death in a riding accident in 1850 Carlyle ceased to look for any good emerging from British Parliamentary politics. It was to his mind all talk, and the talk was cant.

Carlyle abandoned Edinburgh for London, Scotland for England. Edinburgh was insufficient. 'The whole place', he wrote to his brother John in Italy, 'impresses me as something village-like; after the roaring Life-floods of London, it looks all little, secluded, almost quiescent.' 'One must', he told John Stuart Mill, himself a first-generation Anglo-Scot whose father hailed from Brechin, 'put up with much that is spiritually *kleinstädtisch*.' For men like Carlyle, men of gifts and ambition, it seemed that the future lay in London. 'The representative Scot,' wrote Ian Campbell, editor of Carlyle's *Letters*, 'growing up in the last period of the Age of Cockburn and the Age of Scott, works from the heart of British society in London while Edinburgh has only the derivative and essentially outdated work of John Wilson' – the 'Christopher North' of *Blackwood's Magazine's* series of dialogues *Noctes Ambrosianae*.

Carlyle, moralist and prophet in the Old Testament sense of the term, could not fail to write as a social critic. As early as 1829, in his essay 'Signs of the Times', he recognized 'a deep-lying struggle in the whole fabric of society; a boundless grinding collision of the New with the Old'. Sceptical of the Enlightenment assurance of Progress, he questioned the values of the new industrial manufacturing society in which the Poor laboured as miserable wage-earners. For what purpose? Merely to make the Rich richer. Fearing *demos*, he yet had sympathy for the poor and oppressed. In *Sartor Resartus* his (imaginary) German philosopher drinks a toast to 'The Cause of the Poor, in God's name and the Devil's'. Replying to Malthus' warning that the population was in danger of outstripping the means of its support, he suggested, with an irony as lacerating as that of Swift's *Modest Proposal* for reducing population and therefore poverty in Ireland, that there should be an annual three days' hunting season in which the shooting of paupers should be lawful.

Carlyle made his name, and fortune, with his history of the French Revolution. But it was the attention he gave to the social problems resulting from the rapid and unplanned industrialization of the north and midlands of England, and the west of Scotland, that gave him, for a decade at least, the authority of a prophet.

He was not blind – how could he be? – to the grandeur of the achievement. There had been nothing like it in the world before. In his pamphlet *Chartism* he compares the sound of the Manchester cotton-mills in the early morning to 'the boom of an Atlantic tide'; but he saw, none more clearly, the contrast, even the contradiction, between magnificent results and ignoble means: great wealth was produced, prosperity indeed spread, but at the expense of subjecting the workers to a dehumanizing regime, one which reduced them to the status of adjuncts of the machine. Recognizing 'alienation' before Marx defined it, he fulminated against the breaking of the natural bonds that should exist between men, and which had been evident in rural Annandale. Now these were replaced by the 'cash nexus'; and this could be severed at the whim of the employer.

The 1840s were to be remembered as the 'hungry years'. The surging wave of industrialization broke, briefly. There was a slump which none could account for. Unemployment rose sharply, in the midst of unprecedented wealth. Carlyle was no economist. He did not understand what was happening. Nor at the time did economists, whom anyway he dismissed as 'Respectable Professors of the Dismal Science'. But he saw more clearly than an economist might. Unemployment, dearth in the midst of plenty, were to his mind the consequences of the substitution of an economic relationship for what had been, and should be, a personal one. It was the consequence of the refusal of the propertied classes to accept responsibility for the well-being of the inferior classes, their dependants.

A prophet is not someone who offers solutions, rather one who points the finger at what is wrong, who denounces injustice and oppression, who awakens the conscience of his hearers or readers. And this is what Carlyle did. He never denied or reviled the achievements of industrialism; indeed manufacturers, inventors and innovators were among his heroes. But at the same time he told his audience that there was something profoundly wrong with the organization of society and the manner in which it had developed; he articulated, passionately, what thousands obscurely felt.

His message was, primarily, moral. Life, he taught, was in its essence to be characterized by an intense and urgent moral challenge. The world for him, as for his Covenanting forebears, was a battle-ground fought over by the forces of Good and Evil. He might have discarded his inherited and conventional Christianity, but he did not doubt that the universe was, in some way, ordered. He had, he confessed, with some pride even, 'no Morrison's Pill for curing the maladies of Society'. Nevertheless he was certain that 'Midas-eared Mammonism, double-barrelled Dilettantism, and their thousand adjuncts and corollaries, are *not* the Law by which God Almighty has appointed this His universe to go.' 'All reform,' he insisted, 'except a moral one, will prove unavailing.' It was necessary that the ruling classes recovered a sense of social responsibility.

Nowhere was the absence of this more evident than in Ireland:

Ireland has near seven millions of working people, the third unit of whom, it appears by Statistic Science, has not for thirteen weeks each year as many third-rate potatoes as will suffice him. It is a fact, perhaps

the most eloquent that was ever written down in any language, at any
date in the world's history . . . A Government and guidance of white
European man which has issued in perennial hunger of potatoes to the
third man extant, ought to drop a veil over its face, and walk out of
court under conduct of proper officers; saying no word; excepting now
of a surety sentence either to change or to die. England is guilty
towards Ireland; and reaps at last, in full measure, the fruit of fifteen
generations of wrong-doing . . .

(Carlyle, often wearisome to read at length, on account of the intensity and convolutions of his style, is marvellous to quote; and the
temptation is to do so repeatedly.)

This indictment was written and pronounced even before potato
blight caused the famine, the Great Hunger, which reduced the population of Ireland by even more than that 'third unit'. The use of the
word 'unit' is significant, searingly ironic. Carlyle, echoing Swift, with
whom he felt a close affinity – the philosopher–kings and politicians
of the Enlightenment being, in his opinion, spiritual descendants of
Swift's lunatic 'Projectors' in the floating island of Lagado – derided
and despised the tendency of the Utilitarian theorists to reduce men
to the level of a statistical abstraction. For him the fundamental cause
of the Revolution in France had been the inability of the ruling class
to recognize people as individuals:

every unit has his own heart and sorrows; stands covered with his own
skin, and if you prick him, he will bleed . . . Every unit of these Masses
is a miraculous Man, even as thou thyself art; struggling with vision,
or with blindness, for his infinite kingdom, with a spark of the
Divinity, what thou callest an immortal soul in him.

This was the language of Scots Presbyterianism, but also of English
Wesleyan Methodism, the language in which George Whitefield had
preached.

Carlyle's understanding of the social crisis of the 1840s was founded
in experience, not theory. He knew what poor men were, and what
they might be. Those who denied their reality, and reduced the poor
to statistical entities, met with his savage and indignant scorn.

He had no time for the theorists of laissez-faire, heirs, if at a distance, of Adam Smith, when they argued against State intervention intended to correct the mindless working of the economy. Their arguments were dismissed as 'Paralytic Radicalism': 'the public highways ought not to be occupied by people demonstrating that motion is impossible'.

Carlyle's influence, his literary influence at least, was felt more strongly in England than in Scotland. Thoroughly, ineradicably Scotch as he was (though capable of writing 'we English'), his disciples were found south of the Border, partly perhaps because his tone was more familiar north of it. Novels examining the 'Condition of England' abounded in the years after he wrote *Past and Present*: they were written by Disraeli, Dickens, Gaskell, Kingsley, even Bulwer Lytton. There were no comparable 'Condition of Scotland' ones, though society experienced the same stresses there, the same 'boundless grinding collision between the Old and the New'. This is hard to account for, unless or except by the preoccupation of the Scots intelligentsia in that decade with what seemed to them of even greater consequence: the Disruption of the Church of Scotland in 1843, which saw a third of its ministers secede from the established Kirk to set up their own Free Church.

The leader of the Secessionists was Thomas Chalmers, himself certainly not blind to the effects of industrialization. A great preacher, whose 'tones', Carlyle wrote, 'would rise to the piercingly pathetic', Chalmers, as a parish minister in both Glasgow and Edinburgh, had seen the need for the Church to adopt a wider role. His ministry has been described as 'a social experiment which involved pastoral oversight of virtually every aspect of the life of the parish aimed at eliminating poor relief (except for the truly needy) by encouraging independence, self-reliance and self-help'. Pre-Victorian, Chalmers having been born in 1780, this philosophy was to be the essence of mid-nineteenth-century Victorianism, in both Scotland and England. Christopher Smout, English historian who, as Professor of Scottish History, first at St Andrews and then at Edinburgh, revived the study of the social and economic history of Scotland, observed that the reputation of Victorian

Scotland 'for serious philanthropy – like William Collins of the Temperance Movement and William Quarrier of the Children's Homes, was due in no small degree to Thomas Chalmers'.

Carlyle might have been expected to applaud Chalmers's work. To some extent he indeed did so; nevertheless he found Chalmers himself to be 'essentially a man of little culture, of narrow sphere all his life; such an intellect, professing to be educated and yet so ill-read, so ignorant of all that lay beyond the horizon in place or in time, I have almost nowhere met with'. A harsh judgement, not shared by many, inspired, I would guess, by an apprehension on Carlyle's part of a certain complacency in Chalmers, and in the strand of Scottish intellectual life which he represented; it was similar to his response to Jeffrey and the Scottish Whigs. They were too comfortable in the sense of their own virtue, in their social position; exhibiting also what John Buchan, not devoid of it himself, called the deplorable Scots quality of unction.

Be that as it may, the Disruption served as a distraction from social and economic questions. The characteristic Scottish novel of the second half of the century was rural, parochial, occupied with questions of tenant displacement and communal dissension. Its centre was the manse, not the factory or the industrialist's mansion. It offered, in the words of the literary historian and critic Douglas Gifford, an 'anecdotal and episodic sentimental exploitation and distortion of Scottish Life and Character for a bigger British audience'. No later events could rival the Disruption. 'Except for Thomas Carlyle,' J. M. Reid wrote in a history of Scottish literature, 'who belongs to British rather than Scottish literature, Scots writers seemed unable to react to the world around them after 1843.' There was a retreat to comfortable provincialism.

Yet Carlyle's own influence waned in the next decade. This was partly because his contempt for Parliamentary democracy (such as that was) intensified, and his political views seemed increasingly unsympathetic, partly because the return of prosperity following the Great Exhibition of 1851 (itself boosting national self-esteem) made the social–economic questions he had posed seem less urgent, even irrelevant. Things were not after all in danger of breaking up. Chartism had failed. There had been no revolution, and even on the Continent the revolutions of 1848 had all fizzled out. The established order was secure. There was no need of a prophet. Macaulay, celebrating the march of progress and affirming the Whig interpretation of history, caught the mood of the 1850s as Carlyle had that of the 1840s.

Yet there is one other book of Carlyle's and one follower that should be noticed here.

The book was his edition of Oliver Cromwell's *Letters and Speeches*, published with 'Elucidations', these being themselves the length of a fair-sized biography. Carlyle had already treated, admiringly, of Cromwell in his lectures on Heroes and Hero-Worship where he called him 'the strongest soul in England' and 'the one true pre-eminent Statesman England had had in the course of fifteen hundred years'.

Carlyle identified with Cromwell, 'effectively', in the words of his best modern biographer Simon Heffer, 'celebrating the secularization of the Calvinist idea of the Elect'; he:

> would look for its continuance in contemporary England . . . [he] rec-
> ognized he was writing an allegory, a lesson for contemporary Britain.
> That is the note upon which he concludes and, as so often, he cannot
> resist a note of humour:

> > The Genius of England no longer soars sunward, world-defiant,
> > like an Eagle through the storms, 'mewing her mighty youth', as
> > John Milton saw her do: the Genius of England, much like a
> > greedy Ostrich intent on provender and a whole skin mainly,
> > stands with its other extremity Sunward . . . No Ostrich . . . but
> > will be awakened one day – in a terrible a-posteriori manner, if
> > not otherwise! – Awake before it come to that; gods and men bid
> > us awake! The Voices of our Fathers, with a thousand fold stern
> > monition to one and all, bid us awake.

Flattery, castigation, exhortation in a few lines: irresistibly attractive, then as ever.

Carlyle's *Cromwell* is significant for another reason. It offered a revised reading of English, and British, history.

At the Restoration in 1660 Cromwell's body was, understandably, dug up and hung in chains as an expression of reprobation of his career as rebel, regicide and military dictator. Subsequent historians did not dispute this verdict. To the eighteenth century, to David Hume even, Cromwell was a fanatic and hypocrite. The nearest the time could come to admiration was Gray's line in his *Elegy in a Country Churchyard*: 'some Cromwell guiltless of his country's blood'.

Cromwell was indeed something of a fanatic and hypocrite, though perhaps less of either than some of his enemies. The rule of the army which he imposed on both kingdoms, and far more ruthlessly and cruelly on Ireland, left a dark memory, and inspired Britons with a distaste for standing armies that lasted into the twentieth century. That Britain, despite being an imperial power, refused to countenance military conscription, the norm in Continental Europe, until 1916 was one of Cromwell's legacies.

Yet this wasn't his chief significance, which however it took Carlyle to recognize. Cromwell represented, incarnated even, a strain in English life, a response to experience, an ethos, a habit of mind, that ran deep in society, but which was for almost 200 years ignored, one may even say suppressed, by the Establishment, or at the most acknowledged only in the thin diluted form of Whiggism. Cromwell stood for Dissent, for the duty of every man to judge for himself matters of Right and Wrong. Carlyle, by insisting on his greatness, restored him to a central place in an English tradition that stretched from Langland in the fourteenth century, by way of Latimer in the sixteenth, to Lawrence, Orwell and Leavis in the twentieth. Cromwell was the political shadow of Bunyan, author, as already remarked, of the counter-Establishment classic of English literature. It took Carlyle, the Annandale peasant and Scotch moralist, to restore Cromwell – 'God's Own Englishman', in the title of Christopher Hill's biography – to the national Pantheon.

The follower, disciple indeed, was John Ruskin, a Scots-born Englishman, who came to regard Carlyle as his spiritual father. Ruskin, wayward, intense, even fantastic, sometimes childlike, was the pattern of an English eccentric; nevertheless, taking from Carlyle all that was most modern – that is to say, Victorian – in his teaching, 'he evolved,' as G. M. Young wrote, 'and forced his world to accept, a new set of axioms as the basis of all future political science in England' – for a hundred years anyway, one might add. In 1885 a group of economists, escaping for the time being the most dismal elements of the 'Dismal Science', addressed Ruskin as follows, acknowledging their debt to his teaching:

> Political Economy can furnish sound laws of life and work only where it respects the dignity and moral destiny of man: and the wise use of wealth, in developing a complete human life, is of incomparably greater moment both to men and actions than its production or accumulation, and can alone give these any vital significance.

These sentiments were the consequence of Ruskin's teaching, scattered over innumerable books, essays, pamphlets, newsletters and speeches: that teaching which had had Oxford undergraduates, including Oscar Wilde, labouring and breaking stones for the construction of the Iffley Road. This practical demonstration of the virtue of work grew from Carlyle's writings on political economy in the 1830s and 1840s, and from his many conversations, fuelled by tea and tobacco, with Ruskin in Cheyne Walk.

Macaulay would not have questioned the moral value of work; his own industry was prodigious. But his temperament was quite different from Carlyle's, or indeed Ruskin's. Where they were both, to some degree, neurotic (consequence of physical ill-health), Macaulay was blithely serene, confident that human history was proceeding upward and onward. 'The more we study the annals of the past,' he wrote in the conclusion to the third chapter of his *History*, which describes the state of England in 1685,

> the more shall we rejoice that we live in a merciful age, in an age in which cruelty is abhorred, and in which pain, even when deserved, is inflicted reluctantly and from a sense of duty. Every class doubtless has gained largely by this great moral change; but the class which has gained most is the poorest, the most dependent, and the most defenceless.

Moreover, this progress would continue.

> We too shall, in our turn, be outstripped . . . It may well be, in the
> twentieth century, that the peasant of Dorsetshire may think himself
> miserably paid with twenty shillings a week; and that the carpenter at
> Greenwich may receive ten shillings a day; that labouring men may be
> as little used to dine without meat as they now are to eat rye bread; that
> sanitary police and medical discoveries may have added several more
> years to the average length of human life; that numerous comforts and
> luxuries, which are now unknown, or confined to a few, may be
> within the reach of every diligent and thrifty working man . . .

His boundless optimism was not misplaced. Indeed he underesti-
mated the degree to which material progress would accelerate and
transform the lives of all classes. Doubtless, Hugh Trevor-Roper was
right when he wrote that 'Macaulay, in the crude materialism of his
concept of progress, is sometimes positively vulgar.' But this does not
make Macaulay mistaken. Moreover it was not only material progress
that he remarked and approved; he wrote also of the 'moral change'
that had made his time 'more merciful' than previous ages. 'It is pleasing to reflect', he wrote, 'that the public mind of England has softened
while it has ripened, and that we have, in the course of ages, become,
not only a wiser, but also a kinder people.' It disgusted him to think
that, in the seventeenth century, 'husbands, of decent station, were
not ashamed to beat their wives', that 'pedagogues knew no way of
imparting knowledge but by beating their pupils', and that 'Gentlemen arranged parties of pleasure to Bridewell on court days, for the
purpose of seeing the wretched women who beat hemp there
whipped'. He was happy that society no longer looked on misery
'with profound indifference', and he approved:

> that sensitive and restless compassion which has, in our time, extended
> a powerful protection to the factory child, to the Hindoo widow, to
> the negro slave, which pries into the stores and watercasks of every
> emigrant ship, which will not suffer the thief in the hulks to be ill fed
> or overworked, and which has repeatedly endeavoured to save the life
> even of a murderer.

Macaulay's admiration for his own age may seem to us complacent, but it was founded in humanity, and he looked forward confidently to the continuing advance of moral progress as of material.

Whence came this optimism? No doubt it was partly a matter of temperament, partly the result of a childhood in an Evangelical family zealous for the reform of social abuses, and especially for the abolition of slavery. Macaulay would, as an adult, reject much that his father and relations had stood for: his father's Toryism, his mother's Quaker background, for instance. But he stood by their belief in the possibility of moral and social improvement.

Meanwhile, after a Radical interlude while at Trinity College, Cambridge, he became a Whig, an ornament of the *Edinburgh Review* and of the aristocratic Whig sanctum, Holland House, one of those who argued the cause of Parliamentary Reform most cogently in the Commons. No democrat, for he believed that democracy would reduce the United States of America to the condition of 'Barbary or the Morea', a prophecy unfulfilled, perhaps because American democracy has been tempered by respect for wealth, Macaulay saw Reform as his mentors in Edinburgh, Francis Jeffrey and Henry Cockburn, did, as something necessary if government was to command the approval of the educated and the respect of the masses. The unreformed Parliament was in danger of losing both; therefore the franchise must be extended, rotten and pocket boroughs must be abolished, and the new industrial towns and cities brought within the pale of the constitution. There were historical precedents. Hadn't the Roman Senate acted thus when it granted citizenship to the Latins?

Macaulay's Whiggism, Trevor-Roper wrote, 'was distinguished by what we may call his Scottish inheritance. He had absorbed the "utilitarian" philosophy which had made Hume a tory, which had been made whig by Adam Smith, Millar and Mackintosh, and which was now the philosophy of the *Edinburgh Review*.' When he set out to write his *History of England*, it was in opposition to Hume's version, which had held sway for almost a hundred years. He differed from Hume in believing that material progress and enlightened political action were inextricably linked. It was Whiggism – that is, the political courses followed by Whig politicians – which had secured English liberty and progress in 1688, and shielded the country from the bloody and violent Revolution that tore France apart a century later. If this interpretation of history seems complacent today, it nevertheless appeared justified 150 years ago. So Macaulay, the grandson of a bare-legged Highlander whose garb would, before the Union, have been regarded, as he wrote, 'by nine Scotchmen out of ten as the dress of a thief', gave expression in his history to the certainty of English men and women that they lived not only in the most prosperous of countries, but in the best-ordered polity the world had ever known.

Though he entitled his work *The History of England,*

> he was [Trevor-Roper again] the first historian to study the Revolution of 1688 as a British, not purely English, revolution . . . He recognized that each country [of the United Kingdom] had distinct problems, which the Revolution might either settle or inflame; and his analysis of these problems is one of the most valuable parts of his work. He did for the Glorious Revolution of 1688 what nobody, even now, has done for the Puritan Revolution of 1640 to 1660; he saw it as a social and political revolution whose progress and consequences were equally important to all three kingdoms . . .

One influence on Macaulay, as on Carlyle, was Walter Scott. Carlyle recognized as one aspect of Scott's genius the way in which he reminded readers that historical figures were once really men of flesh and blood. He himself sought to give his history of the Revolution in France the vividness and immediacy of a Waverley novel. Macaulay likewise was not unusual in being captivated by Scott, but the use he made of Scott's work, and the lessons he drew from it, informed all his historical writing. In an early essay, published in the *Edinburgh Review* in 1828, he wrote that the historian should not be content to restrict himself to accounts of battles, wars, sieges, politics, diplomatic exchanges. He should also:

> intersperse the details which are the charm of historical romances. Sir Walter Scott . . . has used those fragments of truth which historians have scornfully thrown behind them . . . He has constructed out of

their gleanings works which, even considered as histories, are scarcely less valuable than theirs. But a truly great historian would reclaim those materials which the novelist has appropriated.

And this he set himself to do.

Macaulay's influence was immense. His Whig interpretation of history held sway well into the twentieth century. Winston Churchill, though he would later call Macaulay a 'liar' because of what he wrote about the 1st Duke of Marlborough, nevertheless as a young man believed everything he wrote, took his word as gospel and sought to model his style on the historian's. More to the point, Churchill's own understanding of English and British history, indeed of the history of the English-speaking peoples, deviated scarcely at all from Macaulay's. Politically, he was the historian's heir. He might call himself, at different times, a Liberal and a Tory Democrat. In reality, he was the last Whig, political child of the Enlightenment, the *Edinburgh Review* and Macaulay's essays and history.

6

Royalty

—•—

MEDIEVAL KINGSHIP WAS contractual, in both England and Scotland. Kings reigned and governed with the consent of the 'Community of the Realm' – that is, the political class composed of barons and lesser landowners, and the dignitaries of the Church, the bishops and abbots themselves being great landowners. The Scots barons who affixed their mark to the Declaration of Arbroath in 1320 had affirmed their readiness to dispose of any king who compromised the nation's independence, and choose another in his place. In England the barons had humiliated King John, and compelled him to sign the Magna Carta in which he promised to abide by the laws of the realm. His son Henry III was likewise brought to book and made to attend to grievances as expressed by the first Parliament of England. Later unsatisfactory kings, Edward II and Richard II, were formally deposed, before being murdered to prevent any attempt at their restoration.

Historians used to write of the sixteenth-century Tudor despotism, but even that was conditional on the monarch retaining the confidence of the political class. Henry VIII's minister Thomas Cromwell thought it wise to use Parliament to effect the revolutionary break with Rome; and the later Elizabethan religious settlement was also enacted by Parliament. Nevertheless the Tudors elevated their royal status. Henry VIII was the first to be addressed as 'Your Majesty' rather than 'Your Grace', a title shared with archbishops, bishops, abbots and dukes. The Tudor Court, no longer peripatetic in the style of the medieval monarchy, was more splendid than anything England had previously known.

Scots treated their kings roughly, without ceremony. Shakespeare has the usurper Claudius, in *Hamlet*, speak of the 'divinity' that 'doth hedge a king', and Elizabethan audiences might have nodded in approval. But, north of the Border, the Presbyterian leader Andrew Melville told James VI roundly that in the kingdom of Christ Jesus James himself was 'naught but God's sillie vassal'. Two earlier Stewart kings, James I and James III, were murdered; others, including James VI, were taken and held prisoner by discontented nobles. James's mother Mary was reduced to tears by Knox's scolding (if we are to believe his account). After her surrender to the rebel lords at Carberry Hill, she was brought back to Edinburgh to be met by a mob howling, 'Burn the hoor'; it is not easy to imagine England's Elizabeth being subjected while queen to comparable indignities.

In Scotland kings still lived among their people, the dwellings of poor citizens crowding right up to the Palace of Holyroodhouse, while the abbey attached to the palace served as a sanctuary for debtors and criminals. In July 1593 when Holyrood was invaded by the wild, and perhaps half-crazy, Earl of Bothwell at the head of an armed gang, anxious citizens, gathered round the palace, were appeased only when the king showed himself at a window, dressed in his nightshirt, to assure them he was still alive and safe.

It is no wonder James was happy to migrate to England where the Tudors had accustomed their subjects to treat the monarch with respect, even reverence. Once ensconced there, he showed little inclination to keep his promise to return north every third year to show himself to his people and give even the meanest of his Scottish subjects opportunity to gain access to his royal person. In fact, having discovered that he could rule Scotland more completely with his pen from London than his ancestors had done with the sword, he returned to his native land only once, in 1617. Then he told his Parliament that Scotland contained many barbarities; therefore he wished that his Scottish subjects would copy the good manners of the English, as they already imitated them in drinking toasts, wearing fine clothes and smoking tobacco – which last habit he detested.

In England, perhaps intoxicated by the deference showed them

there, James VI & I and his son Charles I overplayed their hand, insisting on the king's special relationship with the Almighty, and failing to
realize that the king's divine right to rule was at best a polite fiction.
Charles discovered this to his cost, provoking rebellion; he was put on
trial as an enemy of the people, and his claim that 'a sovereign and a
subject are clean different things' was answered by his judges pro-
nouncing sentence of death. Tudor despotism gave way to republican
despotism – in the name of liberty. The Republic failed, but the
restored monarch, Charles II, had learned the lesson.

For the century of the Dual Monarchy Scots seldom saw their king.
Then the Revolution of 1688 gave both countries a king whose title
derived explicitly from the will and approval of the Parliaments. The
Treaty of Union secured the Hanoverian (Protestant) succession,
already determined for England by the Act of Settlement six years previously. From 1714, when George I succeeded Anne, the king was still
the effective, and not merely nominal, head of government, but it was
already established in reality, and was soon acknowledged in theory
also, that the ministers he chose must have the support of the House
of Commons. Those who, like Bute, lacked that support or approval,
or who lost it, as Lord North did in the later stages of the war against
the American rebels, could not be maintained in office, however eager
the king might be to retain their services. It was indeed North himself
who told George III that ultimately the will of Parliament must
prevail, even over his royal wishes.

Eighteenth-century monarchy was popular in the sense that it was
Parliamentary, and Parliament, however unrepresentative, notionally
expressed the will of the people. But it was not popular in the ordinary
sense of the word. The Hanoverian kings were a constitutional necessity. Few regarded them with either admiration or affection. Jacobites
scoffed at George I as a 'wee bit German lairdie'; backwoods English
Tories grumbled about the 'Hanoverian rats'. This was natural enough;
both Jacobites and Tories belonged to the defeated party. But even the
Whigs, thoroughly committed to the Hanoverian succession, felt no
loyalty to the person of their German kings. Loyalty was instead directed
to the constitution and the Revolution Settlement. That sufficed.

It was enough indeed for the kings themselves. They did not seek popularity. Their English world was confined to the Court and the political class. The first two Georges made regular visits to their native Hanover, but neither ventured north of London and the Thames Valley. George III, born and brought up in England, said that he gloried 'in the name of Briton', and indeed felt himself to be British, or at least English. But it did not occur to him to show himself to his subjects in the more distant parts of his kingdom. In the second half of his reign, when afflicted by intermittent madness, he achieved some personal popularity, being called 'Farmer George' and 'the good old king', but this was restricted to the home counties of London. Elsewhere he was at best respected as a symbol of Britain's defiance of the French Revolution and Napoleon.

Instead it was, as recounted in the chapter on Sir Walter Scott, George IV – fat, dissolute, deeply unpopular and despised in London as he was – who pointed the way to a new sort of monarchy, with his visits to Dublin and Edinburgh. If the monarchy was to survive in the new age of revolutions and reform, the king must seek to win the affection of his people. He must therefore show himself to them. It might be absurd for a Highland chief, dressed in the tartan which George's grandfather's government had outlawed, to raise his glass and propose a toast to flabby, indolent George IV as 'the Chief of Chiefs'. Nevertheless in a curious way it made sense. As, over the next century, the political importance of the Crown gradually diminished, so that the Government became His or Her Majesty's in name only rather than in reality, the monarch's function was to be essentially symbolic, embodying the idea of national unity.

To perform this role the king or queen, and indeed all members of the royal family, must be seen to interest themselves in the lives of the people, must identify themselves with good causes and worthwhile projects, must support charities and voluntary organizations, and must be visible in all parts of the kingdom. Given that this kingdom was made up of four nations imperfectly welded into one, each yet retaining its own sense of proud individuality, this new royal role was as difficult as it was important. It would not be performed with complete success. Queen Victoria's indifference to Ireland and her reluctance to follow her uncle George IV's example and show herself there meant that the full Parliamentary Union of Ireland with Great Britain, effected only in 1801, was not strengthened by any royal attempt to win the affections of the Irish people.

It was very different in Scotland. Victoria was of course far more German than Scotch or English, for the Hanoverians had always chosen their brides from among the numerous royal or princely families of Germany; yet she gloried in her descent from James VI, proclaimed herself a Stuart, wrote of Mary Queen of Scots as 'poor Queen Mary' and developed a sincere love for Scotland to which she gave exuberant expression.

She first visited Scotland in 1842, the year after her marriage to her cousin Prince Albert of Saxe-Coburg-Gotha. She found Edinburgh 'quite beautiful; totally unlike anything else I have seen; and what is even more, Albert, who has seen so much, says it is unlike anything he ever saw'. She thought the people 'very friendly and kind', and that was to be her abiding opinion. 'The country and the people', she at once decided, 'have a quite different character from England and the English.' The next day she 'tasted the oatmeal porridge, which I think very good, and also some of the "Finnan Haddies"'. On that first visit she and Albert travelled as far north as Perthshire, and at Scone, where the kings of Scots had been crowned for centuries, signed 'a curious old book in which the last signatures are those of James I [of England] and Charles I'. They stayed at Taymouth Castle, seat of the Earls of Breadalbane, where Albert shot his first stag, and where an old woman told the queen that her people were delighted to see her in Scotland. Victoria was equally delighted to be there, all the more so because Albert was so happy and kept finding points of comparison with the landscapes of Thuringia and Switzerland. As they sailed back to London, she vowed that she would never forget her tour.

Naturally they came back, in 1844 and 1848, and naturally she and Albert decided they must have a house of their own in Scotland. One says 'naturally' because, reading the queen's journal and letters, it seems the most natural and inevitable thing that they should have so decided; but of course it wasn't. It was an unprecedented and almost revolutionary decision. When they leased the little estate of Balmoral on Upper Deeside in 1848, and then, four years later, started to build a castle there (to Albert's design), they were doing something more than establishing a holiday retreat for themselves.

Much has been written about Balmorality, or rather against it. Critics argue that it imposed a false vision on Scotland, and a false vision of Scotland on the world. There is some truth in this. For all the queen's real love for the Highlands, and for the Highlanders, she could never truly be part of Scottish life. There was always an element of comic-opera make-believe about her sojourns at Balmoral. By their example, Victoria and Albert contributed to the transformation of the Highlands into a sporting playground for the aristocracy and the new-rich industrialists. The Highlands became a place to which they resorted for a few weeks in the late summer and autumn to catch fish and shoot deer. With Queen Victoria at Balmoral, we are but a small step from the false romanticism which found expression in Hollywood's Brigadoon.

Yet there is another side to the matter. We have only to ask what might have become of the Highlands in the nineteenth century without this development to realize that their condition might have been very much worse. The castles and shooting-lodges at least provided some employment; their proprietors or tenants poured money into the local economy. Throughout the nineteenth century, agriculture declined even in the most fertile parts of Britain, one-third of arable land in England and Wales going out of cultivation in the half-century after 1880. The decline was still steeper in the Highlands. But for the fashion Victoria set, the depopulation of the north of Scotland would have been even worse.

The queen's example did not create the Scottish tourist industry; it had already been set in motion by 'Ossian' and Scott. But it encouraged it. Victoria herself was a tireless and enthusiastic sightseer, and when in 1868 she published her *Leaves from a Journal of our Life in the Highlands*, she invited her subjects to share her enjoyment of Scotland.

They obediently flocked north to do so. No tourist authority (had one then existed) could have wished for a better advertisement.

The queen's love for Scotland had another consequence. Her eager association with the country and its history – she and Albert decked themselves in Royal Stuart tartan and she incongruously proclaimed herself a Jacobite – served to attach many hitherto indifferent Scots to the Crown. In this way she helped to cement the Union. Her evident love for Scotland and for her Scottish subjects contributed to the assurance that Scotland was a proud and equal partner in the Empire. Scots were pleased to learn that the queen preferred the austere services of the Scots Kirk to those of the Church of England, and that she was happier at Balmoral than anywhere else. It confirmed them in their 'guid conceit' of themselves. They accepted the queen as the honorary Scot she said she was. They were amused and pleased – where the English were offended – by her warm regard for John Brown, who had been the prince's manservant and became hers. They saw nothing odd or deplorable in her affection for him, or even in his overbearing manner. There was many a family in Scotland where the laird's man took comparable liberties with his employer – and if Mr Brown was over-fond of 'a drop of the cratur', that is to say, whisky, why that too was not unusual.

In Ireland the Crown remained remote, and foreign. Thanks to Queen Victoria, the Scottish experience was the reverse. Royalty had been repatriated.

Throughout the twentieth century there was very little difference in attitudes to the Crown and the royal family either side of the Anglo-Scottish Border. The republican movement of the 1860s and 1870s had long since withered. The monarchy was respected, revered in some quarters, everywhere taken at least for granted. Great royal occasions – coronations, weddings, funerals – took place in London, but this was no more likely to distress or irritate Scots than Yorkshiremen or Lancastrians. London was the capital of the United Kingdom, and few Scots till the 1970s had any desire to secede from the Union or thought this practical. Meanwhile members of the royal family were in evidence throughout the kingdom, opening new buildings, attending sporting events, reviewing troops, serving as patrons of charities. Plaques fixed to buildings all over the country attest to their activity.

Society was still deferential. Therefore it was natural to respect both the institution of monarchy and the man or woman who was its incarnation. John Buchan, whose innate Romanticism made him a fervent royalist, told in his autobiography how, when George V visited the Borders in 1923, an old shepherd's wife 'tramped ten miles from a hill glen to greet him. When I asked her why she had undertaken such a journey, her reply was "We maun boo to the buss that bields us"' (We must bow to the bush that shelters us).

It pleased Scots that two of George V's sons had the good sense to choose Scottish wives, the Duke of York marrying a daughter of the Earl of Strathmore, and the Duke of Gloucester a daughter of the Duke of Buccleuch and Queensberry. When the Yorks' younger daughter, Princess Margaret Rose, was born at Glamis Castle in 1930, she was the first member of the royal family since the seventeenth century to have had Scotland as her birthplace. The abdication of Edward VIII passed off as smoothly in Scotland as in England, though Compton Mackenzie, another romantic royalist and post-Jacobite sentimentalist, wrote an indignant defence of Edward, whose determination to marry a twice-divorced American had met with the stern disapproval of the Church of Scotland. More Scots however were pleased to think that the new king's wife, Elizabeth, was the first Scottish royal consort for centuries. The identification of Scotland with the monarchy now seemed complete; even socialists were royalists. This wasn't remarkable. George V's favourite among his prime ministers had been the Labour leader Ramsay MacDonald, born in Lossiemouth in Moray, the illegitimate son of a ploughman and a serving-girl. Monarchy and democracy seemed comfortable bedfellows.

If the second German war, like the first, seemed to strengthen the bond between the Crown and the people, there was in Scotland a slight hiccup when George VI died in 1952 and was succeeded by his daughter Elizabeth. There was first the question of her title. There had never been a Queen Elizabeth of Scotland and there had been no queen of that name since the United Kingdom came into being. Yet she was advised to style herself Elizabeth II, as if the United Kingdom was merely the old Kingdom of England under a new name. There were precedents for the decision. William IV (1830–7) and Edward VII and Edward VIII had all been styled in accordance with the English succession, not the Scottish or British. Likewise the last Jacobite claimant, Henry, Cardinal of York, the younger brother of Bonnie Prince Charlie, had assumed the title of Henry IX, though no Henry had been king regnant of Scotland. It is not therefore surprising that even a prime minister as steeped in history as Winston Churchill did not realize that some Scots would object to the new queen's assumption of a title which suggested that Elizabeth Tudor had been Queen of Scots as well as of England, or that the Treaty of Union represented the annexation of Scotland by England, or that Scottish history was now properly subsumed in English. But some did, and a number of pillar-boxes bearing the legend EIIR were blown up. This however was a nationalist rather than republican act; indeed those Scots who objected most strongly to the designation Elizabeth II were likely to have the highest regard for the institution of monarchy.

They were given further offence the following year when, after her coronation in Westminster Abbey (in which ceremony the Moderator of the Church of Scotland was permitted to play a minor role), the young queen came north to receive the Royal Honours of Scotland; and did so, following the advice of her ministers, in ordinary day-clothes and carrying a handbag, rather than in the ceremonial robes of state many thought fitting to such a solemn and august occasion. Once again it seemed to the sensitive that Scotland's role in the United Kingdom was neither understood nor valued.

Nationalism was already flickering in Scotland, though in a form which offered no necessary threat to the monarchy. A year before the queen's accession three young students from Glasgow University made an audacious raid on Westminster Abbey and removed the Stone of Scone (otherwise known as the Stone of Destiny) from the Coronation

Chair housed in the little chapel of Edward the Confessor. This stone, on which tradition had it the kings of Scots had been crowned from time immemorial, and which was also said to have served the Patriarch Jacob as a pillow the night he wrestled with the angel as recorded in the Book of Genesis, had been removed from Scone Abbey by Edward I of England in 1296.

The taking of the Stone at Christmas 1950 disturbed the Establishment and offended the pompous, but most people in Scotland and a good many in England were amused. They saw it as a student prank rather than as what it was intended to be: a political statement.

When it was reported that the king, George VI, was troubled, the leader of the young conspirators, Ian Hamilton (in later life a QC and Rector of Aberdeen University), was himself dismayed. He was no republican and had indeed a warm admiration for the king: 'he had led us,' he later wrote, 'Scotland as well as England, through one of the most dangerous times in our history. He personally symbolized us all . . . he was one with the nation.'

Accordingly Hamilton and his companions drew up a petition in which they declared that they intended no disrespect to king or Church, but that the Stone was 'the most ancient symbol of Scottish nationality', and therefore properly belonged in Scotland. They promised that they would return it immediately if they received an assurance that 'in all time coming the Stone will remain in Scotland in such of His Majesty's properties or otherwise as shall be deemed fitting by him'. Such an assurance would in no way 'preclude the use of the Stone in any coronation of His Majesty's successors whether in England or in Scotland'.

No such assurance was forthcoming, and eventually the Stone was left on the high altar of the ruined Abbey of Arbroath where in 1320 the declaration of Scottish Independence had been promulgated and signed; and the police were alerted to its whereabouts. It was then returned, under guard, to Westminster Abbey.

This story requires two footnotes.

Almost fifty years later the then Secretary of State for Scotland, Michael Forsyth, hoping to bolster a failing Tory Government, persuaded the prime minister John Major – and he, one supposes, the queen – that the Stone should at last be returned to Scotland, in belated accordance with the promise given in the 1328 Treaty of Northampton. This was duly done. Few paid much attention. The fortunes of the Tory Party in Scotland were not restored. Indeed they lost all their Scottish seats. Now that the Stone reposes in Edinburgh Castle, few – perhaps not even tourists – give it even a passing thought. It seemed important only while it was in London.

Second footnote: it may not be the real Stone. There are some who believe that in 1296 the monks of Scone Abbey hid the real stone, and palmed Edward I off with a substitute, a piece of local grey sandstone. This is an agreeable conceit. If however there was any substance to the story, one wonders why the original Stone was not recovered and used at the coronation of later Scottish kings, after the country's independence had been secured.

In the last half-century attitudes to the monarchy have changed in both Scotland and England. Though there is no overt or organized republican movement, republican views are more frequently expressed, and the Crown seems to many an anachronism in a society that is much more egalitarian and less deferential than Britain was when Queen Elizabeth succeeded George VI. The queen herself remains highly respected, but all her children have come in for criticism in the media of a sort that would have been unthinkable in the first half of the twentieth century.

Though the Scottish National Party eschews republicanism and would provisionally at least retain the queen or her successor as head of state in an independent Scotland, many nationalists see the royal family as essentially English, representative of the British state, and openly express republican sentiments. Socialists too subscribe to the agreeable fiction that sovereignty rests, not with the monarch, but with the Scottish people. No practical expression can be given to this theory, which did not prevent a number of members of the first Scottish Parliament from making such a declaration when taking, under mild protest, the oath of allegiance to the Crown. It is understandable that nationalists should adopt this attitude since the monarchy remains one of the strongest links holding the United Kingdom together. In fact royalists probably exist in much the same proportion in Scotland as in England.

7

Mongrels

— • —

Tony Blair is typically British. His father was born an Englishman, but fostered to Glaswegians whose name, Blair, he took. Leo Blair married a Glasgow girl, the daughter of an Ulster Protestant. Tony Blair himself was born in Edinburgh, but brought up, mostly, in England, till he returned to Edinburgh to be educated at Fettes, where the chief influence he came under was that of his housemaster, Eric Anderson, editor of the most recent edition of the *Journal of Sir Walter Scott*. According to his biographer John Rentoul, Blair's education at Fettes made him 'a member of the British national elite which looked to London as its hub'. Such roots as he has are in County Durham where he spent most of his childhood and where his constituency now is. He thinks of himself as English, but told the House of Commons, 'I'm British, and proud to be British.' Englishmen have sometimes called him a Scot; few Scots would do so. Nobody, I think, has suggested he is an Ulsterman, though Ulster has its part in his heredity.

Nothing in this family background is unusual. Inasmuch as Blair does belong to 'a national elite', this mixed heredity is common. Of the twenty-five prime ministers in the century and a half before Blair, fifteen might be described as English, nine as Scots, with one Welshman, Lloyd George. But in more than half the cases such identification is questionable. For instance, the inter-war Tory Stanley Baldwin seemed to make indeed a cult of 'Englishness', yet was a Macdonald, immediately from Ulster, more distantly from Scotland, on his mother's side. She was sister of Kipling's mother. A recent biographer, Philip Williamson, writes that 'as Conservatives became the dominant party in Scotland, Baldwin made many speeches there on Scottish themes, sometimes invoking his Macdonald ancestors as evidence of shared sympathies'. His Macdonald grandfather was a Methodist minister, and Baldwin said of Kipling, 'we have common puritan blood in us'. English Puritanism and Scotch Presbyterianism were, as earlier remarked, close in outlook and sympathies. Kipling, in *McAndrew's Hymn*, has his ship's engineer see 'Predestination / In the stroke o' yon connecting-rod'. Baldwin's favourite authors were Scott and Dickens. His appeal, Williamson writes, 'to place and roots was far from restricted to English – still less to "southern" English – pastoralism'. He talked of 'the rich variety of our national inheritance'. In speeches in Glasgow and Belfast, and in a St David's Day message published in the *Western Mail*, he expressed his belief that Celtic nationalisms were consistent with British unionism. Blair in his more reflective moments would doubtless agree. Probably no twentieth-century prime minister would have dissented.

Baldwin's political heir was Rab Butler, often described as 'the best prime minister we never had'. One of his biographers, Patrick Cosgrave (a Dubliner), gave his book the subtitle 'An English Life'. Discussing a possible connection with the Norman-Irish Butler clan, Cosgrave wrote, 'there is, however, nothing remotely Celtic about him, though he might claim a more plausible Celtic ancestry than the Irish from his grandmother's close family connections with Cornwall. The truth of the matter is that, not least in its Indian connections, Butler's whole character and background are fundamentally, specifically, and unalterably English.' Well, yes, except that his mother was a Scot, sister of Sir George Adam Smith, Principal of Aberdeen University, author of the *Historical Geography of the Holy Land*, and Moderator of the General Assembly of the Church of Scotland. If on the one hand Butler's family tradition lay in Cambridge and in public service, especially in India, on the other maternal side he belonged to the Scottish intellectual elite (which of course also penetrated Cambridge), and Butler himself spoke of his mother as a major influence in his life, and in the formation of his character and principles. His cousin, the poet Charles Sorley, killed at the Battle of Loos in 1915, 'used to claim', according to Butler himself, 'that he was Celtic, and that the name Sorley was Gaelic for wanderer'. In short, though Rab Butler may indeed have been, as Cosgrave says, 'fundamentally, specifically, and unalterably English', he was that in being half a Scot. He had indeed more right to claim a Scottish identity than his rival Harold Macmillan, for all the play Macmillan made of his crofting ancestors from Arran.

The question 'What determines nationality?' is difficult to answer, so confused are the peoples of these islands. Ancestry? Birthplace? Upbringing? Residence? Any one of these may be deemed sufficient for particular purposes, but there is no legal definition of a Scot, an Englishman, a Welshman, a Northern Irishman. We are all British, citizens of the United Kingdom, subjects of Her Majesty, whether we like it or not. There is only one exception to this generalization. For certain legal purposes domicile will determine whether a case be brought before a Scottish or an English court, and be judged according to Scots or English law.

We are a mixed lot, a mongrel breed. There are doubtless exceptions, especially in country districts, people who can name all their great-grandparents, and possibly even a generation further back, and claim an inability to find anyone who isn't English or Scots. But even those who can do this must admit the probability than in some more remote generation a foreigner may appear. After all, one has to go back only ten generations, perhaps to around 1700, to find upwards of a thousand direct ancestors. It's unlikely that all were true Scots or true English. Purity of blood is a myth.

In reality, there has been so much movement within the United Kingdom as to make any boast of that sort risible. The London telephone directory has columns of Campbells and Camerons, MacDonalds and Mackays, Grants and Gordons, to say nothing of names less immediately recognizable as Lowland Scots. Many of these will be happy to call themselves English; others remain stubbornly attached to the idea of being Scots, even though they may have English mothers and grandmothers.

The author and broadcaster Ludovic Kennedy offers a good example. He was born in Edinburgh, but lived as a child in the south of England (Bedfordshire) after his father retired from the Royal Navy. Till he was seven or eight, he thought of himself as English, learning that he was a Scot – Highland on one side of the family, Lowland on the other – only when taken on a family holiday to Nairn. The news puzzled him. 'I had been English too long to accept instantaneously my metamorphosis into a Scot; and if I thought that this was going to lead to an affinity with those in Nairn who spoke with a Scottish tongue, I was mistaken. To them as to other Scots, I was English.'

In time he concluded that his mother had been wrong in telling him he wasn't English. It seemed to him that any Scot who had been reared and educated in England (Kennedy went to Eton), and whose voice had no trace of a Scottish accent, 'must have a degree of English in his persona'. In short, he was an Anglo-Scot, which hasn't prevented him from campaigning for a Scottish Parliament and from writing a book, the title of which – *In Bed with an Elephant* – expresses his resentment of English domination of Scotland. (The title in fact is borrowed from the Canadian prime minister Pierre Trudeau, who coined the phrase to describe Canada's relations with the USA.) In middle life Kennedy was based for some years in Scotland, first in Edinburgh, then in Roxburghshire. His wife, the ballerina and actress Moira Shearer, is Scottish. I don't know how their children regard themselves. Evidently they have a choice.

In Kennedy's opinion there are many Anglo-Scots living in Scotland – the whole of the hereditary peerage and many landowners. 'In thought processes, attitudes, language, outlook, terms of reference etc, there is virtually nothing to distinguish the English man or woman from the Anglo-Scot, especially when they are products of English public schools.' Many of those so classified wouldn't agree, the founder of the Gaelic College on Skye, Sir Iain Noble, being one example.

One of Kennedy's tests is accent, another knowledge of the old or historic Scots language. Neither is as clear-cut as he supposes. First, there are many different accents in Scotland, probably at least as many as in England. Some of them – that of Buchan, for instance, or of Hawick in the Borders – are incomprehensible to people from other parts of Scotland. Second, the particular 'English' accent to which he refers, and which, speaking with it himself, cost him the chance of any affinity with young people in Nairn, is a class accent rather than a national one. A Scottish duke may speak in the same way as an English duke, but the English duke's accent is no more like a Liverpudlian's than the Scot's is like a Glaswegian's. It would be more accurate to describe this accent as British upper-class, just as what used to be known as BBC English was a British accent insisted on by the first director-general of the BBC, John Reith, a Scot, born in Stonehaven and educated at Glasgow Academy and Gresham's School in Norfolk, who stamped the Corporation with the ethos of Scots Presbyterianism.

Moreover, many who speak with the local accent of some Scottish district are as ignorant of the historic Scots language as any Anglo-Scot or Englishman. They may be able to read Burns, whose Scots is much diluted, without too frequent reference to the glossary, but they will be baffled by the much richer Scots of Burns's predecessor Robert Fergusson, the early-twentieth-century Aberdeenshire Doric of Charles Murray, or the 'synthetic Scots' in which Hugh MacDiarmid wrote his best work. Today's urban demotic Scots is a patois which is not spoken by educated Scots, any more than doctors and lawyers in Liverpool speak 'scouse'. You may hear it sometimes in the new Scottish Parliament, but not from the judges and advocates in old Parliament House.

Kennedy had two cousins (first cousins once removed actually) who serve to illustrate the complications of Anglo-Scottish relations: Henry Dundas and Robert Boothby. They were the grandchildren (Kennedy the great-grandson) of Henry and Margaret Lancaster. Henry Lancaster had gone from Glasgow University to Balliol College, Oxford, where he was a favourite pupil of the future Master of the College, Benjamin Jowett, and then made a career at the Scottish bar. Gladstone proposed him for the office of Lord Advocate, but he died comparatively young at forty-six. There were three Lancaster daughters, Cecil, Ethel and Mabel. Cecil married Neville Dundas, an Edinburgh lawyer (Writer to the Signet) and a descendant of Henry Dundas, Lord Melville, Pitt the Younger's right-hand man, and for years the political master of Scotland. Mabel married Tom Boothby, managing director of the Scottish Provident Life Assurance Company and a director of the Royal Bank of Scotland. Ethel married Sir Ludovic Grant, Professor of Public and International Law at the University of Edinburgh. Their daughter Rosalind was Ludovic Kennedy's mother. All three families sent their sons to prep school in England, and then to Eton.

Henry Dundas died young, being killed in the last weeks of the 1914–18 war. He was then a captain and company commander in the 1st Battalion, the Scots Guards, and had won the Military Cross and Bar. He had served in France for two years and was not yet twenty-two. He was one of countless young men of promise killed in the war, and if we know more about him than about most of them, it is because his father, Neville Dundas, prepared and published a record of his life, with contributions from his housemaster at Eton, C. H. K. Marten (more than twenty years later charged with the responsibility of teaching the Princess Elizabeth British constitutional history), and the future Tory Cabinet minister Oliver Lyttelton, also an Etonian and Guards officer, though in the Grenadiers. Much of the book consists of Henry's letters from France to his parents. These give a vivid and very individual view of the war on the Western Front, as seen by a young infantry officer. Both the letters and his conversation as reported by Lyttelton show him to have been highly intelligent, and in general very engaging. The book itself is of course a work of paternal piety; some today might find much of it cloying. This doesn't detract from its interest. 'War,' Henry wrote on Christmas Day 1916, while on short leave in Paris (and staying at the Ritz in the Place Vendôme), 'always overrated because invariably written about by non-combatants, is entirely played out as a method of settling disputes. Nothing is worth the misery this War has caused . . .' Yet he fought on.

It is tempting to quote more of his views on the war, and military operations, but that would be beside the purpose of this essay. That is best expressed by quoting the first two paragraphs from Lyttelton's memoir:

Scotland to him was an enthusiasm – any patriotism he felt was for that country. He was roused to the wildest excitement by the mere sight of a kilt or a piper, and when the kilts marched and the pipes played he became nothing short of a fanatic.

As for Eton no rival to it ever entered into his ken: he regarded it with a natural unstudied love; his affection for it was filial. 'About Scotland and Eton,' he once said, 'I have no sense of humour.'

Some – some Scots especially – may regard the conjunction in young Henry Dundas's emotions of Scotland and Eton as bizarre, even absurd. Today, a school like Eton is seen by such Scots as purely English and in any case out of tune with our egalitarian society, and sentiment for 'the old school' is less usual than it once was. But such sentiment was common then, and though there were doubtless many like Eric Blair (Orwell) who looked back on their time at Eton quite without nostalgia, there were others, Cyril Connolly among them, to whom in adult life it represented a lost paradise. The prime minister Lord Rosebery even gave instructions that a record of the Eton Boating Song was to be played as he lay dying – more than sixty years after he had left the school. It is not so surprising that young subalterns on the Western Front looked back on their days there lovingly, and were delighted when they had the occasion, frequent enough in a Guards battalion, to indulge in 'Eton shop'.

What cannot be doubted is that Henry Dundas's feeling for Scotland was intense, and it wasn't the Scotland of Highland estates, grouse-moors and deer-forests that delighted him. (He had in any case, I think, no experience of that Scotland.) His father wrote:

Scottish League football and the prowess of Bobby Walker, Jimmy Quinn and their successors were matters of even greater moment to him through all his boyhood than the personalia of English County Cricket and Test Matches – though in this department too his attention to detail was quite unrivalled; and in France many an uncomfortable hour was whiled away in discussions with his platoon as to the rival merits of 'Hairts' and 'Hibs' and 'Celtic' and 'Rangers'.

His letters attest that this feeling was genuine: 'A most strenuous Company football match against "C". I found myself playing left-half in front of Sam Allan, ex-Hibs: it stirred the heart to hear the familiar voices at the ringside, "Come awa, Easter Road", "Poosh 'em, Wullie" etc. It is a pity that with such magnificently Scotch men the officers should be mostly English to a degree.' Even when they weren't English, they tended to have been educated, like Dundas himself, at public schools in England. Later, in August 1917, he mentions three young officers who have just joined the battalion: Erskine (Winchester), Drummond (Harrow) and Macdonald (Beaumont – the Jesuit school in the south of England). All three names are of course Scots.

Dundas's spirits rise whenever he writes about Scottish troops. 'I had tea yesterday with the 7th H.L.I. [Highland Light Infantry], who are next to us – in the Lowland Division. Very good, and more typically Scotch than anything you've ever seen. Little sturdy men with tammies and Harry Lauder faces. It did me good to see them. There was an excellent clergyman at tea, their Chaplain. A most gloriously Scotch man, and I should think damned good.'

One could go on quoting, giving examples of his feeling for Scotland, his love of the music of the pipes (and for Scots music-hall – he knew all the Lauder songs by heart), of Scots literature, especially the Waverley novels and Scott's poems; but it would be otiose. The point surely is clear: here was a young man – still a very young man when he was killed – who found no contradiction between his Scotland and his education in England, and would not, one surmises, have done so if, as was likely, he had gone on to Oxford and then made his career in London, perhaps in politics. The dual loyalties were comfortably accommodated. Being Scottish was a part, by far the most important part, of being British; but being British in no way diluted his consciousness of being a Scot. When he was killed, his batman, by name McIntosh, wrote to his parents to say:

> I have been his servant for over a year and I never had a wrong word from him during that period. The bagpipes, which he loved so well, played the 'Land o' the Leal' when he was laid to rest. I beg leave to express my heartfelt sympathy for the loss you have sustained, but you have the consolation of knowing he was a true British gentleman and an extremely brave man . . .

(Another letter from his commanding officer says that 'the Pipers played "The Flowers o' the Forest" – a lament which he loved – at the end of the service'. Perhaps both tunes were played.)

Henry Dundas was three years older than his cousin Bob Boothby, but they were brought up almost as brothers. Boothby followed him to Eton (though he recalled his time there, unlike Dundas, with no great pleasure) and was on the point of being commissioned in the Guards when the war ended. He went to Oxford and then at the age of only twenty-four was elected Unionist MP for East Aberdeenshire. He held what was never a naturally Tory seat, its tradition being Liberal, for thirty-four years till he became one of the first life peers in 1958. Never averse to controversy, nor untouched by scandal, he yet gained and kept the loyalty and affection of his constituents.

In a speech in 1938 to the London Scots Self-Government Committee – an ambiguous body, since few of its members would have had the intention of removing to a self-governing Scotland should that have come into being – he described his antecedents:

I am rather a rare type. I am an English émigré. I come from Denmark, via Lincolnshire and Derbyshire. When my family had succeeded in losing all its money, my grandfather did a thing few Englishmen have ever had the courage to do. He migrated to Scotland, married a girl from Perth, and settled down at St Andrews. He spent the rest of his life catching salmon, playing golf, and dining with university professors. I cannot think of a more ideal form of existence, this side of heaven, but it was unremunerative. My father, who drove his first ball at the age of two, was an even better golfer. But he had to earn his living. Thank God, he went to Edinburgh to do it. And that is where I saw the light of day.

I may be a mongrel by breeding, but I am a native of the capital city of Scotland. And whatever you may think of my politics, I am as good a Scottish patriot as anyone in this room. As a matter of fact, I often think I combine the best qualities of the two nations!

A mongrel by breeding – it's a good phrase; and for those who insist on making clear distinctions between Scots and English, Boothby may be seen as neither one thing nor the other, a mongrel by inclination.

He called himself a Scottish patriot, and was devoted to his constituency and to the interests of its farmers and fishermen. But he lived all his adult life in London, and his descents on Aberdeenshire, two or three times a year, bore more resemblance to a royal tour than to the regular attendance at constituency surgeries expected of a member of Parliament today. He might declare that his mind, attitudes and opinions had been formed by Scots: 'Hume, Burns and Stevenson have exercised a dominant influence over me – there is an affinity between them which is essentially Scottish; and to them I am principally indebted for the combination of scepticism, tolerance, and an invincible optimism which is the basis of my philosophy.'

But at the same time he was, by reason of his own character and on account of his position in public life, a member of the British Establishment, if a somewhat rackety and at times even disreputable one. He was never his cousin Ludovic Kennedy's typical Anglo-Scot. His biographer, Robert Rhodes James, wrote: 'The English fascinated him, and he was to live his entire adult life in London, but he not only never really understood them, he never really liked them. His spiritual home was in Scotland, where his style and very real erudition and wit were much more appreciated. He occasionally toyed with the idea of settling there, but London was where "the great game" was being played, so that was where he stayed.' This is true, though one might add that some of his fiercest critics were Scots, and some of his most bitter enemies were to be found in that part of the Scottish Tory Party dominated by lords and lairds.

If there are Anglo-Scots, those who, while remaining in certain ways determinedly, even aggressively, Scottish, have nevertheless taken on an English colouring, so intense that to many Scots they have become indistinguishable from the English, then there are others, English in their own mind, who retain, even unconsciously, qualities, elements, which derive from their perhaps distant Scotch ancestors.

In 1951 Evelyn Waugh was invited by a group of students to be a candidate in the University of Edinburgh Rectorial election. Rather surprisingly he accepted the invitation. He was well known as an English novelist, whose *Brideshead Revisited* had been a bestseller in

Britain and the USA in 1945–6; and also as a Roman Catholic convert and apologist. He had no previous connection with the university; the students who had extended the invitation were fellow-Catholics, and not very representative of the student electorate. In the circumstances he thought it expedient to draw attention to his Scots ancestry.

'The Waughs', he advised his supporters,

> were unmixed lowland Scots until the late eighteenth century when they joined the migration south. The last to be born in Scotland, Alexander Waugh, was Doctor of Divinity at Edinburgh. His simple annals may be read in the DNB. He was my great, great, grandfather. A rather more illustrious g.g.g. father on my mother's side is Henry, Lord Cockburn, author of *Memorials of His Time*. He was a considerable figure in Edinburgh, is buried there, was painted by Raeburn, has an hotel named after him. Indeed his portrait appears on the Commercial Bank of Scotland's one pound note (tho' he was no banker).

Cockburn, or at least his name, would have been familiar to some of the students. Edinburgh has its Cockburn Street, running from the High Street down to Waverley Station; and the Cockburn Association is a society formed to campaign for the preservation of Georgian Edinburgh. Some students might have known of Cockburn as a reforming Whig, friend of Francis Jeffrey, contributor to the *Edinburgh Review*, and writer. But they would have been few. Thirty years later they might have been more numerous, after the actor Russell Hunter had a success in the one-man play *Cocky* and Karl Miller had published a ruminative biography.

In *A Little Learning*, the only volume of a planned three-volume autobiography to be written, Waugh treated of these forebears at greater length. The Rev. Alexander Waugh grew up in Berwickshire, where his father, Thomas, 'held the rather bleak upland farm of East Gordon', the fifth generation to do so. This Thomas adhered to the Secession Church of Scotland, which broke away from the established Church in 1733, disapproving acceptance of the landowner's right to appoint a parish minister. Alexander Waugh himself studied at both Edinburgh and Aberdeen, and then, aged twenty-eight, obtained the charge of the Secession Church's London chapel, in Wells Street off Oxford Street. That a breakaway sect had a sufficent number of adherents in London to warrant and maintain a chapel is evidence of the extent of what Evelyn Waugh called 'the migration south'.

Alexander Waugh served as minister of this chapel for more than forty years.

> His sermons and lectures are all in pure English [which he must have gone to some trouble to master] but in private he delighted to resume the dialect of his youth, remaining fervently Scottish throughout his long exile . . . The beauties of Scottish scenery were something of an obsession with Dr Waugh. He seems seldom to have spoken in public without introducing some rhapsodic passage on the subject. He sent all but one of his sons to Scottish schools, but none returned to farm in his homeland; only one entered the ministry, and he died prematurely. The three remaining sons became anglicized and married English women . . . My great-grandfather became a clergyman in the Church of England.

Evelyn Waugh remarks also that, though Dr Waugh's stipend was small, 'he had a childless brother-in-law, John Neill, a Scotchman also, who came to London at the same time as himself, set up as a corn-merchant in Surrey Street, Strand, and did well', eventually leaving '£150,000 entirely to his nephews and nieces in trust to their children'.

It is a common enough story, repeated with variations in innumerable family histories; those of two Archbishops of Canterbury, Tait and Lang, would not be very different. An able Scot comes south, establishes himself and prospers. He may associate chiefly with his compatriots, but his children and grandchildren settle in English life, retaining little more than a sentimental attachment to their country of origin. Sometimes the second generation assiduously keeps its link with Scotland; sometimes, more often perhaps, that withers altogether. This seems to have been the case with the Waughs. Even the pronunciation of the family name was anglicized; it would have been Wauch in Berwickshire. Certainly Evelyn Waugh did not think of himself as other than English.

There are few Scottish characters in his novels, some of the few, like the Laird of Mugg and his half-crazy Scottish Nationalist niece in *Officers and Gentlemen*, purely comic characters; others, Ian Kilbannock and his wife Kirsty who appear in all three parts of the 'Sword of Honour' trilogy, very acutely delineated, Kirsty sympathetically and with some admiration.

It may seem absurd to claim him as in any degree a Scottish novelist, and he might well have first resented, then laughed at, any such attempt. Yet what Byron wrote of Burns, already quoted with regard to Boswell, is, to some extent anyway, applicable to Waugh also: 'what an antithetical mind! – tenderness, roughness, delicacy, coarseness – sentiment, sensuality – soaring and grovelling, dirt and deity – all mixed up in that one compound of inspired clay'. The comparison would probably have displeased Waugh, even disgusted him; nevertheless the description fits him, as indeed it fitted Byron himself. Waugh revered order, revelled in disorder; flew in the manner of Scots poets – Dunbar, Fergusson, Hogg as well as Burns and Byron – from one extreme to the other. The matter is English, but the manner Scots. Even his, to many excessive, reverence for the old Catholic recusant families that kept the lantern of the Faith burning through the centuries of the Penal Laws resembles obstinate and sentimental Scots Jacobitism; Guy Crouchback's father in the 'Sword of Honour' trilogy is not that far removed from Scott's Baron Bradwardine.

If national characteristics are to be discerned in literature, then Waugh, like Byron, fits more easily into a Scottish than an English mould – a certain Scottish mould at any rate.

G. Gregory Smith in his book *Scottish Literature: Character and Influence*, published in 1919, devised the phrase 'the Caledonian antisyzygy' to describe (not very effectively, since the description itself has always to be explained) the 'zigzag of contradictions' which to his mind characterized Scottish literature, and accounted for what he called 'the polemical restlessness' of the Scot. Does any twentieth-century novelist writing in the English language display such a zigzag of contradictions more evidently than Waugh – a zigzag as apparent in his life as his work?

The nature or character of his Catholicism was very unEnglish. There was no room for compromise or half-measures. He was as much of a zealot, as absolute in his dogmatism, as any remote Covenanting Waugh ancestor might have been. To his English contemporaries his Catholicism was wholly unsympathetic, as unsympathetic as Belloc's, in its utter exclusion of doubt. Carlyle would have understood him better, as he understood his own father, James Carlyle, member of the same Burghers' Secessionist Church as the Rev. Alexander Waugh, James Carlyle who 'never meddled with politics . . . to him . . . the whole was of secondary moment; he was looking towards a city that had foundations'. Waugh likewise declined to vote in Parliamentary elections; it was not for him to advise his sovereign on his or her choice of ministers: a ridiculous position, and very Scotch.

Waugh was one of the first to recognize the peculiar and original talent of Muriel Spark, born and reared a Scot, in Edinburgh, but of mixed English and Jewish parentage. Her novels resemble Waugh's in their suddenness, wit, delight in discordancy. She has often spoken of her debt to the Border Ballads, where death is something that strikes abruptly in a single line. It strikes as abruptly in Waugh's novels, sometimes in comic fashion (Apthorpe blown up by his thunder-box; though this fails to kill him, it is as good as a death), sometimes grimly – the child John-Andrew in *A Handful of Dust*.

Like Waugh Muriel Spark was not born a Catholic. Her Catholic characters, like his, exist in an indifferent or uncomprehending world that judges by other standards, and are doomed to be misunderstood, just as, for most of *Brideshead*, Charles Ryder has no understanding of the Flytes, though infatuated with them. Waugh's own Catholicism is an outsider's, though presented, in Calvinist style, as membership of a club of the Elect.

Spark has written that the word 'nevertheless', which she regards as quintessentially Edinburgh, was the pivot of her education. 'I believe myself to be well indoctrinated by the habit of thought which calls for this word . . . I find that much of my literary composition is based on the "nevertheless" idea. It was on the "nevertheless" principle that I became a Catholic.' Waugh might have said the same. The world as it presented itself was meaningless; nevertheless the Church was true. 'Nevertheless' pervades his novels. Ivor Claire in *Officers and Gentlemen* is the fine flower of Englishness, Guy Crouchback's *beau idéal*; nevertheless he behaves shabbily, even disgracefully, when making his escape from Crete.

Waugh's diaries read often like Byron's, at other times like dialogue from a Spark novel: 'poor Mr McGregor turned up having lain with a woman but almost immediately fell backwards downstairs. I think he was killed.' Cut. I once wrote of Muriel Spark – surprising myself in doing so – that 'her concern with style reflects Stevenson, and of all Scottish writers he is the clearest influence on her work; for influence at its most fruitful is to be discerned in manner rather than material'. I have no idea whether Waugh read Stevenson. Yet has there been another novelist whose style in its mingling of lucidity with strength so resembles Stevenson's as Waugh? Like Stevenson Waugh was simultaneously aesthete and moralist. Beneath the elegant surface lay granite.

'The granite was coming painfully through.' Graham Greene wrote that about Stevenson, contemplating his last years. Greene, friend of Waugh, was, as it happens, a cousin, twice removed, of Stevenson, on the Balfour side of the family. *The Times*'s reviewer of his first novel remarked on the connection, saying Greene wrote 'with a distinction and subtlety . . . that Stevenson would, we feel sure, have approved'. The *Daily Telegraph*'s reviewer made a similar point, finding its dramatic tension comparable to 'the best chapters of *Treasure Island*'. Greene retained an interest in Stevenson, was proud of the family connection, and his restlessness, inability to settle in one place, reluctance to put down roots, recall Stevenson, however superficial the resemblance. There was something unEnglish, arguably Scots, in Greene's antinomianism, and his expressed preference for the austerities and intellectual rigidity of the Soviet Union to the comfort and, to his mind, moral indifference of the USA. Hugh MacDiarmid declared that he would 'aye be whaur extremes meet'; Greene sought that position too. Greene made little of his Scots ancestry, showed no especial interest in Scotland, never thought of himself as other than an Englishman; nevertheless . . .

Patrick Hamilton was another English novelist of Scots descent. Author of the West End successes *Rope* and *Gaslight*, his novels, notably *Hangover Square* and *The Slaves of Solitude*, are among the most evocative pictures of the seedier aspects of mid-twentieth-century London and its dreary respectable suburbs. Hamilton, disliking foreigners, lived most of his life in London, Brighton and Norfolk, was indeed very English. Yet his father, alcoholic like himself, a barrister who never practised, and a bad novelist, was immensely proud of aristocratic Scottish ancestry, claiming to belong to a cadet branch of the Dukes of Hamilton and Brandon, and to be in the direct line of descent from Robert the Bruce. Once, returning from a visit north, he was met by Patrick at Euston and declared, 'My boy, if it ever comes to war between England and Scotland, you and I go over the Border.' Fortunately, this determination was never put to the test.

'He had', Patrick Hamilton wrote, 'a "Hamilton" mania. As such he once explained to me, in complete sobriety, that the Hamiltons were the hereditary foes of the Douglases, and that it was really my business, if ever I met a Douglas, "to run him through with my sword".' The elder Hamilton had presumably forgotten, despite that moment of 'complete sobriety', that for several generations now the family name of the Dukes of Hamilton has been Douglas-Hamilton. Ridiculous as his obsession was, it was of a type common enough among anglicized Scots, and among Scots who like to mark their superiority to the English by a claim to aristocratic lineage, to being better born. Stevenson has Alan Breck Stewart boasting that 'I bear a king's name,' and Boswell, like Patrick Hamilton's father, was never slow to remind the world that he was descended from Robert the Bruce.

A Marxist in middle life, Hamilton was introduced to the staff of the *Daily Worker* by the Fife Communist MP Willie Gallacher. It was there that he met Claud Cockburn, a cousin of Waugh's and a friend of Graham Greene since schooldays. Cockburn was several generations removed from his Scottish roots, both his father and grandfather having been colonial civil servants, this a common pattern in Scottish families; two of the sons of the national bard, Robert Burns, became, for example, officers in the Army of the East India Company, and retired, as colonels did, to Cheltenham. Gallacher, a teetotaller like many Scottish socialists of his generation, all brought up painfully aware of the horrors of whisky, explained to Hamilton that it was a great pity Cockburn was a drinker. This was welcome news, Hamilton already galloping hard towards the alcoholism that ruined him as a writer even before it killed him; Scotch enough that. Cockburn never, so far as I know, made anything of his Scots ancestry; yet sent his sons to be schooled there, at Glenalmond.

Angus Wilson was every bit as much a London and home-counties novelist as Hamilton, and like him had a feckless Scots father, heir to a small (but heavily mortgaged) estate in Dumfriesshire. The family name was in fact Johnstone-Wilson, used by Angus till he dropped the first barrel when he began to publish his short stories. How the estate slipped out of the family is not clear, even from Margaret Drabble's admirable biography of Angus Wilson. Drabble, recording Angus's meeting as a schoolboy with Oscar Wilde's Lord Alfred Douglas, remarks that 'slightly depressed and downtrodden, worn out by years of successful and unsuccessful litigation, this descendant of the Black Douglases bore a strange resemblance to that other Lowland Scot, Willie Johnstone-Wilson . . . They had for decades inhabited intersecting worlds, and now these worlds, in old age, converged.'

Angus Wilson himself had few direct connections with Scotland. One short story, 'Totentanz', is set partly in a northern university town, recognizable as St Andrews. A visit to the Edinburgh Writers Conference in 1962 'engendered in him an anti-English mood'; and this was reinforced, as he wrote in *Queen* magazine, by a subsequent Scottish tour and 'the sight of innumerable English middle-class families (Ford Consul to Jaguar, with here and there a Rolls) braving out the Highland rains and mists with Bloody Marys and games of rummy in a series of very expensive, inadequate hotels from Killiecankie to Inverness and Oban' – a picture flattering to neither Scots nor English.

On the other hand, another Wilson, Edmund, the American critic, himself of Ulster Scots descent, ascribed Angus Wilson's 'positive opinions' and determination to make his homosexual habits 'a matter of principle' to 'his strong Scottish moral strain', a judgement that owes something doubtless to Edmund Wilson's own anglophobia.

The list of English novelists, poets and so on with Scotch forebears is a very long one. Some like Emma Tennant, herself once a daughter-in-law of Claud Cockburn, remain in their own mind thoroughly Scots, even if not always recognized as such north of the Border. The Tennants indeed offer a good example of how shifting national identity can be, how difficult any classification is. The family originated in Ayrshire. John Tennant of Glenconner in the late eighteenth century was a small landowner – a 'bonnet laird'. He was a friend of Robert Burns, a witness indeed at the poet's wedding, and the subject of one of Burns's verse epistles: 'My heart-warm love to gude auld Glen, / The ace an' wale of honest men'. His son Charles started a bleachfield in Paisley and later established the St Rollex Chemical Works in Glasgow, in partnership with Charles Mackintosh, the inventor of the waterproof. In the next generation John Tennant expanded the business, but it was his son Charles who became a great imperial figure, making a fortune through a variety of companies engaged in trading, mining of gold and pyrites, as well as chemicals. He lifted his family from the world of provincial business to the heart of British political and social life. Himself a Liberal MP, his daughter Margot married the future Liberal prime minister H. H. Asquith. His sons were sent to Eton and his daughters were members of the social–intellectual group known as the 'Souls'. Charles Tennant himself was made a baronet; when he died, he left an estate in Britain alone valued at £3 million. The Tennants married into English aristocratic families, without ever becoming absolutely English or losing their sense of being Scots. Emma Tennant's brother Colin, the 3rd Lord Glenconner, socialite and close friend of Princess Margaret, was for a time anyway a member of the Scottish National Party.

Naturally, England being the richer country, more Scots have come south than Englishmen have travelled north in search of a living. Nevertheless some do, and also many Scots have taken themselves an English wife. So just as we find Englishmen whose ancestry is Scots, so too there are Scots who owe something in their character to an English heredity.

Eric Linklater was one such. The best Scottish novelist of the mid-twentieth century, he was Orcadian on his father's side, and proud of it, identifying himself with Orkney all his life, though, as it happens, he was born in Wales, something he did not dwell on. But Orkney itself is only reluctantly Scots, having been Norse till the late fifteenth century; and the Linklaters were themselves probably Norse – that is, Norwegian – in origin. The people of the Northern Isles remain aware of their Norse heritage, and jealous of it, though the Orcadian poet and writer of wonderful short stories George Mackay Brown once said to me sadly, 'There's really not a lot of Norse blood left.' Be that as it may, Linklater was Orcadian-Scots only on the paternal side, for his mother was half Swedish, the daughter of a sailor whose own father had a sawmill a hundred miles north of Stockholm, and of a girl called Sarah Dodd, 'whose father, and several fathers', Linklater wrote, 'had been farmers in Northamptonshire', one member of that family all but succeeding 'except for a worrying lacuna during the Wars of the Roses, in tracing his descent from the Countess Judith, a niece of William the Conqueror'.

Linklater never thought of himself as other than a Scot. But then again, though he once light-heartedly stood as a Scottish Nationalist candidate in a by-election, he never thought of himself as other than British. Tony Chisholm, the narrator of his masterpiece *The Dark of Summer*, Scots on his father's side, as his name indicates, English on his mother's, writes, 'I grew up in the knowledge that "we had come down in the world"; and by "we" I mean, quite simply, all of us who by birth are British.' That was Linklater's own position: a British Scot. He ended, in his son Magnus's opinion, as an idiosyncratic Tory and imperialist – even after the Empire was no more.

Linklater was educated in Scotland, at Aberdeen Grammar School (like Byron) and Aberdeen University, and he served in a Scottish regiment, the Black Watch, in the 1914–18 war; but his mother had told him that, after his father's death, 'the only reason for our living in Scotland is that a university education is cheap here'. His wife Marjorie was the daughter of a Writer to the Signet; but they sent one son to Eton and the other to Winchester, thus offering them entry to the British Establishment. Both sons became writers themselves, Andro the biographer of his father's friend Compton Mackenzie, Magnus editor first of the *London Daily News*, then of the *Scotsman* before becoming chairman of the Scottish Arts Council.

Eric Linklater, living by choice in Scotland, nevertheless had London publishers and was a member of London clubs. Some of his novels are set in England with, mostly, English characters, though to my mind the best are essentially Scottish. That said, his own favourite among them was *Position at Noon*, which, with grace, wit and rare economy, tells the story of an English family over three centuries.

English literature was his passion: 'in its swim', he wrote, 'I could watch the planets of all human experience. I found a full table for my hunger.' I can't recall that he ever wrote harshly of the English, rarely even disapprovingly. Aware certainly of differences between them and the Scots, he could yet, like Buchan, lump the two peoples together: 'it is of course characteristic of us – of the English and the Scots, I mean – to form a deep attachment to some distant people in a little-known land'.

Drawing general conclusions from a few individual examples is usually futile. Nevertheless two such may be offered.

First, mongrelism is so common that its products are only to be properly described as British, even though many of them may choose to identify themselves more narrowly as English, Scots, Welsh or Irish. For many people in the British Isles, nationality, other than a British one, is a matter of choice. This choice may be determined by birthplace, upbringing or simply personal predilection. Vast numbers of people have this choice, though it is perhaps only with sportsmen who aspire to play at international level that it becomes of great moment. Among them dual, or even triple, qualification is common. Two recent Scottish rugby captains, David Sole and Rob Wainwright, might both have opted for England. The England footballer Michael Owen is Welsh on his father's side, Scots on his mother's; nevertheless he chose to be English.

Second, mongrelism permeates all levels of society. If it is more evident at certain of them – among, for instance, politicians, academics, writers, sportsmen – this is first because the lives of such people are likely to be, or have been, better documented; and second, because some of them will have given public expression to their position, or have left, perhaps without intention, written evidence from which one may draw conclusions about national characteristics.

Many mongrels become thoroughly assimilated, casting off their ancestral skins, only perhaps a family name pointing to their origin. It may take very little time for a Scot or a Scottish family to become English, and vice versa. On the other hand there are those who retain a loyalty to their forefathers' native land, even after an exile lasting two or three generations. This merely serves again to emphasize the degree to which personal choice determines nationality. The same personal choice may also lead some to deny that they have any British identity at all, no matter in how many ways the reality of a common British culture manifests itself in their way of life or habit of thought and speech.

8

Cultural Influence: Two-Way Traffic

IN *BRITONS*, LINDA Colley wrote: 'Great Britain was an invented nation superimposed, if only for a while, onto much older alignments and loyalties.' The invention, as I have suggested, was only partial. Scots and English had much in common, notably commitment to the Protestant religion, in one form or another, long before the Treaty of Union was signed. Moreover, inasmuch as Great Britain was an idea superimposed on older alignments and loyalties, the experience of Britishness itself changed these. Neither Scotland nor England is what it might have been if there had been no Union. The Union influenced the development of both nations.

That Scotland was changed as a result of the Union is generally accepted, with resentment by Scottish cultural nationalists, whose own habit of mind is nevertheless formed to a great extent by the experience of being British – and not only because they customarily, though not invariably, express their resentment in English rather than Scots or Gaelic.

The process of influence is called anglicization. There has been a deal of it. That is incontrovertible. The most obvious example is that just mentioned: language. As a result of the Union, the language of Scotland is English. People may speak some variety of Scots; many of them do. But the language of public business, of government, law-courts and official documents, is English. Scottish newspapers are published in English. Scottish broadcasters may speak with a Scots accent, but they speak English. There is no longer a coherent Scots language, suitable for all purposes. Nobody writes a scientific thesis in Scots, and, though nothing is impossible, for languages can be revived, it's improbable that anyone ever will. Attempts at writing expository prose in Scots almost always fail. The Scottish Parliament produced a booklet in Scots, or what passed for Scots, describing its work; it was merely embarrassing. As for Gaelic, the number of people identifying themselves as Gaelic-speakers is now as low as 60,000. The language will survive, but only just, because there are enough people, and a sufficient number of vested interests, to keep it on a life-support system. But it will never be again the language of general or public discourse; it will survive as a hobby language.

Other evidence of anglicization is all around us. The Scottish universities are still distinct, but they are much more like English universities than they were a hundred or a hundred and fifty years ago. Though there are many indigenous small businesses and family firms, there are now very few public companies which retain their head office in Scotland. (In the case of public companies, there is no point trying to link ownership to nationality.) Scotland has not quite become a 'branch-line economy', but, with a few exceptions like the Royal Bank, which took over the National Westminster, public companies operating in Scotland mostly have their head office in England – if not in the USA, Japan, Korea, Germany.

Likewise high streets and shopping centres are dominated by English-based British companies or multi-nationals. A Scottish store or large retail business is now a rarity. John Menzies, for instance, sold all its shops to W. H. Smith. Independent Scottish booksellers, John Smith in Glasgow and James Thin in Edinburgh, could not survive competition from Waterstone's and the American firm Borders. Successful Scottish companies often move south. Long before the Distillers' Company was taken over by Guinness to become Diageo, its headquarters were in London and most of its directors lived in Berkshire.

Meanwhile the anglicization of Scotland continues and seems even to gather pace. In the late 1980s a journalist Chris Baur coined the word 'Anglocracy' to describe the Englishmen holding senior positions in Scottish universities and cultural institutions. Paul H. Scott, former (British) diplomat, nationalist and sometime Rector of Dundee University, wrote:

what really worries us is the fact that there has been a virtually complete English take-over in many aspects of our national life, including especially the top jobs in the Arts. Can this really be healthy in a country with a long and valuable cultural tradition of its own? Would any other country stand for it?

At the time he wrote this, 1988, the editor of *The Times* was a Scot, Charles Wilson, and so was the editor of the *Sunday Times*, Andrew Neil. Another Scot, Alasdair Milne, had retired the previous year from the director-generalship of the BBC. Yet another, Neil McGregor, had just become Director of the National Gallery in London, thus cancelling out, so to speak, the Englishman Timothy Clifford who was Director of the Scottish National Gallery in Edinburgh. Innumerable university posts in England were held by Scots, and of course since 1997 Scots have been disproportionately numerous in the New Labour Cabinet. Even then in 1988, despite the Tory decline in Scotland, there were several Scots in Mrs Thatcher's Cabinet (and there would be still more in John Major's), while the Scots lawyer Lord Mackay of Clashfern held the office of lord chancellor. Rupert Murdoch, the most influential media figure of the last quarter-century, is an Australian Scot, his grandfather having been a Free Kirk minister in Aberdeenshire.

Scots cultural nationalists are inclined to discount the Scottish influence on England. To their mind, the Anglocrats create, as Paul Scott puts it, 'a colonial atmosphere with all that implies in the breeding of an inferiority complex, alienation, irresponsibility and a sense of helplessness'. Scots who go south and succeed seem to cultural nationalists to be absorbed into the English mainstream. There is something in this of course, but only if you deny that that English mainstream is in reality British, and if you disregard the centuries-old influence of Scots on England and English life. Yet that influence has run deep. Modern England has in many respects been formed by Scots. It would be an exaggeration to say that England is a Scottish creation, but no more of an exaggeration than to speak of a 'complete English take-over' of Scotland.

It is curious that Paul Scott, like other cultural nationalists, doesn't appear to recognize this – especially curious in his case, because, in the same book of essays, *Scotland Resurgent*, where his 'Open Letter to the Anglocrats' appears, he quotes a passage from John Gross's book, *The Rise and Fall of the Man of Letters*:

> It would be hard to exaggerate the part played by Scotsmen in the development of the English periodical press. They helped to create not only the great quarterlies and monthlies, as is well known, but the weeklies as well: the first editors of the *Spectator*, *The Economist* and the *Saturday Review*, for example, were all Scotsmen. And right through the nineteenth century critics and essayists made their way south across the border. Lockhart, Masson, Andrew Lang, William Archer are a few random instances, the list could easily be extended – and it would become positively daunting if one were allowed to include the second generation of the diaspora: men like Ruskin, who still spoke with traces of a Scots accent, or Macaulay, whose features in repose struck Carlyle as those of 'an honest good sort of fellow, made out of oatmeal'.

Now it's possible of course to see this merely as Scotland's loss and England's gain; but inasmuch as it was England's gain, that took the form of the imprinting on England of Scottish ideas, Scottish ethics and what Stevenson called 'a Scots accent of the mind'.

To take only one example from Gross's list: William Archer, though now largely forgotten except by historians of the theatre, was, as a drama critic, immensely influential. According to the *Dictionary of National Biography*, he 'largely contributed to raising the standard of the English stage'. He was indeed its great modernizer, championing Ibsen and Shaw; he was Ibsen's first English translator. In 1907 he produced, along with Harley Granville-Barker of the English Stage Company, the first detailed proposals for a National Theatre, and after the 1914–18 war he was instrumental in the establishment of the New Shakespeare Company (now the Royal Shakespeare Company) at Stratford-upon-Avon. Archer may be fairly regarded as the father of modern British theatre.

Much that is finely, typically English will be found to have Scottish roots, or at least connections. What could be more serenely English than the neo-classical Senate House in Cambridge and the Fellows' Building that stands at right-angles to King's College Chapel. Yet both are the work of James Gibbs (1682–1754) from Aberdeen. A friend and disciple of Sir Christopher Wren, he also designed St Mary-le-Strand and St Martin-in-the-Fields in London and the Radcliffe Camera in Oxford. His *Book of Architecture* popularized the Palladian style to which he had been introduced while studying with the Italian master Carlo Fontana.

Gibbs, it may be argued, owed little to Scotland but his birth. Nevertheless, even if this be granted, his work in England offers, like the poet James Thomson's, evidence that even as early as the Treaty of Union there was sufficient cultural community between Scotland and England for a Scots artist to work comfortably and acceptably south of the Border. In any case, though Gibbs may have learned his Palladian style directly from Fontana, he was working in what was already a Scottish tradition established by Sir William Bruce of Kinross and James Smith, son of a master-mason from Tain in Ross-shire, who together worked in the reigns of Charles II and James VII & II on the Palace of Holyroodhouse, while Smith designed Hopetoun House by South Queensferry, a Palladian masterpiece.

Gibbs influenced William Adam (who also worked on Hopetoun), and Adam's sons Robert and James, who established a practice in London in 1758, became the most successful architects and interior decorators of the time. The English country houses and the London townhouses of the English aristocracy, most now sadly demolished, were very often Scottish creations. Robert Adam decreed the taste of the day just as surely as Adam Smith, born like him in Kirkcaldy, taught English politicians from Pitt the Younger onwards a new way to stimulate the wealth of the nation.

From the eighteenth century onwards Scots have permeated English cultural life. William Smellie, an Edinburgh printer, devised and produced the first edition of the *Encyclopaedia Britannica*, that compendium of knowledge which, by its fourth edition of 1801–19, already ran to twenty volumes. This most thoroughly British of undertakings, to which leading scientists, philosophers, historians, economists and geographers contributed, remained a Scottish publication till the early twentieth century when the tenth and eleventh editions appeared under the auspices of the Cambridge University Press.

An equally remarkable and necessary publication was the *Dictionary of National Biography*, begun in 1882. This was the brainchild of the publisher George Smith. Smith's father had founded a publishing firm in partnership with Alexander Elder soon after coming as a young man to London from his home town, Elgin. George Smith became head of the firm in 1846 and made it one of the most successful in the country. His authors included Ruskin, Thackeray and Charlotte Brontë. He founded the *Cornhill Magazine* with Thackeray as editor, and the *Pall Mall Gazette*, a high-quality London evening paper. But it was the *Dictionary of National Biography* that remains his monument. No work compares to it as a record of the centuries. 'National' in the title means British, the term employed in the widest possible sense: the first entry is for a French Huguenot who became Dean of Killaloe in Ireland and died in Westminster. Its first editor was Leslie Stephen, father of Virginia Woolf; he himself was three or four generations removed from his family origins in Aberdeenshire where they had held the tenancy of the farm of Conglass by Inverurie since around 1600.

To the *Encyclopaedia Britannica* and the *DNB* may be added the great repository of the English language, the *Oxford English Dictionary*. In the form it took it was the creation of James Murray, a tailor's son from the village of Denholm near Hawick in the Scottish Borders. Murray, whose own first book was *The Dialect of the Southern Counties of Scotland*, was an exceptional linguist; he used to teach himself a new language by studying translations of the Bible. Too poor to go to university, he became a schoolteacher, was at the age of twenty headmaster of the Hawick Union School. He removed to London, at first working in a bank, but was soon teaching again at Mill Hill School, a Dissenting Academy founded as a rival to the great Anglican public schools; again one may note the community between English Dissent and Scots Presbyterianism. He joined the Philological Society and worked as an editor for the Early English Text Society. In 1879, when he was forty-one, he was appointed editor of the Philological Society's proposed new 'Dictionary of the English Language'. The Society thought it might run to 6,000 pages. This alarmed its prospective publishers, Macmillan in London and Harper in New York. The Oxford University Press took over the project, and the result was the *OED*. It occupied the rest of Murray's life, though he had reached only the letter T when he died in 1915. The *OED* may be compared to a medieval cathedral, always in the making and never assuming a final form. But Murray was its architect.

His approach was modern and scientific: a dictionary recorded words as they were used; moral judgements did not apply. Meanings changed and the changes must be illustrated. In other words, his idea was that a dictionary described; it did not prescribe. Murray was in general so admirable that it is agreeable to note that he wasn't always consistent. 'Browning', he said, 'continually used words without regard to their proper meaning. He has added greatly to the difficulties of the Dictionary.' But Browning's usages could become part of a word's meaning.

Murray had been reared speaking Border Scots. He had, perhaps for this reason, no time for notions of the necessary correctness of standard English. Dialects could not be classed as 'incorrect' speech. That was nonsense; they were survivals of other and older forms of languages. If English, despite the efforts of generations of schoolteachers, has never been frozen in attitudes of correctness, if the meaning of words still fluctuates, if new words are admitted easily and without recrimination, if it remains rich and flexible and yet of an infinite subtlety, we owe much of this to Murray and to the principles that informed his work. Everyone who speaks and writes the English language is in his debt, and it is pleasing to think that the fullest description of our language was given by one who came from a poor family and a country district where polite English was spoken by few.

The *Britannica*, the *DNB* and the *OED* were great enterprises, inspired and largely created by Scots, their effect on national – British, English and Scots – culture vast, if incalculable. But there is more to it than that. The prominence of Scots in publishing has been extraordinary. The list of London-based firms founded by Scots is long: John

Murray, Macmillan, Smith Elder, Constable, Collins, A. & C. Black. No less influential, in the nineteenth century, were publishing houses that remained in Scotland: Blackwood's, Chambers, Blackie, Nelson. Apart from their contribution to the dissemination of imaginative literature, Scottish publishers excelled in the production of works of reference and school textbooks. Several of the founders of publishing houses started out as poor boys, apprenticed to printers. Their subsequent careers testified to the Presbyterian zeal for education that made Scotland for a time the nation in Europe which had attained the highest general level of literacy.

This impressed the English clergyman Sydney Smith, who came to Edinburgh in 1798 and remained to be one of the founders of the *Edinburgh Review*. He was impressed to find that:

> the common people are extremely conversant with the Scriptures, are really not so much pupils, as formidable critics to their preachers; many of them are well read in controversial divinity. They are perhaps in some points of view the most remarkable nation in the world, and no country can afford an example of so much order, morality, oeconomy, and knowledge among the lower orders of Society. Every nation has its peculiarities, the very improved state of the common people appears to me at present the phenomenon of this country.

No wonder it produced a Murray.

This zeal for education survived into the twentieth century and was carried into England. Scots were early in recognizing the importance of teacher training. Sir John Adams, for example, born in Glasgow in 1857, became successively Rector of the Free Church Colleges, first in Aberdeen, then in Glasgow, lecturer in education at Glasgow University, Principal of the London Day Training College, and then, 1902–22, London University's first Professor of Education. Adams taught that verbs of teaching take two accusatives: you teach the pupil and the subject simultaneously, and one cannot be divorced from the other. His influence on teacher training in England was considerable.

No institution in the twentieth century did more to shape Britain, and a sense of national identity, than the BBC. Its ethos was determined by its first director-general, John Reith, a pragmatic Calvinist son of the manse, in many ways a difficult and often disagreeable man. Malcolm Muggeridge summed up his achievement: 'in other countries, the voice [of broadcasting] might be monopolized by a party, and made to utter only its slogans, or put up for sale, precious moments purchased to praise a pill, explain a soap's excellence, but in England, in Sir John Reith's words, what was aimed at was "an expression of British mentality at its best"'. This was no mean ambition, and if, in the decades since Reith left the BBC in 1938, it has been so diluted as to be now scarcely recognizable, it remained for a quarter of a century at least Reith's BBC. Under his authority it became a national asset. Refusing to allow it to be used for any party political purpose unless the other side was given a fair hearing too, he made it appear as impartial as the Crown. At a time when, too often, people already said, 'You can't believe what you read in the papers,' 'I heard it on the wireless' became an asseveration of ultimate truth. That was Reith's achievement. Though many in Scotland have come to see the Corporation as centralist, metropolitan in tone and outlook, despite the regional network existing since Reith's time, it contributed to the development and dissemination of a truly national British culture – which is indeed what Scottish cultural nationalists dislike.

But such a culture does actually exist. This does not imply that other distinct national and regional cultures do not survive within and beyond it. They very evidently do. But there is an over-arching British culture which has been created by the interaction of the different national cultures within the United Kingdom, by the influence of England on Scotland, Wales and Ulster, and by their influence on England, that of Scots especially being pervasive and profound.

To deny the reality of a British culture is folly, refusal to look reality in the face. This culture exists at all levels. It is pointless to pretend otherwise, to pretend for instance that sitcoms and soaps, even when they have an English setting, are not as much, and as agreeably, part of television viewers' cultural experience in Scotland as in England. A Scottish cultural nationalist may bridle when the BBC speaks of 'national institutions like *Test Match Special*', but Scottish cricket-lovers, of whom there are many, would be dismayed not to be able to receive it.

Of course, for those sufficiently determined, it is possible to see, and deplore, English-based sitcoms and soaps, *Test Match Special* and so on, as examples of the insidious anglicization of Scotland. But it is more reasonable to regard them as evidence of a common British culture – one which can for example admit the very Glaswegian Billy Connolly, recently voted in a predominantly English poll the third funniest television comedian of all time. If the very Scottish Connolly is acceptably British, then so are the very English *EastEnders* and *Coronation Street*.

British is a widely inclusive term. It comprehends English, Scottish, Welsh and Irish, and, within these, regional peculiarities and differences too. So Shakespeare and Dickens are as much part of Scottish culture as Scott and Stevenson are of English; they have gone to form the way we feel and think; they are what we have all inherited. My grandfather, an Aberdeenshire farmer, had two books to which he turned when bored or depressed: *The Pickwick Papers* and *Three Men in a Boat*. Both might be described as very English, and southern suburban English at that. But I do not think this can be fairly described as an example of anglicization. He talked a fairly broad Scots, and his favourite poet was Charles Murray, who wrote in the Aberdeenshire Doric.

The experience of being British for 300 years at least has formed us all. Paradoxical as it may seem, the experience of a political union may even have checked a process of assimilation, Scots, conscious of their status as junior partners, cultivating their difference and individuality. Without political Union it is improbable that Lowland Scots would have consented to adopt Highland dress as their national garb. 'Highlandism', the historian Tom Devine has written, 'answered the emotional need for a distinctive Scottish identity without in any way compromising the Union', which by the early nineteenth century, when the cult of Highlandism was established, was bringing about a Scottish economic miracle. More Lowlanders than Highlanders served in the British army, but Scotland was so associated with the Highland regiments that Lowland ones like the Royal Scots and the King's Own Scottish Borderers wore tartan trews as their ceremonial, or dress, uniform. 'The tartan cult', in Devine's words, 'is also a reminder that Britishness is a part of Scottishness.' Highlandism created the British Scotland that Queen Victoria adored, a Scotland which Englishmen could recognize and respect.

Modern Scotland is therefore a creation of the Union; but so in its different way is modern England.

9

Two Novelists

JOHN BUCHAN WAS born a Scot, married into the English aristocracy, and died as Governor-General of Canada and a distinguished member of the British Establishment. Compton Mackenzie was born an Englishman, brought up as a Londoner; in middle life he removed to Scotland, became one of the founding members of the Scottish National Party, and died the Grand Old Man of Scottish letters and one of the sights of Edinburgh. Both were very successful and popular novelists. The young Mackenzie was hailed by the elderly Henry James as the great hope of the English novel. In Scotland today he is remembered as the author of Highland farces, such as *Whisky Galore* and *The Monarch of the Glen*. (The BBC television series with that title claims to be 'inspired by Compton Mackenzie's Highland novels', but bears no relation to them.) Buchan dismissed many of his own novels as lightweight 'shockers', written for his own entertainment, and that of his readers. Yet his work has lasted better than Mackenzie's.

They were near-coevals, Buchan being born in 1875, Mackenzie in 1883. Each had a wide circle of friends which didn't, surprisingly, include the other. Both were classicists, Buchan inclining to Rome, Mackenzie to Greece. Like so many Scottish writers, both engaged in public life, as comparatively few English novelists have done. Their politics were sharply opposed.

Buchan was thoroughly Scots, in family and upbringing. His father, from an Aberdeenshire family now established in the Borders, was a minister in the Free Church of Scotland. In Buchan's childhood, the Rev. John Buchan was called to a slum parish in the Glasgow Gorbals. As a young man, the future governor-general taught in its Sunday school. His mother came from a farming family in Tweeddale. Married young, only eighteen when John, her eldest son, was born, 'her world', he wrote, 'was the Church, or rather a little section of the Church. Public affairs affected her if they affected her Kirk.' Buchan remained a Presbyterian all his life, if less narrowly than his mother. For many years he was an elder of St Columba's in Pont Street, the principal Scots kirk in London. He would serve as Lord High Commissioner, the king's representative, to the General Assembly of the Church of Scotland – his mother's proudest moment, he thought. But, though strongly marked by Calvinism and deeply imbued with the Protestant work-ethic, he was, as a historian, severely critical of the narrowness and fanaticism of the seventeenth-century Covenanters. A recent biographer, Andrew Lownie, called him a 'Presbyterian Cavalier'. It is an accurate description, to be applied also to his hero James Graham, Marquess of Montrose, a signatory of the National Covenant of 1638, subsequently Royalist commander in Scotland as the king's Lieutenant-General in the Civil War. Buchan saw Montrose as a man passionate for moderation. Other heroes were Scott, Cromwell, the Emperor Augustus and Abraham Lincoln. He wrote biographies of the first three, and gave Lincoln a fine imaginary heredity in a novel entitled *The Path of the King*.

The young Buchan was zealously ambitious, a Scotsman on the make and in a hurry. Educated at Hutcheson's Grammar School and Glasgow University, he began publishing while still a student. He was a natural writer, but he wrote also with the immediate purpose of making himself financially independent. From Glasgow he went with a scholarship to Oxford, and fell in love with it.

He had been reared as a narrow patriot. 'Against our little land there had always stood England, vast, menacing and cruel . . . Even when we grew older and the intolerance abated, England remained for us a foreign place, not too friendly, to be suspected and even dreaded.' Oxford changed all that. It represented his 'first true visit to England, when I came under the spell of its ancient magnificence and discovered a new loyalty'.

Many Scots, descending with like prejudices on Oxford or

Cambridge, have had the same experience, only a few continuing to feel strangers in a foreign land. Oxford and Cambridge are English certainly, but, by Buchan's time, were also British. A little earlier Benjamin Jowett, Master of Balliol, had been asked by the Scots classical scholar J. S. Blackie, 'What do you think of us?' and replied, 'Sir, we never think of you at all.' But that was a joke. As the historian Christopher Harvie has remarked, 'by Jowett's time you couldn't throw a stone in Balliol without hitting a Scot'.

Buchan soon found friends among the sons of the English Liberal Establishment, chief among them Raymond Asquith, son of the future prime minister. But he also noted that 'Oxford was full of Scots – studious Scots, orgiastic Scots, rhetorical Scots who talked in the Union, robustious Scots from the football teams.' He became a founder member of a new Caledonian Club. 'It was limited to members with a proven Scots descent on both sides for at least three generations; an English club in the university, which adopted the same principle, could find only two who passed the test conditions.' The Establishment had become British. In passing, I observe that some sixty years later at Cambridge I drew up a list of twenty close friends, only three of whom had two English parents; and as for the grand-parents, who knows?

Soon after Oxford Buchan became one of the proconsul Lord Milner's *Kindergarten* in South Africa. They were bright young men charged with the responsibility of settling the affairs of the country after the Boer War. It was the happiest non-literary work of Buchan's life, and it made him an imperialist. 'I began to see that the Empire, which had hitherto been only a phrase to me, might be a potent and beneficent force in the world.' He remained an imperialist to the end, but when he spoke and wrote of the Empire, he meant chiefly, almost exclusively, what were then known as the White Dominions: South Africa, Canada, Australia, New Zealand. Although a much loved younger brother entered the Indian Civil Service, India played little part in John Buchan's imaginings. He never travelled east of Suez where so many Scots made their careers as soldiers, administrators, planters and merchants, or served as missionaries or doctors.

Buchan scarcely lived in Scotland as an adult. Either side of the 1914–18 war, he was a partner in the Edinburgh publishing house Nelson's, recruited by an Oxford friend, Tommy Nelson, a Scottish rugby international. So he spent a few days every month at their Edinburgh office. Eager for a political career, he was adopted as Unionist candidate for Roxburgh, Selkirkshire and Peebles, a Liberal seat. He loved that, felt at home there, but never fought an election, stepping down as candidate when in poor health after the war.

So, for the greater part of his life, Scotland for Buchan, as for the royal family and many members of the English upper class, was a place for holidays – for walking, climbing, fishing, shooting and reading. His home after the war was the manor house of Elsfield in the Cotswolds, four miles north of his beloved Oxford. There, he wrote, 'I "took sasine" of English soil and learned to know intimately what I had hitherto only admired.' Characteristically, while saying that he had acquired 'a new loyalty and a new heritage, having added the southern midlands to the Scottish Borders', he employed a Scots law term to announce this new allegiance, 'sasine' being the act of giving and taking legal possession of feudal property.

Nevertheless he remained intensely and proudly Scottish. He was President of the Scottish History Society and was closely involved in the creation of the National Library of Scotland. From 1927 to 1935 he was Member of Parliament for the Scottish Universities, and argued for the devolution of political and administrative power and responsibility from London to Edinburgh. (Like Labour politicians from the mid-1970s, he thought this would forestall any inclination towards separatism.) Like Scott, he worried that 'in language, liter-ature and art we are losing our idiom, and . . . [are] in danger very soon of reaching the point where Scotland will have nothing dis-tinctive to show the world'. These words come close to echoing the fears expressed by Scott in the Preface to the *Minstrelsy*. It doesn't seem to have occurred to Buchan that a dismal prospect first iden-tified more than a century previously, and not yet realized, might be chimerical.

Like Scott Buchan accepted the Union as a fact, and found no

difficulty in combining a Scottish and British patriotism. He detested
and despised Irish Nationalism. In *The Three Hostages* Sandy
Arbuthnott has this to say of the villain, Dominick Medina: 'There's
a faraway streak of the Latin in him, but he is mainly Irish, and that
never makes a good cross. He's the *déraciné* Irish, such as you find in
America . . .' Medina has:

> that venomous hatred of imaginary things – an imaginary England, an
> imaginary civilization, which they call love of country. There's no love
> in it. They think there is, and sentimentalize about an old simplicity,
> and spinning wheels and an uncouth language, but it's all hollow.
> There's plenty of decent plain folk in Ireland, but his kind of *déraciné*
> is a ghastly throwback to something you find in the dawn of history,
> hollow and cruel like the fantastic gods of their own myths . . . Did
> you ever read the old Irish folk-lore? Very beautiful it is, but there is
> always something fantastic and silly which mars the finest stories. They
> lack the grave good-sense which you find in the Norse sagas, and, of
> course, in the Greek.

This is a pretty damning assessment. That novel was published in
1924, two years after the Treaty which established the Irish Free State.
The extreme Nationalists, the Republicans, had refused to accept that
settlement, and were engaged in a civil war with their own Irish
Government. The leader of the extremists was Eamonn De Valera,
whose mixed Spanish–American–Irish ancestry resembles Medina's.
This can hardly have been unconscious on Buchan's part.

One shouldn't, as I have remarked, ascribe the sentiments or opinions expressed by a character in a novel to its author. Yet it is hard not
to think that this is Buchan the Glasgow-reared Scots Presbyterian
Unionist speaking his mind. Many Scots, and not only nationalists,
feel far more warmly towards the Irish than towards the English.
Buchan was not one of them. In the same novel he has another character, Macgillivray (Scotland Yard, Special Branch), say this: 'Look at
the Irish! They are the cleverest propagandists extant, and managed to
persuade most people that they were a brave, generous, humorous, talented, warm-hearted race, cruelly yoked to a dull mercantile England,
when God knows they were the exact opposite.' 'Macgillivray',

Buchan's narrator Richard Hannay has the grace to remark, 'is an Ulsterman, and has his prejudices . . .'

Fair enough, but one cannot help concluding that they were Buchan's also, as they were Kipling's, for whom, as a recent biographer David Gilmour has written, 'no crisis could justify negotiation with the Irish gunmen. The Irish Free State', he believed, 'was the precursor of "Free States of Evil" throughout the Empire. India was no doubt on the list.'

Buchan, cannier than Kipling, might not have gone so far. Yet I can think of nowhere that he expressed any sympathy with Irish Nationalism or Sinn Fein. Before 1914 he differed 'violently' from the Liberal Government on the matter of Ulster, 'for, though a federal home ruler, after the fashion of my friend, F. S. Oliver, their blundering in the treatment of Ulster roused some ancient Covenanting devil in my blood', a remark which demonstrates yet again how Scots may contrive to be half-Jacobite, half-Covenanter, containing these opposites in some sort of equilibrium. On the other hand it is simpler to regard Buchan's hostility to the Irish as an expression of the innate prejudice of a Glasgow Protestant.

His second love, unquestionably, was England. He came to Oxfordshire as a stranger, much as Kipling came to Sussex; and, like Kipling, he was captivated.

'England', he wrote in his memoir, *Memory-Hold-the-Door*,

is full of patches which the tides of modernity have somehow missed, and Elsfield was such an one. Though only fifty-five miles by road from London, and an hour's walk from Oxford, it was as set in its ancient ways as an isle of the Hebrides. When I first went there my gamekeeper had never been in a railway train. At that time it was the only side of Oxford where there were no suburbs, for the college towers could be seen from our hill rising sheer from meadows, and there was the same moat of deep country between its mind and the outer world. Startling experiences passed from its people like water from a duck's back. My gardener had fought through the East African campaign and nearly died of fever, and another of my men had had four years in France, but for all the effect those adventures had had on them they might never have left the parish.

That is a lover speaking, a lover of both the place and the people. It delighted him to think that:

> the manor had had few owners since the days of the Saxon Aella: the Norman grantee, the Pudseys from Yorkshire, the Hores from East Anglia, and then until nearly the end of the last century it was a kind of dower-house for the North family at Wroxton, further up the Cherwell. It was a clearing in the forest at the time of the Conquest, and a clearing it remained . . .

Again like Kipling, Buchan's view of England was romantic. Both felt the strong attraction of the timelessness of the place where they had settled. Kipling wrote *Puck of Pook's Hill* to give words to this love that had come to him in middle life. Buchan, in one of his best historical novels, *Midwinter*, has the eponymous character say:

> There is an Old England which has outlived Roman and Saxon and Dane and Norman and will outlast the Hanoverian. It has seen priest turn to presbyter and presbyter to parson and has only smiled. It is the land of the edge of moorlands and the rim of forests and the twilight before dawn, and strange knowledge still dwells in it. Lords and Parliament-men bustle about, but the dust of their coaches stops at the roadside hedges, and they do not see the quiet eyes watching them at the fords.

This, doubtless, is fanciful, but it is also the England of Shakespeare's Forest of Arden and *A Midsummer Night's Dream*. It is the England inhabited by Chesterton's 'people . . . who have not spoken yet'. It is the England which Scott sketched in the opening chapters of *Ivanhoe*. It is indeed an England that many Scots have fallen in love with, a gentle England that carries no burden of history. That said, it is also an England which bears very little resemblance to the England in which millions live. Like Stevenson, Buchan knew nothing directly of the England of the great industrial cities of the north and midlands, nothing either of the suburbs and dormitory towns from which tens of thousands commuted to work in London offices; his England was inhabited by aristocrats, scholars, yeomen and peasants. But it was also the ideal England of contemporary English poets such as Housman, Rupert Brooke and Edward Thomas.

That England is to be found also in some of Compton Mackenzie's early novels, though the young Mackenzie was essentially a Londoner, and his world one of gas-lit streets, theatres, music-halls and Anglo-Catholic parsons.

Mackenzie was born into a theatrical family, his father, Edward Compton, being an actor–manager, more successful in the provinces than in London. There was always something theatrical in Mackenzie himself; he was a born actor. Indeed his biographer, Andro Linklater, has suggested that his only wholly successful work of art was the persona he constructed for himself.

He was given the education of an English gentleman, at St Paul's and Magdalen College, Oxford; and his early novels are very English, dewily English, the best of them, *Sinister Street*, an autobiographical portrait of the artist in making. They were hugely popular, admired by critics also, captivating, among countless others, the young Scott Fitzgerald, whose own first two novels betray their influence.

It was a couple of generations since any of his family had lived in Scotland, but Mackenzie delighted in his Highland heritage. As an adolescent he was already the sentimental Jacobite which he would remain, though his powerful sense of the ridiculous was excited by the freaks and inadequates who frequented obscure societies that professed an undying allegiance to the long-vanished Stuarts and supported various European monarchist claims.

From an early age he was a passionate defender of small nations that might be deemed oppressed: a pro-Boer in the South African War; an enthusiast for Irish Nationalism who detested the Ulster Protestants with whose cause Buchan identified. During the 1914–18 war he served as Director of British Intelligence in the Aegean, and, a Greek scholar, became an enthusiastic pan-Hellenist. He conceived a hatred of imperialism, power politics and bureaucracy. He loathed Germany, and, a convert to Roman Catholicism, blamed Martin Luther for everything that had gone wrong in Europe since the sixteenth century. His detestation and distrust of Germany were equal to Kipling's – almost the only thing they had in common.

Mackenzie's career went into a decline after 1918. Scott Fitzgerald, meeting him – 'my old idol' – on Capri in 1925, reckoned that 'he's just tired. The war wrecked him as it did Wells and many of that generation.' The severe judgement was premature. He was a long way from being wrecked. But he was ready to shift direction. Within a couple of years of that meeting, he was reinventing himself as a Scot. He made his home on the island of Barra, was elected Rector of Glasgow University on a Nationalist ticket, and became in 1932 one of the founders of the Scottish National Party. A few years later he embarked on what was intended to be his *magnum opus*, *The Four Winds of Love*.

This is a huge novel, running in the most recent (1968) edition to eight volumes. Much of it follows the course of Mackenzie's own life. One key episode recalls his first visit to the Mackenzie homeland of Sutherland where he sees out the last night of the nineteenth century. It is a novel of moods and ideas. It has never been fashionable, in its own time on account partly of Mackenzie's distrust of Freudian psychoanalysis. It has also one of the most tiresome heroes in English or Scottish literature, John Ogilvie, named after one of the few Roman Catholic martyrs of the Scottish Reformation. He is a successful playwright, is loved by a succession of beautiful women, and is also an argumentative, opinionated and often boring preacher and polemicist, a vehicle for Mackenzie's own ideas rather than a truly realized character.

Few people, probably, have read the whole novel. Yet it is remarkable and has had its admirers, chief among them the American critic (and friend of Fitzgerald) Edmund Wilson. Much of it remains interesting, though inevitably many of the then topical arguments are now either dead or of only historical significance. Parts are still funny.

More to my present purpose, much that he says about Scotland and England, the Scots and the English, merits notice.

Mackenzie was critical of English (British) politics, but never anti-English. That would have been ridiculous. Ever in love with his own youth, he could not forget how much he owed to England. Ogilvie tells a Cornish cousin (who himself denies his own Englishness): 'I can afford to love England in all that is most English because the fight is

not for spiritual independence [only?] but for material independence
as well. And who would not love England and the English once one
had convinced them that, however ridiculous it might seem to them,
there were quite a few nations that did not want to be English.' It is
then the comfortable assumption that all the world aspires to the condition of Englishness that irks him; this is what many Scots would now
call 'English arrogance', in reality an unthinking sense of their own
virtue and superiority, galling to their smaller neighbours who,
however, have much the same sense as regards themselves.

Mackenzie disliked and distrusted the City of London and its 'loan
capitalism', though the merchant banks that devised and developed
this were as likely to be Jewish (Rothschild) or Scots (Robert Fleming)
as English (Baring). Like Scott and Buchan, Mackenzie resented what
he saw as a process of assimilation, as a result of which it seemed that
Scotland was losing its singular identity. What, to his mind, made this
worse was that the chief agents of assimilation were Scots themselves.

Ogilvie, like Mackenzie a man who has chosen to become a Scot,
has this to say of his adopted fellow-countrymen:

> We are a nation of ferocious individualists in Scotland. Hence the con-
> spicuous success of the Protestant Reformation. Hence the appeal of
> Presbyterianism. Hence the economic triumphs of the Scot. Hence
> the disgraceful show Scotland makes beside co-operative societies like
> Norway or Finland or Denmark [all, one may observe, Protestant
> countries themselves], all three of which enjoy less natural advantages
> than our own country. The same was once true of Ireland, which lost
> every war by sacrificing the cause to the individual and usually follow-
> ing that up by sacrificing the individual, until those young men of 1916
> [the men of the Easter Rising] redeemed their country from the curse
> of excessive individualism with their own blood . . . We have no men
> like that to shame our country out of its individualism.

This reads oddly today, so oddly indeed as to seem nonsensical.
During the 1980s, the years of the Thatcher governments, the opposite argument was commonly advanced, setting an inherited Scottish
sense of community and attachment to communal co-operative values
against the 'excessive individualism' of the English.

Mackenzie's was an ideal nationalism, divorced from realities. It was essentially sentimental. In his Rectorial Address to Glasgow University, he explained how, at the age of eight, he was given a copy of Scott's *Tales of a Grandfather* and how:

> it happened that soon after I came possessed of this talisman to live in the past of the race from which I sprung that I travelled northward alone. It was near dusk on an evening of earliest Spring. Somebody in the railway-carriage announced that we were crossing the border, and I craned my head out of the window to enjoy the magical sensation. Down the long train came a faint sound of cheering and from windows far ahead I could see hats being waved. An austere landscape in the fast-fading dusk, a stream of flamy smoke from an engine, a few cheers ringing above the roar of the train, a few hats waving; not much perhaps, but enough for a child of eight to sit back again in a dim railway-carriage and dream over, his heart blazoned like a herald's tabard with the bright symbols of his country's life, his heart draped like a hatchment with the sombre memories of defeat upon defeat. Thence onward I lived secretly in the past of my country . . .

This is fine rhetoric, but strange fanciful stuff; and not only because the landscape, either side of the Border, whether you come by the east- or west-coast route, is equally 'austere'. It would be unkind to question Mackenzie's sincerity, though the temptation to do so is strong, but this passage reminds me of nothing more surely than of some of Enoch Powell's rhapsodies about the essence of England: this, for example, from an address given in 1964 to the Royal Society of St George:

> There was this deep, this providential difference between our empire and others, that the nationhood of the mother country remained unaltered through it all, almost unconscious of the strange fantastic structure built around her . . . England [*sic*] underwent no organic change as the mistress of a world empire. So the continuity of her existence was unbroken . . . Thus, our generation is like one which comes home again from years of distant wandering. We recover affinities with earlier generations of English, who feel no country but this to be their own . . . We find ourselves once more akin to the old English . . . From brass

and stone, from line and effigy their eyes look out at us, and we gaze into them, as if we would win some answer from their inscrutable silence: 'Tell us what it is that binds us together; show us the clue that leads through a thousand years; whisper to us the secret of this charmed life of England, that we may in our time know how to hold it fast.'

This may be called lyrical; it may be called guff. It bears some resemblance to Mackenzie's (Scottish) 'heart blazoned like a herald's tabard with the bright symbols of his country's life', more perhaps to Buchan's view of immemorial 'Old England'. It is characteristically English also in Powell's evident ability to forget what Buchan could never have forgotten: that the Empire was a British, not English, enterprise.

Mackenzie too could not forget that, though, unlike Buchan, he had moments when he was ashamed of Scotland's part in the winning and retaining of Empire. It had to his mind contributed to the anglicization of Scotland, inasmuch as the aristocracy and the service upper-middle class acquired loyalties that went beyond Scotland, and were infected by English manners and attitudes. The clan chiefs and lairds in his Highland farces may profess a reverence for tradition, but they have been educated as members of the Anglo-Scots aristocracy, typically at Harrow and Sandhurst, and have only a few words and phrases of Gaelic, abominably mispronounced, at their command. They are quite certain they are not English, are indeed convinced of their innate superiority to the English, yet appear less than wholly Scottish. Mackenzie regards them with a mocking affection.

Orwell in an essay on nationalism remarked how common it was for leaders of nationalist movements to be either peripheral members of the nation with which they identified or outright foreigners. Mackenzie, lacking the pertinacity and capacity to endure boredom of the professional politician, was only sporadically engaged in nationalist politics. But he belongs to the category Orwell described. He idealized an imaginary Scotland and had little time for the Scotland that actually existed. He saw Scotland as properly a Celtic nation, and disliked almost everything that was characteristic of Lowland Scotland. He dreamed of a pan-Celtic association to be formed by

Scotland, Ireland, Wales, Brittany and Cornwall, and has Ogilvie out-lining such a scheme to the Irish prime minister Eamonn De Valera. (He was practical enough and a sufficiently honest novelist to show De Valera quite unimpressed by the idea.) His pan-Celtic fantasy was entertained also by the poet Hugh MacDiarmid; and, again like MacDiarmid, Mackenzie was for a time attracted to the Social Credit ideas of the Scots-Canadian Major Douglas, as an alternative to the 'loan capitalism' of the City of London. In short, everything he wrote about nationalism and the spiritual rebirth of Scotland appeared absurd to men and women who prided themselves on their practical good sense, and who, like Buchan, felt much closer to England than to Ireland, and much closer to Protestant Ulster than to the Roman Catholic Free State.

For a long time I saw, and wrote of, Buchan and Mackenzie simply as opposites. So in a sense they were, though each also contained opposites within himself, Buchan being the Presbyterian Cavalier, Mackenzie the Englishman who had identified with Celtic Scotland as other Englishmen identified with the desert Arabs. Buchan drew strength from his immersion in the timelessness of his England, Mackenzie from his rejection of the England of his youth.

For Buchan civilization was a thin crust, because man was by nature mischievous, and ready to listen to the message of dark and malignant gods. His heroes in fact and fiction are all conscious that civilization has been constructed with difficulty, and can be wrecked with ease; his villains are lonely egoists. *Witch Wood*, the finest of his historical novels, centres on the choice of evil in the name of good. It may be read as a condemnation of the excesses of Calvinism, with echoes of James Hogg's *Justified Sinner*, but it could not have been written if he had not been equally conscious of the rigorous grandeur of that faith. Buchan was wary of idealism. It was not only his commitment to imperialism and the Union which inspired his hostility to Sinn Fein and Irish Nationalism. Where Mackenzie saw individuals 'redeeming their country from the curse of excessive individualism', Buchan saw destructive egoism and the enacting of the pernicious doctrine that the end justifies the means. He was suspicious of all talk of rights, agreeing with Stevenson that 'there are no rights and plenty duties' – this being an expression of the Calvinist habit of mind, if not of Calvinist theology. He has been charged with placing too great a value on worldly success. Yet to him this was a sign that you had worked well – very Scottish, of his generation anyway. It is a misreading of Buchan to see him simply as a bastion of the existing order, for he believed that, to survive, that order must repeatedly justify itself. If it failed to do so, then it rotted from within. So he distrusted cleverness without character, one reason for his love of England, for the English, he thought, valued character first, way before cleverness.

Mackenzie in contrast rarely penetrated below the surface of human nature, perhaps shy of what might be discovered there. Possessed of a wonderful vitality, he was a stranger to both doubt and Calvinist gloom. Whatever his opinions might be – and, since he was inconstant, they shifted – he retained to the end the happy certainties of his English Edwardian youth. He rejected political Liberalism as expressed by the Liberal Party, but still adhered to its ethos. He remained thirled to Enlightenment ideas of progress and the natural goodness of man; if only man would employ his intelligence, anything might be possible. This was perhaps the consequence of an admirable digestion; Buchan suffered from a duodenal ulcer for more than twenty years.

Buchan revelled in new experience, yet was fundamentally hard and pessimistic, taking a suspicious view of our nature, if it was not anchored by religious faith and a sense of duty. Mackenzie, forever amused, if also irritated, by human folly, nevertheless remained essentially optimistic. Apply intelligence to the world, respect small nations and their inherited culture, and the sun will shine.

Mackenzie, the self-created Scot, was in truth an English empiricist to the last. Buchan, proud to be accepted as a member of the British Establishment, delighting in his acquaintance with royalty and prime ministers, found in himself towards the end of his life something of the temper of a seventeenth-century Covenanter. He looked on the Europe of the 1930s and it seemed to him 'as if a mature society was being assailed by diseased and vicious children', carrying an infection to which fortunately, or rather on account of their inherited character and values, England, Scotland, the White Dominions and the USA were immune.

He ended his autobiography with a quotation from the New Englander Henry Adams: 'after all, man knows mighty little, and may some day learn enough of his own ignorance to fall down and pray'. He added his own conclusion: 'Dogmatism gives way to questioning, and questioning in the end to prayer.' The English country gentleman, secure in his ownership of the manor of Elsfield, had come back to the Free Kirk manse. But there was no book he quoted from more often than *The Pilgrim's Progress*, written by an English Dissenter in Bedford Jail.

IO

Empire

— ❦ —

THE ENGLISH CAME late to empire overseas, the Scots later still. There had been English empires of a sort in the Middle Ages, when the kings of England held dominion over various provinces of France, but these had little to do with the English people, brought them small benefit, and were transitory. Attempts by the English kings to conquer the other parts of the British Isles were more significant. They subdued Wales, which was incorporated into England, established uneasy dominance in Ireland and were defeated in Scotland. In the seventeenth century Ireland would become an Anglo-Scottish colony, with the native Irish reduced to subordination, their lands confiscated, the practice of their religion proscribed.

The Continental ambitions of the English Crown withered in the fifteenth century. The end of the Hundred Years War in 1453 saw France triumphant, England humiliated; of all the conquests of Edward III and Henry V only the port of Calais now remained in English possession. It would soon be time to look westward, to seek opportunities in the wider world now being revealed to Europeans by, initially, Portuguese and Spanish adventurers.

Though Henry VII helped finance the Genoese entrepreneurs John and Sebastian Cabot, who sailed from Bristol to the North Atlantic and 'discovered' Newfoundland, the English part in the new age of European expansion remained insignificant till the end of the sixteenth century. By then Spain had conquered the Inca Empire of Peru and the Aztec Empire of Mexico, while Portugal had established itself in what is now Brazil and controlled Europe's trade with the Indies.

English imperial ambitions awoke in the reign of Queen Elizabeth,

with Sir Francis Drake's circumnavigation of the globe, the exploitation
of the slave trade from Africa, and Sir Walter Raleigh's attempt to found
a colony (Virginia) in North America. Raleigh's first effort failed, but
success was not long delayed. With all the other European powers
engaged in the Thirty Years War (1618–48), with Spain in economic
decline, and its government exhausting its credit with European
bankers, opportunities opened for England. By the mid-seventeenth
century there were English colonies in North America; and several West
Indian islands, valuable on account of the sugar trade, had been annexed.
War with the Dutch resulted in the capture of New Amsterdam, which
was renamed New York. England was on the way to becoming the dominant power in North America and the Caribbean, though France
would dispute supremacy for another hundred years. Meanwhile
English merchants had already established a foothold in India.

Scotland shared in none of this, even though the two kingdoms
were now united under one monarch. Admittedly some enterprising
Scottish merchants were trading with the English American colonies
by the 1630s; the earliest cargo of tobacco from Virginia entered the
Firth of Clyde in 1640 (where indeed it was confiscated by the
Covenanters who had rebelled against Charles I). But Scottish
attempts at colonization in that part of Canada optimistically styled
Nova Scotia came to nothing, and after the Restoration of 1660 the
Scots found themselves excluded by the terms of the Navigation Acts
passed by the English Parliament from all legitimate trade with English
colonies. So, by the time of the Revolution of 1688, England was an
imperial power, if still only in a small way; and Scotland was not.

It was difficult to see how it might become one. English mercan-
tilist theory stressed that no economic or political gain could result
from allowing foreigners to convey goods between the mother
country and its colonies. This theory, adopted in response to the
success of the Dutch in dominating the carrying trade between
Europe and the wider world, blocked Scottish participation in the
English Empire – as long, that is, as the Scots were defined as foreigners. That exclusion, however, was not in practice complete. By the
1680s perhaps as many as a dozen vessels were trading regularly, if illi-

citly, between Scotland and England's American colonies; one Lord Provost of Glasgow, Walter Gibson, flew the flag of St George on his ships bringing sugar and tobacco into the Clyde.

Nevertheless the restrictions were irksome. There was vast wealth to be won, if only Scots could find a means of getting into the game. In 1695 the Scottish Parliament passed an Act to establish the Company of Scotland trading to Africa and the Indies, in imitation of the success both the English and the Dutch had had with chartered companies. This was vague enough, yet the mere floating of the Company was sufficient to alarm the English Parliament, for it seemed that this upstart Scottish company (which had, originally, some English directors) was seeking to infringe the monopoly enjoyed for almost a century by the English East India Company.

The king, William III, expressed his displeasure. The House of Commons impeached the Company's English directors. But enthusiasm in Scotland still ran high, partly because Scotland's economic plight was severe; the 1690s saw a succession of poor harvests. At this point the Company was, in effect, seduced by a remarkable man, a visionary called William Paterson.

Paterson, born in Dumfriesshire in 1658, had himself settled in London and become a merchant trading with the West Indies, thus as an English resident circumventing the restrictions of the Navigation Acts. Very little is known of his early ventures. It was not till after the Revolution of 1688 that he became prominent.

That Revolution and the subsequent war with France put a great strain on the public finances, and made a high level of Government borrowing necessary. Various schemes to expand and stabilize credit were advanced; none cogently. Then Paterson secured the support of the Chancellor of the Exchequer, Charles Montague, and a leading London merchant, Michael Godfrey, for his solution to the problem. His scheme was that £1,200,000 should be borrowed by the Government at 8 per cent. To encourage subscription of the loan, the subscribers were to be incorporated as the Governor and Company of the Bank of England, with the power to trade in bills of exchange, bullion and forfeited pledges; the Bank was also forbidden to lend money to the Crown without the authority of Parliament. It is not too much to say that Paterson's device secured the Revolution Settlement; it gave all who bought Government stock as issued by the Bank an interest in the survival of the New Order. Paterson had devised the most effective means of securing public credit then to be found anywhere in Europe.

He became one of the first directors of the Bank, but quarrelled with his colleagues and was not re-elected. So he returned to Scotland where he persuaded the promoters of the Company of Scotland to abandon thoughts of establishing a trading post in Africa, and instead plant a Scottish colony at Panama on the Isthmus of Darien.

His project was of the utmost simplicity, and should perhaps have been distrusted for that very reason. Yet his argument was seductive: enormous profits might be made if trading vessels between Asia and Europe could avoid the long route round Africa. A colony established at the narrowest point of the Americas, where the strip of land was no more than a bridge between the Atlantic and the Pacific, could capture the bulk of the Indian trade. He had himself been to Darien and averred that there was no serious obstacle to the establishment of a colony. This was rash, mistaken indeed, for Spain claimed the land and retained the monopoly of trade.

Paterson's plan aroused great enthusiasm in Scotland. Men tumbled over each other to invest. Eventually something between a third and half of the money wealth of the country was invested in the project. The result was a disaster. Success depended on English support and the protection of the Royal (English) Navy. This was not forthcoming; the directors of the East India Company saw Paterson's project as threatening to their monopoly. They lobbied the City and the Court successfully.

Scotland's first attempt at empire was inauspicious, an abject failure. Yet it was also significant, for two reasons. First, it prefigured the Scottish concept of imperial endeavour. Though Scottish soldiers would play a conspicuous part in the winning of empire, and then in its defence, for Scots the object of empire was always commerce rather than conquest. Wars might have to be fought – but primarily to open up or protect markets. So for instance and most notoriously the Scottish merchant adventurers William Jardine and James Matheson forced a war on China in 1840 to compel the Celestial Empire to allow them to trade in opium. Their success made Hong Kong one of the great trading outposts of the British Empire.

Second, the Darien failure concentrated Scottish minds. Within ten years William Paterson himself was advising those Scotch politicians who were in favour of the Treaty of Union with England, and was invited to assist in framing its fiscal provisions. Union made sense to him. As a young man he had had to move to England in order to be able to share in the opportunities offered by the new English Empire. He had then seen his boldest project founder as a result of English hostility. He drew the logical conclusion; if you can't beat them, join them. In his magisterial study *The Scottish Empire*, Michael Fry writes that the Empire 'beckoned Scots to exotic climes where they did their business and left, content that they had achieved what they could, for they knew commerce to be the vehicle of progress. In a sense it turned out that the great advantage of the Union was to make more Dariens possible, now successful because of English co-operation.'

The knowledge that commerce is the vehicle of social progress was one of the discoveries of the philosophers and philosophic historians of the Scottish Enlightenment. The hydrographer and explorer of the South Seas Alexander Dalrymple declared in 1770 that discovery was important 'not with a view to colonizing; not with a view of conquest; but of an amicable intercourse for mutual benefit'. One of the founders of the *Edinburgh Review*, Henry Brougham, later Lord Chancellor in the Reforming Whig Government of the 1830s and one of those responsible for the creation of London University, published in 1804 an *Enquiry into the Colonial Policy of the European Countries*, in which he argued that colonies should be regarded as provinces of a single large empire: 'The commerce which a country carries on with its colonies is, in every respect, a home trade.' This was evidence perhaps of the *Romanitas* characteristic of Scotch education.

As for the justification of empire, Scottish philosophy taught that social development was the most important aspect of human affairs, and its promotion the mark of a wise politics. Often, inevitably, empire-builders fell below the lofty and idealistic standards enjoined by this belief; nevertheless at its best the promotion of social development of the native races was the imperial aim. The methods by which this was to be achieved were sometimes questionable. Macaulay's famous Minute on Indian Education of 1835 displayed a contempt for oriental learning and culture which now seems shocking. Nevertheless his certainty that exposure to European thought would contribute to the social and political development of India, so that eventually Indians would resume self-government, was not only itself, as Fry puts it, expressive of 'the cosmopolitan spirit of the eighteenth century', it was progressive and eminently practical – so practical indeed that just over a century after Macaulay wrote that minute the first prime minister of an independent India, Jawaharlal Nehru, educated at Harrow and Trinity College, Cambridge (Macaulay's own college), was the very model of an eastern Whig, a latterday Edinburgh Reviewer, as it were, who would have been welcome to dine at Holland House.

As for the Scottish impetus to imperial adventure, Adam Smith remarked: 'it is a sort of instinctive feeling to us, that the destiny of our name and nation is not here, in this narrow island which we occupy'. Kipling couldn't have put it otherwise, though he would not have restricted consciousness of that destiny to the Scots.

Empire is a portmanteau term, concealing differences and distinctions. The most obvious of these is between the settler colonies and those where the British came only to work, trade, develop, govern and, when necessary, fight. The first group comprised the American colonies (which achieved independence in 1783), Canada, Australia, New Zealand, South Africa and parts of East Africa; the second, India and all other imperial territories on the Asian landmass, West African colonies and some of East Africa. A few imperial possessions, notably the West Indian islands, were in a hybrid state. The first group would, with the exception of the East African settler colonies (Kenya and Southern Rhodesia), be granted Dominion status early in the twentieth century. They proceeded easily and with little argument to the point where they were fully independent countries, legal entities capable of making treaties, and member-states of the United Nations – all this while, in most cases, retaining a nominal allegiance to the British Crown.

For the second group progress to independence would be slower, less certain, at times resisted by the imperial power. In retrospect, however, the eventual independence of colonies, and the transformation of Empire into Commonwealth, appears natural, even inevitable, the logical consequence of an imperial mission properly regarded as stewardship.

No one expressed this idea of stewardship more compellingly than David Livingstone, the greatest hero of Victorian Scotland. Born in 1813, in the small town of Blantyre in Lanarkshire, Livingstone was put to work in a cotton mill at the age of ten. He pursued a path of self-education and self-improvement, and at the age of twenty-three was admitted to Anderson's College in Glasgow to train as a medical missionary. The following year he joined the London Missionary Society and was sent, as he wished, to Africa. He would become the most famous explorer of the age.

Explorers were heroes to the British public, opening up what Joseph Conrad called 'the dark places of the earth'. Travelling with the Bible in one hand and a compass in the other (with a breech-loading rifle slung across the shoulder), they exemplified the British sense of civilizing destiny. Critics of imperialism have found it easy to denigrate their achievement: their concept of 'discovery' was European arrogance, for the lands they discovered were already known to their inhabitants. This is a futile argument: they were not known to the explorers, who therefore did indeed discover them for themselves and their compatriots. Moreover, the explorers mapped them and revealed their relation to other lands. Critics then accuse the explorers of having been 'exploiters' – the charge most consistently levelled at imperialists. So the explorers opened up parts of the world to pillage; they destroyed native cultures which they did not trouble to understand; their civilizing mission was a fraud; and their assumption of superior moral standards intolerable. This is a curious argument, for it assumes that morality is relative, and that there is no possibility of any real moral superiority; yet the very criticism directed at Victorian explorers is itself an expression of the critic's own assumption of that same moral superiority.

Nevertheless, Western post-imperial guilt has ensured the triumph of such criticism. Even in Scotland, which gave so much to the Empire, and took so much from it, the Scottish imperial role is now commonly regarded as a matter for shame. Inasmuch as children are taught anything about the Empire, they are taught that it was nothing to be proud of.

For this reason it is worth looking more closely at Livingstone, both legend and reality. Early biographers, Fry writes, aimed to create the image of a Protestant saint who would 'vindicate to the public the causes of the age: Free Trade, rule of law, abolition of slavery, defeat of barbarism, diffusion of Christianity, global distribution of the British stock, reconciliation of scientific and religious truth in progress practical and moral'. So Livingstone's became 'not just a personal story but an epic of Britain's greatness and an apologia for her imperial state'. Livingstone, archetypal Scot, with both Highland and Lowland strains in his heredity, nevertheless was made into a British hero to be honoured with a resting-place in Westminster Abbey. 'He affirmed', in Fry's words, 'an order both British and imperial, both liberal and hierarchical.' He remains also 'the one imperial figure of the nineteenth century to be honoured in the independent Africa of today'.

There is good reason for this. Livingstone not only loved Africa and Africans; he respected the people he moved among and came to know. He understood why Africans resisted missionary attempts which, to their mind, were 'reducing them and their much-loved domestic institutions'. A Christianity which destroyed native culture would make for alienation. Africa must be made Christian, but the act of conversion must run with the bias of African traditional culture, not against it. He believed, as an heir of the Scottish Enlightenment, in the civilizing influence of commerce. 'I go back', he told a Cambridge audience, 'to make an open path for commerce and Christianity.' 'Commerce', he said, 'has the effect of speedily letting the tribes see their mutual dependence. It breaks up the sullen isolations of heathenism.' The promotion of commerce in material goods would liberate Africans from the principal commerce then practised: trade in human beings.

The slave trade, outlawed on the high seas half a century before, still flourished in Africa, and corrupted all affected by it, for it reduced individuals to the status of commodities. Livingstone properly saw it as an abomination, but understood also that attempts at mere suppression were not enough. Substitutes must be found. Commerce in goods would lead, he believed, to the promotion of 'a preparation of the raw materials of European maufactures in Africa for by that means we may introduce the negro family into the body corporate of nations'. This was still the language of the Scottish Enlightenment, the language of Hume, Smith and Adam Ferguson. Livingstone believed that the planting of settler colonies – 'Christian families' – might be necessary as the means of effecting social and economic improvement. There must however be no racialism. He looked forward to 'the fusion or mixture of the black and white races in this continent'. The history of Africa might have been happier if that hope had been fulfilled.

The Empire could not however escape the curse of racialism. So much evidence pointed to the superiority of Europeans in so many different ways – militarily, educationally, commercially – that only a few could fail to regard the native peoples as inferior, either savages or children. In those settler colonies which would become White Dominions, the British soon outnumbered the natives; the only exception was the future Republic of South Africa. In Canada, Australia, New Zealand, the British followed the American example, subduing the indigenous inhabitants and pushing them to the margins of society. In this no distinction is to be found between Scots and English. Intellectually the more intelligent might accept that some day, in Asia and Africa, the British would relinquish power and return it to those who were now the subject races; but that day was distant. Others – missionaries, army officers, district commissioners and colonial civil servants – might feel a deep affection for those to whom they ministered, those whom they led or governed. But that affection was generally paternalist. For almost a century, the decades either side of Victoria's Diamond Jubilee, the fact of empire, Britain's right to empire, could be questioned only by disaffected radicals.

But could the Empire endure as it was? That was the question which occupied the minds of many towards the end of the nineteenth century, as the white settler colonies grew in self-confidence, and the Irish, agitating for Home Rule, conjured up the spectre of the American disaffection which had led to the War of Independence and the dissolution of the first British Empire a hundred years previously.

One politician who addressed the question more acutely and more persistently than others was the most enigmatic public figure of the day, Lord Rosebery. Intelligent, hugely rich (thanks to his marriage to Hannah Rothschild), excessively sensitive, easily bored, sometimes preferring the Turf to political life, he was a difficult, at times impossible colleague. Intensely Scottish, yet also a product of Eton and Oxford, he was both a Liberal and an Imperialist. A world tour in 1883–4 convinced him that the Empire was 'the greatest secular agency for good the world has ever seen'. It was held together by a 'single red line, and that red line is the communion of races'. The Empire was 'a Commonwealth of Nations'. Among these nations the Scots had a special role, partly on account of their historical experience. He defined imperialism as 'a larger patriotism', as the Union had been for Scotland. The Scots could lead the English to a better understanding of empire, as partnership rather than domination. Scotland had been transcended by Britain, had achieved a new self-understanding by absorption in a larger whole: now the same prospect opened before England. Like the Scots in 1707 the English might be wary, fearful of what they would surrender in the imperial federation he saw as the logical development. Therefore it was the Scots' duty to 'mould the Empire', even while the English hesitated to submit to 'the vigorous embrace of the new world'.

'Rosebery', Fry writes, 'became a catalyst for new Scottish values rising to compete with the old ones: collectivist, elitist, perhaps racialist, certainly imperialist values, hard to dismiss because they seemed to offer a way through baffling problems where otherwise an impasse had been reached.'

With imperialism went decentralization, or Home Rule all round. Originally sceptical of Gladstone's scheme of Irish Home Rule, Rosebery came to believe that it might be fitted into a programme of constitutional reform of benefit to all. 'I detest separation', he wrote, 'and feel that nothing would make me agree to it. Home Rule, however, is a necessity for both us and the Irish. They will have it within two years at the latest. Scotland will follow, then England. When that is accomplished, Imperial Federation will cease to be a dream.'

Rosebery had good reason for his urgency. The economic and commercial supremacy which Britain had enjoyed throughout the nineteenth century was being challenged, was indeed slipping away. The United States of America and imperial Germany, Bismarck's Reich, which had come into being only in 1871, were now great industrial powers. Germany's steel production would soon surpass Britain's. Within thirty years, at 16,200,000 tonnes, it would be twice as large. In chemicals and the new electrical industry too, Germany was forging ahead. Something – but what? – must be done.

Imperial federation was Rosebery's answer. In 1886 he became President of the Imperial Federation League. Canada, which had become a Confederation of very diverse provinces in 1867, seemed to offer a model. Some Canadians certainly thought so, among them the architect of the Confederation, Sir John Macdonald, born in Dornoch and prime minister since 1878. The first Canadian High Commissioner to the United Kingdom, Alexander Galt, another Scot, son of the Ayrshire-born novelist John Galt, was even more enthusiastic. He advocated the establishment of an imperial Parliament with representatives from legislatures in the settler colonies and from England, Scotland and Ireland.

Rosebery's imperialist ideas aroused some enthusiasm in Scotland, less in England. Practical Tories, hostile to Irish Home Rule, saw schemes of imperial federation as chimerical. The Liberals themselves were divided. The party split over Home Rule, Joseph Chamberlain leading those who were to become Liberal Unionists into alliance with the Tories. Then the South African War of 1899–1902 discredited the idea of empire; the Radicals in the party, Lloyd George among them, were pro-Boer. Rosebery himself, now in semi-retirement, only inter-mittently active in politics, thought the war unwise, the means by which it had been forced on the Boers deplorable, but he nevertheless clung to his imperialist ideal.

The war was popular in Scotland, as the war memorials raised after it throughout the country suggest. Volunteering was patriotic. In the Khaki Election of 1900 the Liberals tainted by opposition to the war lost their majority in Scotland for the first time since 1832. The Liberal imperialists had their last chance to regain control of the party. They failed, partly because Henry Campbell-Bannerman (son of a Lord Provost of Glasgow, MP for Stirling Burghs and since 1899 party leader) outmanoeuvred them. A moderate pro-Boer, he denounced not the war but the 'methods of barbarism' employed in the winning of it. Liberal imperialism fizzled out. There would be no moderniza-tion of either the Union or the Empire. Both would still be adminis-tered from London, until the White Dominions went their own way, and India and the imperial territories in Asia and Africa eventually demanded and achieved independence.

Rosebery failed. So also did his sometime friend, sometime rival, Joseph Chamberlain. Transformed as a result of his opposition to Gladstone's Irish Home Rule policy from Radical to Liberal Unionist and quasi-Tory imperialist, Chamberlain, having been one of the architects of the South African War, launched in 1903 a campaign for tariff reform, the end of Free Trade and its replacement by what would be in effect an imperial customs union. Rosebery, while not believing that 'Free Trade is part of the Sermon on the Mount', was sceptical; he nevertheless concluded that, far from strengthening the Empire, Chamberlain's plans would tend 'to dislocate, and in time dissolve, its Unity'. On the face of it, his logic is hard to follow. Wouldn't his own scheme for imperial federation have led to just some such arrangement as Chamberlain was proposing? Perhaps yes, but Chamberlain was offering a policy imposed by London, in contrast to Rosebery's pro-posals for Home Rule all round and an imperial parliament. It may be this was never practical politics; certainly it doesn't appear to have been so in retrospect. But nor, as it happened, was Chamberlain's.

The idea of empire occupied the attention of many thinking Scots. Two of the young men who worked with Milner in the reconstruction of South Africa after the war were Philip Kerr (later the Marquess of Lothian) and John Buchan. Kerr founded the Round Table, a think-tank with a magazine of the same name to foster discussion of the means to create 'an organic union to be brought about by the establishment of an imperial government constitutionally responsible to all the electors of the Empire, with the power to act directly on the individual citizens'. Buchan wrote a novel, or rather a conversation-piece, *A Lodge in the Wilderness*, examining and promoting the idea of imperialism. Later his commitment dissolved into mere wordiness. He no longer believed in imperial federation. He had come to 'distrust any large scheme of formal organization'. Instead he 'dreamed of a world-wide brotherhood with the background of a common race and creed, consecrated to the service of peace: Britain enriching the rest out of her culture and traditions, and the spirit of the Dominions like a strong wind freshening the stuffiness of the old lands'. This was, sadly, guff, mere waffling. More interestingly, Buchan's view of empire apparently excluded India and all those colonies where, for generations, we had come to trade, administer and develop, but not to settle. Yet for many India was the Empire, famously the 'jewel in the crown'. It was indeed only in India that the monarch was king–emperor.

It was perhaps neither surprising nor shameful that Buchan's philosophy of empire should have so degenerated. The project of imperial federation had been a bold one, and characteristically Scots. It was provoked partly by the realization that Westminster was tightening its authority within the United Kingdom even while the settler colonies were beginning to assert their independence. 'How', Fry asks, 'were the positions of Scotland, Ireland and Wales to be reconciled with those of Canada or Australia?' Proposals for imperial federation 'aimed at a rational result dispelling imperial absence of mind. The result would not have been an English sort of Empire but a Scottish sort of Empire. The notion was a spectacular example of contemporary Scottish self-confidence. As so often, though, Scottish self-confidence outreached reality.' Imperial federation died because its advantages were evident to so few, the difficulties of establishing and maintaining it all too obvious. It withered too because its establishment would have required the English to have surrendered something of their primacy. The prospect appealed as little as full incorporation within the European Union does today – and ultimately for the same reason: England would not be governed even in part by institutional bodies over which it could not exercise full control.

Imperial federation was an idea conceived in the afternoon of empire. With its failure, followed by the moral shock of the 1914–18 war, enthusiasm for empire faded. In the next war, Winston Churchill might protest that he had not become prime minister in order to preside over the dissolution of the British Empire; nevertheless that dissolution could not be long delayed. The jewel in the crown was surrendered; two new states, India and Pakistan, came into being. The poet and prophet of empire, Kipling, had despondently foreseen it. 'I hate your generation,' he told a young lawyer, 'because you are going to give it all away.' Few cared. George Orwell thought, correctly, that 'the mass of the people, in the nineties as now, were anti-militarist, bored by the Empire'. By the 1940s this was generally true, in Scotland as well as in England.

In the generation that came to maturity after the 1939–45 war, enthusiasm for empire faded, then died. Some felt ashamed of our imperial past. This was the case even in Scotland. There was still the occasional flicker of pride, as when for example the exploits of the Argyll and Sutherland Highlanders ensured that withdrawal from Aden was orderly, but this was rare. The socialist equation of empire with exploitation was accepted by many. Others turned with some relief from the problems of disengagement from empire to the opportunities offered by the project for European Union.

That disengagement from empire was the principal, the only enduring, achievement of Macmillan's premiership. It was the work, controversial at the time, of his colonial secretary Iain Macleod. In it this Yorkshire-born child of the Hebrides and of two Gaelic-speaking parents was assisted by his under-secretaries, both Scottish aristocrats, the Earl of Perth and Hugh Fraser, son of the 16th Lord Lovat.

The speed with which Macleod brought about this disengagement made him unpopular with the Tory right, and may have cost him the leadership of the party a few years later, but, though criticized by the leader of the so-called Die-Hards, Lord Salisbury, as 'too clever by half', his commitment to what he called 'one of the great dramas of history, as so many countries thrust forwards through nationalism to independence', was absolute.

In his final speech as colonial secretary in October 1961, he said that he believed:

> in what our grandfathers would have called the British Imperial mission. It is not yet completed. Since the world began, empires have grown and flourished and decayed, some into a sort of genteel obscurity, some leaving little heritage and culture behind them, some even no more than stones covered by sand. They are one with Nineveh and Tyre [a Kipling quotation], but we are the only empire leaving behind us a coherent political scheme of development. We are the only people who, with all the hesitations and failures that there have been, are genuinely resolved on turning, to use Harold Macmillan's phrase, an empire into a commonwealth, and a commonwealth into a family . . . I believe quite simply in the brotherhood of man – men of all races, of all colours, of all creeds . . . And now what lies ahead in this event? It is perhaps strange to an English and to a Welsh audience to quote the greatest of our Scottish native poets, but nobody has put this in simpler or finer words than Burns:
>
> > It is coming yet for a' that,
> > That man to man the whole world o'er,
> > Shall brothers be for a' that.
>
> And this is coming. There are foolish men who will deny it, but they will be swept away; but if we are wise then indeed the task of bringing these countries towards their destiny of free and equal partners and friends with us in the Commonwealth of Nations can be a task as exciting, as rewarding, as inspiring and as noble as the creation of empire itself.

That hope may have faded in the near half-century since. The task may not have been completed. Yet the Commonwealth has not dissolved.

In Macleod's articulation of his belief in the 'brotherhood of man', one can catch echoes of the Scottish Enlightenment with its trust in reason and its confidence that sympathy and benevolence can make for a better world. The Empire to which so many Scots had given so much may be seen now as a staging-post on the road to the realization of the aims of the Enlightenment.

11

Economy and Industry

'**O**ATS: A GRAIN, which in England is generally given to horses, but in Scotland supports the people.' Johnson's definition is well known. He admitted to Boswell that it was intended to vex the Scots. One rose finely to the tease, Patrick Murray, Lord Elibank, asking, 'but where will you find such horses, and such men?' Elibank's rejoinder was taken up and expanded a century later in a dialogue, or imaginary conversation, written by John Stuart Blackie, Professor of Greek at Edinburgh and early Scottish Nationalist.

> MACDONALD: The oatcakes, you remember, Dr Johnson says, are food for men in Scotland and horses in England, and you see the reason here both how Scotchmen are so superior to Englishmen, and English horses to all other horses. If beer and beef-steaks have made Englishmen, oatmeal cakes and oatmeal porridge have made Scotchmen.
>
> HILARIUS: Specially Scotch brains. There is a notable seasoning of phosphorus in oats which produced the *perfervidum ingenium Scotorum*.

In the Middle Ages the French chronicler Froissart had attributed the hardiness and endurance of Scottish soldiers to their ability to sustain themselves on campaign on a diet of oatmeal mixed with a little water.

Such observations and such fooling are now only of antiquarian interest, oatmeal, though still doubtless eaten in the form of oatcakes and porridge more often in Scotland than in England, no longer being the staple of the Scottish diet. Yet Johnson's joke, Elibank's and Blackie's rejoinders and Froissart's remark all point to the same conclusions: that Scotland was, in comparison with England, a country of few resources; and that whatever Scotsmen achieved was in response to a harsh and demanding environment, much having to be made of little.

Pre-Union Scotland was, and had long been, a poor land, its chief export, like nineteenth-century Ireland's, being people. Admittedly this poverty was more marked on account of the succession of miserable harvests in the 1690s and of the failure of the Darien Scheme in which so large a part of the money wealth of the country was invested and lost. Admittedly too, recent historians have demonstrated that the country was not as economically backward as was thought for the best part of two centuries after the Union. They have shown that the conditions, or preconditions, for economic expansion existed before 1707.

Yet the poverty was real, and it was extreme. Sir William Menzies, who farmed the Excise of Scotland, fell into arrears and was prosecuted for payment by the Privy Council. In his defence he alleged that famine, whether arising from natural causes or the will of God, annulled all contracts; and argued that from 1697 to 1705 the harvests had failed and their produce could not support the people: thousands of the poor had died of starvation, thousands more had emigrated, 'and multitudes were compelled to have recourse to unnatural food, such as wild spinage, snails, etc.'.

Menzies doubtless had a case to make, but others support his evidence. The 'Patriot', Andrew Fletcher of Saltoun, wrote in 1698 of there being 'two hundred thousand vagrants begging from door to door, half of these belonging to the wild, brutalized, savage race of nomads, the other half families whom poverty and famine had driven to want, while thousands of our people are at this day dying for want of food'.

Yet within a hundred years Scotland had transformed itself, and was on the way to being one of the first of the industrialized nations. Within 200 years it enjoyed one of the highest *per capita* incomes in the world, ill and unevenly distributed though this was, so that abject poverty existed in the midst of plenty.

How did this transformation come about? How did a society that had been poor for so long finance industrialization? Professor

Tom Devine in his history, *The Scottish Nation 1700–2000*, offers four answers.

First, the big landowners, 'the elite of the old society', not only undertook schemes of agricultural improvement, which banished the fear of famine and produced a food surplus capable of feeding the rapidly growing towns and cities, but were also active in financing industrial expansion, especially in coal, lead and ironstone mining. They built roads and canals, and members of the nobility were prominent among the directors of the three chartered banks: the Bank of Scotland, the Royal Bank of Scotland and the British Linen Bank.

Second, the Treaty of Union admitted Scots to the Atlantic trade, and it was on the back of the sugar and tobacco trades that, as Scott's Bailie Nicol Jarvie observed, Glasgow flourished.

Third, 'Scottish society mobilized capital more efficiently through the banking system'. Banks responded to the shortage of coin by pioneering the issue of banknotes; and it was in the eighteenth century that Scottish banks invented that useful, if occasionally perilous, device – the overdraft.

Fourth, new industries were built up by men of enterprise and originally modest means, who prudently reinvested their profits to fund expansion. They did not hesitate to borrow ideas and technology from the English. 'Technology transfer', Devine writes, 'on a remarkable scale took place from south to north, reflecting Scotland's relative backwardness and also the strategy of English businessmen who were on the lookout for cheaper labour and low-rented factory sites.' This too was a consequence of the Union.

There was another, at least as important as the opening of the American trade, technology transfer, inward investment and the convenient availability of coal and iron deposits. Throughout the eighteenth century, and well into the nineteenth, Scotland enjoyed a remarkable freedom from politics and from Government interference. As long as the country was peaceable (which it was after the end of the Jacobite threat) the Government in London was happy to let Scotland alone. Indeed, as Scott wrote, it was precisely on account of this neglect that Scotland was able 'to win her silent way to wealth and prosperity'.

The nineteenth century is the odd one out in the history of both England and Scotland. There was a remarkable shift in the balance of the economy. For most of English history the south and east had been the prosperous and progressive regions, the north and north-west backward. That changed. Though London remained the largest and richest city, it was challenged by Manchester, Liverpool, Leeds, Newcastle and, in the west midlands, Birmingham. The textile industries were located in Lancashire and Yorkshire, the new heavy industries in the north-east, while Birmingham and the towns of the Black Country became producers of consumer goods and of machine-tools. The north bred advanced economic thinkers. Free Trade was a Manchester doctrine; the Anti-Corn Law League was formed there by Richard Cobden and John Bright. 'What Manchester thinks today, London will think to-morrow.' As England changed from a predominantly agricultural land to an industrial power, the impetus came from the north.

Something similar happened in Scotland. Edinburgh surrendered its primacy to Glasgow, which, like the industrial cities of the north and midlands of England, grew at an unprecedented rate, until by the middle of the Victorian Age it could justifiably boast of being 'the Second City of the Empire', a title that only Manchester and Birmingham might dispute.

Commerce in the form of the American trade made Glasgow, but in its nineteenth-century heyday it became one of the workshops of the world, and its great ships were the city's most glorious work. Henry Bell launched the first steamship on the Clyde in 1812, and thereafter the advance of the industry was remarkable. The secret of its success lay in engineering superiority; the stages in marine-engine design associated with John Elder, James Howden, A. C. Kirk at Fairfield's and Walter Brock at Denny of Dumbarton secured world leadership for the Clyde. In percentage terms the peak was probably reached by 1870 when 70 per cent of all iron ships and two-thirds of all steam ships were built there. Yet even these figures are less impressive than the fact that in 1914 the Clyde launched one-third of all British tonnage, 18 per cent of world tonnage and more than the total shipbuilding production of either the United States or Germany, though these were by then the most advanced industrial nations in the world with the fastest-growing economies. Some forty firms were engaged in shipbuilding on the Clyde. 'Clyde-built' meant quality.

It was not only ships. Three of the four largest locomotive-building companies in Britain were in Glasgow; they exported railway engines all over the world. Civil engineering followed logically: Tower Bridge in London, the Forth and Tay railway bridges, and most of the bridges on the uncompleted Cape-to-Cairo railway were made in Glasgow, by the firm of Sir William Arrol & Co., Engineers and Bridge-builders.

It could not last, or at least it did not last. The economic historian Sydney Checkland, an American who taught at Glasgow University, wrote that:

> The evolution of Glasgow between 1875 and 1914 is a classic example of the limitation of business-time horizons. It illustrates also the tendency, where circumstances have permitted, to develop a high level of mutually confirming specializations, to press the advantages of such a situation, to be blind to warnings of its precariousness, and to seek opiates that will allow it to continue. In this way it was possible to ignore the erosion of the fundamental basis of the Clydeside economy brought about by changes in demand, the rise of foreign rivals, and the refusal of other nations to continue in a state of dependence upon British suppliers.

What Checkland wrote about Glasgow might be written, with only minor variations, about the cotton industry of Lancashire and the textile industry of Yorkshire. Coal-mining throughout Britain would also seek, as the twentieth century entered its second half, 'opiates that would allow it to continue'.

Checkland provided a metaphor to explain the decline of Glasgow, one applicable also to the north of England:

> The Upas tree of Java (Antiarius Toxicaria), entering European legend through Erasmus Darwin, was believed to have the power to destroy other growths for a radius of fifteen miles . . . It is taken as a symbol

of the heavy industry that so long dominated the economy and society of Glasgow . . . The Upas tree of heavy engineering killed anything that sought to grow under its branches . . . Now the Upas tree, so long ailing, was decaying, its limbs falling away one by one. Not only had it been inimical to other growths, it had by an inversion of its own condition before 1914, brought about limitation of its own performance.

The brilliant metaphor may dazzle rather than illuminate. There were other reasons for the shift in economic balance after the first German war. Glasgow, like Manchester and Liverpool, had been the classic free-trade city; their market was the world, and their wealth had grown from their ability to service that market in the expanding global economy of the nineteenth century. But the Depression of the 1930s saw world trade contract. In two years it fell by as much as a third. Alarmed and puzzled politicians responded to cries for Protection; global trade contracted still more sharply. The conditions which had allowed the great industrial cities of the Victorian Age to flourish disappeared. Decline ensued, inexorable and distressing.

Nineteenth-century Glasgow had found itself in the industrial avant-garde: its ships, locomotives and bridges were the symbols of the age. Between the wars the new age's symbols were to be found elsewhere: in the English midlands and in the light-industry towns such as Slough and Stevenage that surrounded London. Though the Scottish Office and forward-thinking industrialists and politicians understood that light industries must be developed in Glasgow and the Central Belt of Scotland, the 1930s were, in the economics of Glasgow, as of the north of England, the years the locusts ate. The 1935 Census of Production reported that two of the growth industries of the time, car manufacturing and electrical goods, had only 2 per cent of their British workforce in Scotland.

The moral effect of the loss of primacy was as significant as the material. It was not just that the old industrial cities and regions lost their footing in the new economy, not just that they failed to seize the opportunities offered by the rising demand for motor cars and consumer goods; they also suffered from the consciousness of failure. They had flourished while they knew themselves to be in the van of progress; they withered when they felt that they were dragged at the tail of the twentieth-century chariot.

Shipbuilding in Glasgow contracted so severely between the wars that Sir James Lithgow, chairman of one of the most famous firms, established with the financial support of Montagu Norman, Governor of the Bank of England, a new company, the National Shipbuilders Security Ltd, to take over loss-making yards, cut construction capacity and share out work among the smaller number of yards that survived. Rearmament, war and the demands of post-war reconstruction afforded the industry a temporary reprieve. But this expired in the mid-1950s. The Clyde was brought up hard against reality. Bedevilled by restrictive practices, distrust of innovation and the insistence on parity of wage rates (already higher than those of foreign competitors), it lurched from crisis to crisis, from short-lived expedient to shorter-lived one. In desperation, to keep cash flowing, managements tendered for contracts at prices that brought no profit, and offered delivery dates which they could not meet. Consequently, winning a contract could prove more damaging than failure to win one, for it might only increase indebtedness. John Brown's of Clydebank, the yard famous for building the great liners, the *Queen Mary* and the *Queen Elizabeth*, lost £3 million on the *Kungsholm*, the difference between the contracted price and the actual cost of construction.

'Clyde-built' had been a synonym for quality; now the Clyde seemed to represent all that was worst in British industry: restrictive work practices, obsolete ideologies, weak, unimaginative and ever more desperate management, inefficiency, over-manning, short-sightedness. Glasgow, which had flourished as the supreme example of the market economy in action, as befitted the city where Adam Smith had developed the theory of how the wealth of nations came about, now struggled along with the help of subsidies supplied directly by the state, indirectly by those other regions of Britain which had adapted more successfully to twentieth-century realities.

Shipbuilding was only one industry, though that which had long dominated the west-of-Scotland economy. Glasgow likewise was only one city in Scotland. But it had been the motor of the Scottish economy, its continuing importance in Scotland so much greater than the importance of comparable Victorian cities in the twentieth-century economy of England. Its decline accordingly took on profound significance. It was both a cause and a symptom of the Scottish malaise.

Nineteenth-century Scotland had been expansionist; twentieth-century Scotland was defensive. From being the proud leader of the first Industrial Revolution, Scotland now tagged along behind, consuming more wealth than it created. The same mood of resentment and self-pity might be evident in Manchester, Liverpool, Leeds and Newcastle, but they did not represent, could in no way be thought to represent, England, as Glasgow did Scotland.

Too long dependent on the heavy industries which had made Victorian Scotland rich, slow in adapting to changed circumstances, the Scottish mind seemed to lose its native vigour in the years after the Hitler war. Instead of setting the pace, Scotland fell behind. Enterprise – indeed capitalism itself – became suspect. The national mood was defensive. The old industries looked to the state for support, and only the state, it seemed, was ready to invest in new ones. Attempts by the Macmillan and Wilson Governments to 'rationalize' the economy and to implant new large-scale industries – a car factory at Linwood, a pulp mill at Fort William, a huge steel plant at Ravenscraig, an aluminium smelter at Invergordon – foundered. Private enterprise had failed; public investment was no more successful. Nineteenth-century Scotland had invested all over the world; towards the end of the twentieth century the belief prevailed that only inward investment, from the USA, from Germany, from Japan and even from Korea, could regenerate the Scottish economy.

There were admittedly some successes. The Scottish financial sector, almost the only area of the economy free of Government direction and support, flourished, especially in Edinburgh; but found opportunities for investment of its profits beyond Scotland. The policy of attracting inward investment did lead to the creation of an electronics industry, but the so-called Silicon Glen consisted mostly of assembly-plants, while research and development remained with the parent companies domiciled elsewhere. Moreover, it was not long before many of these assembly-plants themselves were closed and production transferred to countries with lower labour costs.

The discovery of oil in the North Sea brought new hope, and certainly stimulated the economy of Aberdeen and the surrounding district. Indeed the servicing of the oil industry transformed the north-east and made Aberdeen one of the most prosperous – and expensive – cities in the United Kingdom. But the refusal of successive governments to set up a Scottish Oil Fund like that established in Norway meant that Government revenues from the oil industry were used to finance current expenditure rather than for long-term investment. The belief that the oil wealth was being dissipated in this way stimulated political nationalism.

The nationalists had one other, and rather better, argument, though they made less of it than they might have. Monetary policy, whether in the hands of the interventionist Macmillan and Wilson governments, or of the Thatcher Government with its commitment to the free market, was, doubtless inevitably, determined by the needs of the UK economy rather than those of Scotland. So, characteristically, a brake would be applied to the economy, and interest rates raised, whenever it was deemed to be overheating. That judgement was made on the evidence of the economic performance of the south-east of England and the west midlands. But there was never a time in the post-war decades when the Scottish economy was overheating. Inasmuch as it existed as an individually identifiable entity, it was rarely even warm. Consequently Scotland tended to be first into recession and last out, precisely because it was never in need of the higher interest rates and restriction of credit thought necessary for the restraint of too rapid growth in the richer parts of the United Kingdom. Growth in Scotland was never too rapid; indeed it was never rapid enough.

Thrown on the defensive, thirled to the belief that only the state was capable of regenerating the economy, Scotland was particularly vulnerable when the Thatcher Government abandoned the policy of propping up failing industries, and instead exposed them to the cold wind of market economics. The 1980s therefore resulted in the closure of old industries, the long-resisted crumbling of Scotland's Victorian economy, and mass unemployment on a scale not experienced since the 1930s. It was harsh medicine, a purgative, and though eventually it might be argued that the patient recovered, emerging from the experience with an economy better suited to the modern age, the treatment had been so painful that the Scottish electorate deserted the party responsible for administering it. Measures undertaken to regenerate the British economy contributed to the political disenchantment with Scotland's position in the United Kingdom.

In general of course Scotland, like England, like indeed the whole of the Western world, became more prosperous in the second half of the twentieth century, and wealth was more widely distributed than had been the case when Victorian Scotland was a market leader and a global economic power. The days when Scots lived on a diet of oatmeal were long past. The second agricultural revolution raised production to unprecedented levels; unlike England, Scotland was a net exporter of food, producing more than was consumed at home. Other sectors, notably banking, did well; the Royal Bank of Scotland took over one of the biggest English banks, the National Westminster, and became one of the largest banks in the European Union. But at the same time the Bank of Scotland lost its independence in a merger with the Halifax, which was the dominant partner in the new group. This was all too characteristic of a trend that had been evident since at least the end of the 1914–18 war, Scottish companies being swallowed up by English ones, losing not only their independence but head-office functions. By the end of the century most even of the whisky industry (Scotland's largest exporter in terms of value) was owned by companies based outwith Scotland.

Finally, though Scotland became richer, it did so more slowly than England, more slowly than most of the member-states of the European Union, and more slowly than the rapidly expanding economies of much of Asia. The comparative advantage it had enjoyed in the nineteenth century was lost; instead it now stood at a comparative disadvantage to partners who were also competitors. Comparative economic failure engendered a national mood that was defensive. The demand for political devolution, even independence, was the consequence. If we could no longer compete on equal terms within the unitary state that Britain had become, then the temptation to withdraw, in part at least, became irresistible.

12

Politics

I N 1886 THE future Liberal prime minister H. H. Asquith, a Yorkshireman by birth, was adopted as his party's Parliamentary candidate for the East Fife constituency. In his biography of Asquith, Roy Jenkins remarked: 'It was not then as great a disadvantage in the circumstances to be an Englishman as it would be today, when English members for Scottish seats are very rare birds indeed.' (Jenkins himself, twenty years after the publication of his life of Asquith, was to become such a bird himself, though of course Welsh by birth, if not conviction or habit, when he was elected to the constituency of Glasgow Hillhead. Nevertheless the observation holds generally good.)

> Apart from Asquith himself, John Morley, Augustine Birrell and Winston Churchill, to cite only Liberal politicians of the first prominence, all sat for Scottish constituencies during the next twenty-five years. Birrell was MP for the other part of the County of Fife, and on one occasion in about 1900 when he and Asquith and Haldane had climbed to the top of a hill near the Firth of Forth which commanded a wide view over both Fife and East Lothian, he turned to the others and exclaimed: 'What a grateful thought that there is not an acre in this vast and varied landscape which is not represented at Westminster by a London barrister!'

Actually Asquith had been jobbed into the position of Liberal candidate by Haldane, a Scot himself, later Secretary of State for War in Asquith's Cabinet, and Labour's first Lord Chancellor; he had, as Jenkins writes, 'extensive family connections over most of the eastern half of the Scottish Lowlands' – further than that indeed, for the Haldanes were lairds of Gleneagles.

Asquith's election was significant for two reasons. The first has been remarked by Jenkins. There was no feeling then that Scottish constituencies should be represented by Scotsmen, any more than there was, even today is, a feeling that only Englishmen should sit as MPs for English constituencies. Nineteenth-century Scotland was comfortably British.

Second, the emergency had arisen because of the first split in the Liberal Party over Gladstone's proposal to grant a measure of Home Rule to Ireland. The sitting Liberal member, a local laird called Boyd Kinnear, had voted against Gladstone's bill and been disowned by the East Fife Liberal Association, which was firmly Gladstonian. A section of the Liberal Party hived off, to become the Liberal Unionists, eventually indistinguishable from the Conservatives. Well into the 1950s the Scottish Tories were generally known as the Unionists, the Union referred to being that not of Scotland and England, but of Great Britain and Ireland. It was only with the rise of Scottish Nationalism in the early 1970s that the name Unionist took on a different significance.

Scotland, since the expansion of the electorate by the Reform Act of 1832, had been solidly Liberal. In the General Election of 1865, for instance, the Liberals won forty-two Scottish seats and the Conservatives only eleven. Every burgh seat was Liberal. The disgruntled Tory leader Disraeli said: 'The Scotch shall have no favours from me until they return more Tory members to the H. of C., and of all parts of Scotland the most odious are the Universities. They have always been our bitterest and most insulting foes.' Many Scots, if invited to identify the author of these words, would undoubtedly plump for Margaret Thatcher. Indeed nineteenth-century Scottish Tories were in almost as miserable a condition as their successors in the Thatcher and Major years. Like them, they had their moments, but they were few. One was when Alexander Whitelaw of Gartshore became in 1874 the first Conservative elected for a Glasgow seat since 1832. (His great-grandson would be Margaret Thatcher's deputy prime minister.) More characteristic however was the boast that Gladstone was able to make in 1880. This was the year of his Midlothian campaign, and he wrote to his host in Scotland, the young

Lord Rosebery, to express his delight: 'The romance of politics, which befell my old age in Scotland, has spread over the whole land . . . I suppose the Conservative Scotch will fill a first-class compartment, or nearly so, but no more.' Scotland was a Liberal fief.

What was this Scotch Liberalism, and did it differ in any respect from the English variety?

It subscribed to the same economic creed: Free Trade and minimal state interference with the processes of the economy. This was the doctrine of laissez-faire, often ascribed to the Manchester school of Liberals; with some reason, as we have seen, for it was in Lancashire that Richard Cobden and John Bright had formed the Anti-Corn Law League, which, in the 1840s, had succeeded in eradicating Protectionism, and replacing it with its own nostrum, Free Trade. But Glasgow was in no way less enthusiastic for Free Trade than Manchester, and in any case the argument derived from Adam Smith. Free Trade was an Anglo-Scottish or British doctrine, in which eventually even Tories had to acquiesce.

Beyond that it was very difficult, it is very difficult, to say exactly what Liberalism meant. The English-born Scots Tory historian Michael Fry is probably right when he suggests that it stood for 'a view of Man as a free independent being, and for not much else'. Yet that itself is quite a lot, a considerable philosophical statement: that the individual has the responsibility of making his own life, and is capable of exercising that responsibility. It derives in part at least from the Protestant insistence on Bible-reading, no priest needed as intermediary between Man and his Maker. Though the Calvinist doctrine of Predestination, whereby the Elect, arbitrarily chosen, were distinguished from those doomed to damnation, might seem to run counter to the principle of free choice inherent in ideas of personal responsibility, in practice Scots Presbyterians, though doubtless convinced of their own virtue, were more likely to believe with Carlyle's father that work, well and dutifully performed, was what gave meaning to existence. There were hypocrites, Holy Willies among them, as among the adherents of every faith, but the nineteenth-century Scottish mind was, for the most part and at its best, serious, responsible, honest and, politically, liberal.

The fullest expression of that Liberalism is to be found in John Stuart Mill's *Essay on Liberty*, essentially a plea for free discussion of serious matters. Mill himself was a first-generation Anglo-Scot, his father James Mill, a utilitarian philosopher, journalist, educationalist (one of the founders of London University) and economist, having been born in Brechin and educated in Edinburgh. John Stuart Mill (1806–73) was a friend of Carlyle (remaining so despite losing the manuscript of Carlyle's *History of the French Revolution*) but did not follow Carlyle as he drifted towards authoritarianism. Like his father he preferred to apply the utilitarian test, proposed by the Englishman Jeremy Bentham, to all political questions and established institutions: 'what's the use of it?'

Utilitarianism derived from the principles enunciated by the philosophers and political economists of the Scottish Enlightenment, and was to be one of the bases on which Victorian Liberalism rested, in England and Scotland alike. It respected the material improvements brought about by applied science. It believed in progress. How did it express itself? The historian G. M. Young suggests:

> something like this: 'Frame your institutions so as to give the utmost scope to these new pioneers and this new power. Throw down everything that may obstruct the progress of industry and the march of mind. And that means, bring your laws and your administration by means of free discussion into accordance with the findings of public opinion. Then there will be no subversion, no revolution, because the people will be on the side of the law; the Government will govern with their consent; and the process of improvement will be working everywhere and all the time, because political freedom and material progress are two sides of the same medal.' That, one may say, is standard mid-Victorian liberalism.

That, one may also say, is the natural corollary of the thinking of the Scottish Enlightenment. Liberal England was a Scottish invention.

The message indeed was to be carried even further: to India, and the empire won there. It was James Mill, an official in the India Office in London, and Macaulay serving on the Board of Control in India and writing his Minutes on Indian education, who established the policy whereby native Indians were to be educated for positions of responsibility in Government service. That education was to be conducted in English, to open to them all the riches of Western knowledge. In time this would lead, inevitably, to the administration of the Empire becoming Indian. Macaulay accepted this with equanimity:

> The sceptre may pass from us. Victory may be inconstant to our arms. But there are triumphs which are followed by no reverse. There is an empire exempt from all natural causes of decay. Those triumphs are the pacific triumphs of reason over barbarism; that empire is the imperishable empire of our arts and our morals, our literature and our laws.

David Hume might have expressed some scepticism at the assertion that any empire might be 'exempt from all natural causes of decay'. Nevertheless Macaulay here showed himself to be the heir of Hume and the other great figures of the Scottish Enlightenment. His confidence was that of the *Edinburgh Review*, in the pages of which indeed he had first established his reputation: that reason could defeat the forces of obscurantism and prejudice, and allow, in Young's words, 'the process of improvement' to work everywhere.

In the second half of the nineteenth century political Liberalism was incarnate in Gladstone. Once described by Macaulay as 'the rising hope of the stern and unbending Tories', Gladstone in his long political journey arrived at the point when he considered that the essential element of a wise or right policy was that it should satisfy what an earlier liberal Tory Canning had called 'that public opinion which, embodied in a free press, pervades, checks, and in the last resort nearly governs all'. Again and again in his mature years Gladstone drew attention to the number of matters on which public opinion, the people, had been right, and the governing classes, the Conservatives, the West End of London, had been wrong. Gladstone was no enemy of the aristocracy – his Cabinets were packed with dukes, earls, barons and the sons of peers – but he came to put his trust in public opinion. To quote Young again, 'The General Will is true, public opinion is right, if it is informed, elicited, and directed by men trained from youth in the business of government by the "invisible education" of home, of school, of the Universities, and by the open conflicts of the House.'

This was a view of public affairs that accorded well with Scottish opinion. Scotland was an argumentative society. Serious men and women debated the matter of the long sermon to which they had listened on Sundays, ministers of religion were learned men expounding the meaning of Biblical texts; yet their interpretation would be challenged if it did not satisfy. Scots liked to argue from first principles; so did Gladstone. They took, like him, a highly moral stance on public questions. His great Midlothian campaigns of 1879–80 saw him assert, with copious examples, the first place that moral principle, as opposed to mere expediency, must have in politics.

But there was another strain in the Scottish temper. On the one hand was the conviction of the equality of all men and women in the sight of God, the conviction expressed by Burns that 'a man's a man for a' that', that 'rank is but the guinea stamp'. Yet at the same time Scotland was, in important respects, a deferential society. Servants might be outspoken, were nevertheless servants. A minister of the Kirk might find his arguments dissected, was nevertheless a figure of authority. Villages and small towns deferred to the triumvirate of the minister, the doctor and the dominie; and a politician such as Gladstone was, in a sense, an amalgam of all three: spiritual guide, social healer and teacher.

'Eton and Oxford on top, Liverpool underneath' was one judgement of Gladstone. Fair enough; the family fortune was made from Liverpool, in West Indian trade and plantations. But there was a deeper stratum yet, and that was Fife, most obdurately Scotch of counties, one with centuries-old links to the Continent, yet rendered a peninsula by the Firth of Forth to the south and the Firth of Tay to the north. The Gladstones originated there, and Gladstone in old age had the look of a Fife fisherman.

He was in religion a High Church Anglican, strongly influenced by the Tractarian movement of his Oxford youth. In his fondness for hair-splitting, his refinement of every argument, his mastery of ambiguity, he resembled Newman, the inspiration of the Tractarians and future cardinal. But this manner of arguing a case was Scotch also. The novelist Muriel Spark has already been quoted as saying that her education in Edinburgh had been founded on the word 'nevertheless'. Gladstone was a 'nevertheless' man. His interest in Scotland long preceded his adoption for a Scottish constituency, which arrived only late in life. But his father had bought the estate of Fasque in Kincardineshire, and, as related in my Introduction, Gladstone was one of the founders of my own school, Trinity College, Glenalmond.

Gladstone, the High Anglican, appealed to Presbyterian Scotland on account of his moral fervour; equally of course to Nonconformist England. Liberalism was the creed of the great industrial cities of Victorian Britain. In the twentieth century Liberalism would give way to socialism, itself developed in an all-British form, very different from the socialism of Continental Europe.

Yet, if Gladstone was the inspiration and representative figure, his Irish policy provoked the first split in the party he led. Disraeli had identified the Conservative working man, but it was Gladstone's conversion to the cause of Irish Home Rule which drove a large part of the working class away from Liberalism, and enabled the Conservatives to become the One Nation party of Disraeli's imagining. For more than fifty years the Orange vote was securely Conservative, or rather Unionist. Ties between the west of Scotland and Protestant Ulster were close. The greatest of Glasgow scientists, William Thomson, Lord Kelvin, was born an Ulsterman, though of a family with Scottish roots, as its name suggests. Andrew Bonar Law, born in Canada, reared in Glasgow, as Tory leader brought Ireland to the brink of civil war by the intensity of his opposition to Asquith's proposals for Irish Home Rule in the years before the outbreak of European war in 1914. Scots Unionism was anti-Catholic, imperialist, business-like, fearful of socialism.

The historic Liberal Party cracked as a result of the 1914–18 war and its aftermath. The Catholic working class in the west of Scotland, Irish in origin, deserted it for Labour; this stiffened the Protestant working class's commitment to Unionism. There was of course a deeper reason for the Liberals' decline. The Liberal ethos could not satisfy the demands of organized Labour. Its essential individualism was at odds with Labour's corporate spirit. Moreover, though Liberalism and free-market economics had delivered wealth, that wealth was inequitably shared. Scotland, like the northern counties of England, might have one of the highest *per capita* incomes in the world, but the statistics were deceptive. Living conditions in the industrial cities were appalling. Glasgow was said to have the worst slums north of Naples, though those who had seen Dundee might question the judgement. Be that as it may, as late as 1886 one-third of Glasgow's families lived in single-room flats. The poet Edwin Muir, transported from an idyllic childhood in Orkney to a Glasgow tenement, found as he made his way to work as clerk in a shipping office that his daily journeys filled him 'with a deep sense of degradation: the crumbling houses, the twisted faces, the obscene words heard casually in passing, the ancient, haunting stench of pollution and decay, the arrogant women, the mean men, the terrible children, frightened me, and at last filled me with an immense, blind dejection'. He might, true, have had the same experience in Liverpool or Manchester, Leeds or Sheffield. The Industrial Revolution had been a British phenomenon; its social consequences were British too.

Scottish politics changed between the two German wars. The years of expansion were over. Retrenchment, shoring up the fabric while alleviating the social distress, became the aim of all political parties. The Liberals were pushed to the fringe, their economic doctrines discredited. The battle now was between Labour and the Unionists, and both inclined to Protectionism.

Though Labour, in its various forms, was committed to Home Rule for Scotland, that commitment was lukewarm. The trade union movement was British, and Labour was a British party. Early leaders might be Scots, but Keir Hardie was returned to Westminster for a Welsh constituency and Ramsay MacDonald for an English one.

Actually, Scottish workers had been slow to turn to socialism. In 1892 only a quarter of shipyard workers belonged to unions. Beatrice Webb lamented that 'the Scottish nature does not lend itself to combination' – an opinion which less than a century later would have astonished

Scots who asserted that the individualism promoted by Thatcherism was inimical to the Scottish communal ethos. But at the end of the nineteenth century things were different. The tradition among the skilled working class was one of self-help and self-improvement. A man who had mastered a trade was his own master, no matter who he worked for.

Yet in 1923 the ILP (Independent Labour Party) won ten of Glasgow's fifteen constituencies. The myth of the Red Clyde was born. Exultant crowds saw the newly elected MPs off from St Enoch's Station. They sang the Red Flag, but also, significantly, two Psalms, the 23rd and 124th – 'Had not the Lord been upon our side / When cruel men / Against us furiously / Rose up in Wrath / To make of us their prey'. Just as English socialism owed more to Methodism than to Marx, so in Scotland the greater debt was to the Calvinist Presbyterian inheritance. In 1918, John Maclean, hero of the Scottish Revolution that never was, told the Durham Miners Gala that 'the mantle of Jesus Christ has fallen on the Bolsheviks'.

One of the Red Clyde MPs, James Maxton, promised the crowd at St Enoch's Station that the atmosphere of the Clyde would get the better of the House of Commons. The reverse happened. The Commons won hands down. Scottish Labour soon lost whatever revolutionary zest it might have had. Maxton himself became one of the ornaments of the House, a much admired orator – whose speeches changed nothing. Another of his comrades, David Kirkwood, ended in the House of Lords. Scottish Labour was soon intensely respectable, and unequivocally British. This was eventually to its advantage. Fifty years after that day at St Enoch's a large part of the salaried middle class in Scotland, many employed in the large public sector, was voting Labour. By the 1970s the Scottish political Establishment was as firmly Labour as it had been Liberal a hundred years before.

In the interim however, with the exception of the Attlee years 1945–51, the Government was usually Tory (Unionist), and the pattern of Scottish politics was no different from England's. There was no feeling that the Unionists were an 'English party'. The governments of Baldwin, Chamberlain, Churchill, Eden, Macmillan, Douglas-Home were generally no less acceptable in Scotland than in England. This was not surprising. They stood mostly for industrial protection and moderate social progress. The welfare state was the creation of successive administrations, from Asquith's Liberals onwards. Everyone accepted that the state had a necessary and growing role to play. In Scotland it was a Tory secretary of state, Walter Elliot, who in the 1930s set up the Scottish Special Housing Association, the Scottish National Development Council and the Scottish Economic Committee, all examples of Government intervention. Corporatism and Keynesianism came to rule either side of the Border, and Scottish politics and political attitudes remained indistinguishable from English. The second half of the twentieth century was well advanced before they began to diverge.

The clearest evidence of this divergence was the gradual crumbling, eventually disintegration, of the Tory–Unionist vote in Scotland. No one has satisfactorily accounted for this; any explanation must be tentative. Yet the facts are clear. In 1955 the Tory–Unionists secured 50 per cent of Scottish votes in the General Election, and half the Scottish seats. In 1997 their share of the vote fell below 20 per cent and not a single Tory–Unionist was returned from Scotland as a member of Parliament.

Only one thing is certain: no single reason can be offered which will satisfactorily explain this collapse of support. To some extent it was not a peculiarly Scottish phenomenon. In the 1980s and 1990s the Tory vote crumbled as completely in Wales and in the old industrial cities of the north of England. Wherever adaptation to the new services-based economy was slow and painful, Tory support withered. Where that adaptation was comfortable and led to immediate prosperity, it held up.

But there were factors peculiar to Scotland. The Tories had been the party of the Empire, with which Scotland had identified itself so strongly; and now the Empire was no more. At the same time the character of the Tory Party itself changed. Its leadership had been upper class, British and imperial. Churchill, Eden, Macmillan and Douglas-Home had all belonged to the old governing class, though Macmillan's membership of that class owed more to his marriage to

Lady Dorothy Cavendish, a daughter of the Duke of Devonshire, than to his education at Eton and Oxford, and his commission in the Grenadier Guards during the 1914–18 war.

Macmillan is however interesting, and relevant to the subject of this book, as an example of the Anglo-Scot. His biographer, Alistair Horne, wrote that 'In the 1960s one fact every schoolchild knew about Macmillan, next to his being author of the remark "you've never had it so good", was that he was the grandson of a Scottish crofter and the son-in-law of an English duke.' (Strictly speaking, it was his great-grandfather who was the crofter, but pride in his origins caused Macmillan habitually to skip a generation.) The grandfather, Daniel, brought up on the family croft on the northern tip of the isle of Arran, removed first to Irvine on the Ayrshire coast where he became apprentice to a bookseller, thence to Glasgow, and then to Cambridge, where he married the daughter of a pharmacist, and at last to London. There he established the publishing firm, Macmillan and Co., in partnership with his brother Alexander. 'The career of these remarkable brothers', Horne writes, 'was a typical Victorian success story, with all its stern precepts and morality.' A typically Scottish one also, not least in the transfer in the next generation of their religious allegiance to the Church of England. This was accomplished by Harold's father Maurice, who nevertheless continued to regard the English as being 'rather snobbish, compared with the essential nobility of the Scots'.

Nevertheless, despite the references after he became prime minister to the crofting grandfather – references, one would guess, more frequent on public platforms than when visiting his Cavendish in-laws at Chatsworth – Scotland played very little part in Macmillan's public life. Indeed the north of England where he was MP for Stockton 1924–9 and 1931–45 mattered much more to him. His experience of the misery there of the Depression years pushed him to the far left of the Tory Party, so far left indeed that the Labour leader Clement Attlee believed that, but for the Hitler war, Macmillan would have crossed the floor of the House and joined Labour. It was from Stockton that he eventually took the title of his earldom.

As for Scotland, Macmillan's attachment was purely sentimental and literary – he delighted in the Waverley novels throughout his life. But he seems rarely to have come north of the Border until he was prime minister; 'Scotland' doesn't feature in the index of the first volume of Horne's biography, which takes Macmillan's life up to 1956. When he did come north, it was to shoot grouse or play golf at Nairn or Gleneagles.

Consequently his inherited Scottishness scarcely impinged on Scotland. The references to the crofting grandfather impressed few. Indeed Macmillan seemed in his years as premier an example of the 'grouse-moor Toryism' that was both out of date and resented or despised, almost as complete an example as his brother-in-law, the Hon. James Stuart, the deplorable and ineffective Secretary of State for Scotland 1951–7.

After Macmillan, Rab Butler and Alec Douglas-Home, the Tory Party became obsessed with the idea of modernization. The old landed aristocracy was on the way out; it was the hour of the new class, the meritocrats. The upper-class Establishment became an object of the new fashionable satirists, and few noticed that most of the satirists themselves had been educated at public schools and Oxford or Cambridge. So the Tories chose as their new leader the state-school-educated Edward Heath (though he had admittedly been to Oxford and had long ago discarded the vowel sounds of his Kentish childhood), and when Heath failed he was replaced by the Lincolnshire grocer's daughter Margaret Thatcher (whose own vowel sounds had travelled far from Grantham), and she in turn by John Major, who had been reared in a poor London suburb and had escaped, or been denied, a university education.

All had their merits, and in England Margaret Thatcher was, electorally, the most successful Tory leader since Stanley Baldwin between the wars. But all three were, in the eyes of Scots, unmistakably English, and southern English at that. Nobody could seriously doubt that all three were British patriots, Margaret Thatcher even stridently so. Nevertheless to Scots they did not seem British, as Churchill, Eden, Macmillan and Douglas-Home had seemed British. The decline of the Tory Party in Scotland coincided with the rise of the suburban meritocrats, may even have been a consequence. Margaret Thatcher was eager to claim a Scots authority for her economic policies; Scots sourly responded that she had misunderstood Adam Smith, or, if they were more generous (which was rare), conceded that her misunderstanding was the result of coming to Smith by way of the Austrian apostle of the free market, Friedrich Hayek. Her emphasis on individualism offended. She was denounced as crassly materialistic. She did not understand the importance Scots placed on 'community and communal values', and so on. This was at least the opinion of the left-inclining Scottish Establishment, itself predominantly middle class. When she had the temerity to deliver an address to the General Assembly of the Church of Scotland, her suggestion that the Good Samaritan would not have been able to be of such help to the man who fell among thieves if he had not himself been a rich man was ill received, though the observation was self-evidently true.

The hostility she provoked seemed odd to some Scots however, myself among them. The emphasis she laid on thrift, self-reliance, enterprise, the duty of 'getting on, making good', was familiar to, at least, Aberdonian ears. In north-east Scotland – and doubtless other parts of the country – in the 1940s and 1950s, the 'Victorian values' she preached were practised. There was indeed little that she said which did not repeat the teaching of Samuel Smiles, Haddington-born writer and social reformer, whose *Self-Help* (1859) and *Thrift* (1875) expressed the prevailing morality of nineteenth-century Scotland. There was indeed a case for saying that Margaret Thatcher was less a Tory than a nineteenth-century Scottish-style Liberal with a 'view of Man as a free independent being, and not much else'.

But Scotland had changed, and since her Government's policies led to a high rate of unemployment, unmatched since the 1930s, if only temporarily, and accelerated the decline of heavy industry and of Scotland's excessive reliance on manufacturing, she was rewarded with a degree of unpopularity unequalled by any other twentieth-century prime minister. Other things contributed to this: her refusal to countenance devolution, and, perhaps, the mere fact that she was a woman.

It was suggested that some Scots resented her because she reminded them of the teachers under whom they had suffered at school. Undoubtedly however her Englishness, and the nature of her Englishness, were chief causes of the dislike, even loathing, with which she was regarded.

She became associated with a crass materialism, with a worship of wealth, and a careless, even harsh, selfishness. 'Essex man', uncultured, concerned only with self-advancement, indifferent to social values, became the symbol of Thatcherism. Of course there were Scottish equivalents of 'Essex man', for the type is universal, but many voted SNP rather than Tory, for the Tories were now seen more and more as an English party; and the weaker they became in Scotland, while flourishing in England, the more English they appeared. Accordingly, while Thatcherism was as disliked in the north of England and the old manufacturing cities of the north and midlands as it was in Scotland, that dislike in Scotland acquired a sharper, nationalist note. When the poll tax, devised by Scottish intellectuals and forced on an initially reluctant prime minister by the Scottish Office, was introduced a year earlier in Scotland than in England, the conviction that Margaret Thatcher and the Tories were anti-Scottish became fixed.

As the Tories declined, Labour flourished. It presented itself as the defender of Scottish interests against the anti-Scottish Thatcherite Government; Tory secretaries of state were seen as quislings, agents of an alien ideology. Yet Labour also remained a Unionist party.

More remarkably, for the first time since the 1920s, Scots came to dominate the British Labour Party. The Attlee Government had been so short of talent among its Scottish MPs that it had been hard put to it to find a competent Secretary of State for Scotland, and failed to find an impressive one. None of the leading figures of that 1945–51 Labour Government was a Scot. The only Scottish MP to hold Cabinet office unrelated to Scotland was John Strachey, Old Etonian and former Communist, who sat for Dundee 1945–50, then Dundee West 1950–63. Strachey, close friend of the Tory MP Bob Boothby, and former parliamentary private secretary to Sir Oswald Mosley, was an upper-class Englishman, his father having been proprietor and editor of the *Spectator*, but had Scottish connections, his grandmother having been a Grant from Inverness-shire.

Harold Wilson's Cabinets were almost equally bereft of Scots, though he did have a strong secretary of state, Willie Ross, MP for Kilmarnock and a former schoolmaster. Ross, firmly Unionist, contemptuous of the nascent Scottish National Party, whose members he dismissed as 'Tartan Tories', nevertheless jealously practised administrative devolution and, according to Richard Crossman, tried to prevent Scottish business from being discussed in Cabinet, and usually succeeded. Yet despite the sizeable Scottish contribution to Labour's Parliamentary majorities (very thin except in the years 1966–70), the Scottish influence in Labour Governments was small. Indeed that influence had arguably been stronger in Macmillan's Cabinet when the Earl of Home (Sir Alec Douglas-Home) was foreign secretary and Iain Macleod, a Lewisman, brought up in Yorkshire, educated at Fettes and representing a London suburban seat, was first colonial secretary and then Chairman of the Conservative Party.

In contrast Scottish Labour members in the Attlee and Wilson years were mostly lobby-fodder. They were representatives of the authentic working class, many trade unionists assigned by their unions to an industrial seat that was effectively in the union's gift. The Scottish electorate in the 1950s was polarized, seats being either solidly Labour or securely Unionist, few changing hands.

This began to change in the second half of the 1960s. The slow decline of Scotland's enterprising nineteenth-century industrial economy resulted in the ever greater reliance on the public sector, with even privately owned businesses, like the shipbuilding firms on the Clyde, looking for Government aid to enable them to remain active. Consequently the Scottish economy came to be dominated by the state, and the Scottish middle classes, once contemptuous and fearful of socialism, seemed now happy to creep under the state's umbrella. It helped of course that Labour Governments since 1951 had sidled away from any intention to impose real socialism on the country.

From the mid-1960s a Scottish university graduate with political ambitions was most likely to be Labour. In a sense Scots had been slow to make this move. Harold Wilson had aspired to make Labour 'the natural party of government', and his Cabinet had been stocked with men who had won a First at Oxford – Denis Healey, Roy Jenkins, Anthony Crosland, Richard Crossman and the lord chancellor Geoffrey Gardiner, for example. Few would have forecast then that in less than thirty years, or one political generation, Scots would dominate in the Cabinet of the next but one Labour prime minister. But that is how it turned out.

There were two reasons, apart from individual talent. After the General Election defeat in 1979, the Labour Party in England was pulled to the left, first by the Bennite agitation, and then in the town halls. The Tory press and politicians began to talk about 'the Loony Left', which nevertheless really did flourish. There was no Loony Left in Scotland, or at least none of any significance. The Scots party kept on an even keel. Its leaders, John Smith and Donald Dewar, were moderates, prudent men, both lawyers (Smith an advocate, Dewar a solicitor), reassuring, eminently sensible; they frightened nobody.

Then, whereas in England Labour's right wing, alarmed by the Bennite ascendancy and despairing of the party's future, broke away to form the new Social Democratic Party (later to amalgamate with the Liberals as the Liberal Democrats), they found few followers in Scotland, where from 1979 Labour still saw itself as the natural party of government, albeit one condemned to opposition by the Tory majority in England. This posed a certain difficulty: how to assert Labour's right to govern Scotland without sliding into hostility to England. Gradually Scottish Labour which had originally adopted the policy of devolution, or Home Rule for Scotland, hesitantly, suspiciously, was pushed towards a firmer commitment. It began to speak of the 'democratic deficit', as a consequence of which Scotland was denied the government for which it had voted, and condemned to suffer one imposed on it by the English electorate. Naturally, in the eighteen years of Tory government from 1979, the Labour Party in England had no such argument to support it. It might have a majority in the north and midlands, but there could be no suggestion that these English provinces constituted a nation deprived of self-government, nor even a coherent political entity. So the experience of prolonged Tory rule pushed not only Scotland and England some way apart, but opened up a division within the formerly united British Labour Party; its Scottish wing now had its own distinct agenda, one which was viewed without enthusiasm, even with suspicion, by many north-of-England Labour MPs and councillors, already resentful of the higher levels of public spending per head of population in Scotland. Yet by 1997 the Scottish dominance in the upper reaches of the Parliamentary party was such that there was no likelihood that English Labour MPs would not acquiesce in the plan for devolved government in Scotland (and also Wales).

Scottish Labour had an old commitment to Home Rule for Scotland, dating back to the early years of the Labour Representative Council and the Independent Labour Party. But this had withered as Labour displaced the Liberals to become one of the two parties competing for government. For twenty years more after 1945 this commitment seemed moribund. The rise of the SNP, evidence of Scottish discontent with the unitary state, revived it. The loss of a by-election at Hamilton in 1967, and the SNP surge in the two 1974 elections, in the second of which it took around 30 per cent of the vote and won eleven seats at Westminster, persuaded Labour leaders that nationalist feeling in Scotland must be appeased, and that this required the creation of a Scottish Assembly or Parliament. Though the first attempt to provide this failed, being rejected in the 1979 referendum, when the majority for devolution failed to reach the figure of 40 per cent of the electorate imposed by an amendment to the Scotland Bill, proposed by a Scottish backbencher George Cunningham who, however, represented a London constituency, the experience of the Thatcher and Major Governments convinced Labour and a majority in Scotland of the necessity, or at least desirability, of devolution.

Yet this imperative was widely misunderstood. Idealists saw devolution as offering an opportunity for radical change in policies and in the style of politics. Labour saw it as an essentially conservative measure: 'Things will have to change', as Tancredi says in Lampedusa's novel, *The Leopard*, 'if we want them to remain the same.' During the referendum campaign of 1997 I asked Dewar what he would be able to do as first minister of a devolved Scotland that he could not achieve as secretary of state. He offered no convincing reply. This was not surprising, because the truth was at that moment unspeakable: that the real purpose of devolution as seen by Labour was to be able to prevent change being forced on Scotland from London.

John Smith, Labour leader 1992–4, had called devolution Scotland's 'unfinished business'. It was certainly his; as a junior minister in the Callaghan Government, he had helped devise the 1978 Scotland Act and steer it through the Commons. By the 1990s almost all Labour doubts had been laid to rest. Devolution was the agreed way forward. The policy originally adopted to check the SNP had, as a consequence of the long period of Tory rule, become the political equivalent of the Ark of the Covenant for Labour.

The relationship between devolution and nationalism was nevertheless equivocal. The SNP would back Labour in the referendum of September 1997, even though, a few months earlier, the then Labour Shadow Secretary of State for Scotland, George Robertson, had asserted that devolution would 'bury the SNP'. Now, with the SNP the second party in Scotland, as it has been for a dozen years, it is too soon to say whether Robertson's prophecy will be fulfilled.

The rise of Scottish nationalism since the 1960s has been the most significant development in British politics. The adjective is deliberately employed. For most of the twentieth century there was little difference in politics either side of the old Border. Politics indeed were British. There were regional variations in both England and Scotland, but, by and large, the two countries voted as one. Support for the Conservatives or Labour followed very much the same pattern in Scotland as in England. Scots voted, like the English, for the National Government in the 1930s, for Labour in the 1940s, and for the Conservatives in the 1950s. The emergence of the SNP as a political force broke the mould.

Common experiences had made Scots and English alike British. These included the winning and administration of the Empire, the conviction that the United Kingdom was a Great Power, the two world wars, the creation of the welfare state after 1945. All these were significant. It was easy to be proud of being British. Scots who fought and died on the Somme or in Normandy did not think they were fighting an English war.

There were cultural bonds too: the possession of a common language (whatever the variation between regions) was obviously one, reinforced by the new medium of broadcasting, first radio, then television, which ensured that the same programmes were listened to or watched from Shetland to Cornwall. National institutions, notably the monarchy and the armed forces, formed another bond, as did the sense of a shared history. Moreover, regional variations did not disguise the fact that there was a single coherent British economy.

In the second half of the twentieth century many of these bonds slackened, some were severed. The Empire, in which Scots had played a disproportionately large role, dissolved. The memory of the two great wars receded, began to grow dim, except when stimulated by television programmes and commemorative anniversaries. With the weakening of the habit of deference, respect for the monarchy diminished. Britain lost its status as a Great Power; it was either a lackey of the USA or a component part of the European Union. Economic decline made it more difficult to retain the sense of pride in being British. It was not surprising that an increasing number of Scots began to question the continuing value of the Union.

At the same time the renascent sense of Scottish identity was, paradoxically, stimulated by the fear that that distinct identity was in danger of disappearing. Cultural nationalism in Scotland was provoked less by an awareness of differences between Scotland and England than by the evidence that such differences were evaporating. It was, of course, an old fear, articulated (as we have seen) in earlier times by Walter Scott and John Buchan. But in the age of what the English novelist and social critic J. B. Priestley had called 'Admass', when, for example, the same chain stores were to be found in Edinburgh's Princes Street, Glasgow's Sauchiehall Street and Aberdeen's Union Street as in London's Oxford Street and the principal streets of every English provincial city, that fear seemed well founded. It was not that

Scotland and England were moving apart, but rather that they were coming together, in danger of seeming indistinguishable one from the other. Creeping uniformity provoked a reaction: the more we were alike, the more urgent the desire to assert differences.

Moreover the mass media made Scots more aware of Englishness than ever before. English voices, expressing English viewpoints, articulating English hopes, making English boasts, now came into every Scottish home. Even Unionists found this irritating, disliking for instance continual reminders that England had won football's World Cup in 1966, resenting what appeared to be English ignorance of Scotland and the English tendency to equate England with Britain. The campaigners against devolution in 1978–9 took as their slogan, 'Scotland is British'. They would never have said 'Scotland is English'; yet, for many Englishmen, the formulation still appears to be 'Britain is English'. Even the most intelligent and sensitive of them insensibly make this confusion.

Take this, for example, from the military historian John Keegan. It comes from his excellent book, *The Face of Battle*. He has just quoted a long passage from Napier's *History of the Peninsular War*, as an illustration of one style of writing battle-pieces. He continues:

> Napier was trying . . . to describe what by any reckoning was one of the high points of the British effort in the wars against Napoleon – which had, for Englishmen of his own time and class, the same quality of national epic as did the struggle to overthrow Hitler for their descendants five generations later . . . No Englishman before him had written such energetic, many-sided, informative and explicative military history.

Perhaps no Englishman had, but Keegan fails to remark that Napier was not an Englishman but a Scot, a descendant of John Napier of Merchiston, the inventor of logarithms and brother of the great imperial general Sir Charles Napier, their father George being himself a pupil of David Hume. Note too how, for Keegan, 'the British effort in the wars against Napoleon' becomes, by a transition so smooth as to be, one assumes, utterly unconscious, 'for Englishmen of his [Napier's] own time and class', 'a national epic'. Thus, any distinction between English and British is obscured and a Scot like Napier becomes an Englishman of a certain class.

Inevitably, in reaction, Scottish nationalism can never entirely free itself of a tinge of anglophobia. Hugh MacDiarmid, not wholly in jest, gave 'anglophobia' as one of his recreations. But mostly this is too strong a word. We need a weaker suffix than 'phobia'. Irritation and resentment are the emotions, rather than hatred.

In general Scottish nationalism was mild, restrained. The SNP was quick to disown, and disembarrass itself, of extremist groups which preached an ethnic nationalism, in a form actually which seemed ridiculous and offensive to the vast majority of Scots. Instead the party spoke, sensibly, of a civic nationalism, including all resident in Scotland who identified themselves with the country. It steered clear of any association with Irish nationalism, though by the 1990s Scottish nationalists were looking to the Republic of Ireland as an economic model for an independent Scotland. At the same time, eschewing the attitudes of early-twentieth-century Protestant Scots, the SNP showed no sympathy for 'Loyalist' Ulster. This was natural enough since Ulster Protestants identified themselves by their commitment to the United Kingdom, from which the SNP wished to separate Scotland. But the lack of sympathy for those whom Americans had known as the Scots-Irish who, in the cultural field, were seeking official status for the dialect known as Ulster Scots, had its own local justification. Scots Catholics, for long suspicious of the nationalist movement in Scotland, had to be wooed from their Labour loyalties. So the SNP kept its distance from the Orange Order in Scotland, and when the party president William Wolfe was discovered to have had Orange links, he was quietly removed to the sidelines.

In the 1970s the Royal Commission on the Constitution, chaired by the Scottish judge Lord Kilbrandon, had concluded that:

> The greatest significance of the Scottish Nationalist movement lies not in its advocacy of separatism but in the means which it has provided for the people of Scotland to register their feelings of national identity and political importance. Nationalist voters, and the obvious sympathy

they have attracted from many others who would not themselves be prepared by their votes to endorse a separatist policy, have drawn attention to an intensity of national feeling in Scotland which people outside that country were not generally aware of.

This seemed fair comment at the time; it does not appear unfair more than thirty years later.

There was always the possibility, danger even, that this display of a previously unremarked 'intensity of national feeling in Scotland' would provoke a backlash in England. English nationalism, some, including the Tory prime minister John Major, believed, was the sleeping beast of British politics. What would happen if one day the English said, 'Enough,' and told the Scots to go their own way?

But English nationalism was slow in arising. There was xenophobia certainly, but that wasn't directed at Scots, and in any case was generally smothered by reticence and decency. It found expression in mild anti-Americanism, tetchy Euroscepticism, suspicious resentment of immigrants. The first two were respectable enough, the third not at all. Scots came low on the list, tiresome 'subsidy-junkies' perhaps, but nevertheless British, and therefore family.

13

Identities: Through the Looking-Glass and into the Next Room

THE UNITED KINGDOM will have its 300th birthday in 2007. This is now certain. The political timetable ensures it; there simply isn't time to engineer even the smoothest of divorces before the tercentenary. A few years ago this seemed possible. 'Free by '93' was an SNP cry in the run-up to the 1992 General Election. But the SNP breakthrough was, once again, postponed. Now, in wet and windy December 2004, the moment at which I write, it looks as distant as ever; and not only because the electoral system for the devolved Scottish Parliament was devised to make it difficult for one party to achieve an overall majority.

Of course the Union may founder. Scotland may choose independence. It may even have independence thrust upon it. The journalist and historian Neal Ascherson has found it 'not hard to imagine a "velvet divorce" on the Czech/Slovak model. Slovakia's independence was not achieved by Slovak patriotic fervour. Instead it was dumped on the table by the Czechs, who grew tired of negotiating endless Slovak demands and walked away. As births of nations go, it was undignified.' But so was the Treaty of Union itself.

Still Ascherson thinks the Union will end for other reasons: on account of 'Scotland's sense of European identity, as a small North Sea nation which needs to encounter the world directly rather than through the priorities of "Great Britain"'. The inverted commas round the words Great Britain are his. He may be right, but that loaded verb 'needs' – this time the inverted commas are mine – invites the question: how many Scots feel that 'need'?

Then he says there is 'Scottish constitutional doctrine, now slowly re-emerging . . . This tradition . . . relies on the notion that there is a supreme law which is above monarchs and parliaments.' He refers back to the Declaration of Arbroath and the seventeenth-century Covenants. But then in that century it was an English court which, in the name of the people of England, sentenced a king to death, rebutting Charles I's claim that 'a sovereign and a subject are clean different things'. Ascherson writes that 'Scotland is gravitating towards a constitutional view of public life and popular sovereignty which is European rather than British.' Does he mean 'English' there, rather than 'British', for what is 'British' is also, unavoidably, Scottish in part? And even if he does mean 'English', it was an English Whig, Charles James Fox, who proposed a toast to 'our sovereign, the People'.

Finally, Ascherson falls back on what he admits to be a subjective generalization: 'there is the particular, apparently indelible colouring of Scottish society . . . I suggest that the Scots are communitarian rather than individualist, democratic in their obsession with equality, patriarchal rather than spontaneous in their respect for authority, spartan in their insistence that solidarity matters more than free self-expression . . .'

No doubt there is truth in this, but couldn't the same be said, with equal truth, about at least some sectors of English society? Were Scots miners more communitarian than English miners? Any more convinced that 'solidarity matters more than free self-expression'? And isn't the great mass of English society today just as keen on equality as the Scots? Moreover, the qualities that Ascherson ascribes to the Scots were to be found also among English Nonconformists. That the Labour Party, in England and Wales, 'owes more to Methodism than Marx' was an observation that has become a truism.

More than a century ago a French political scientist Emile Boutmy was, according to the Scottish historian Christopher Harvie, 'intrigued to find that the so-called United Kingdom consisted of four nations in a state of permanent irritation with each other'. Irritation, and, one might add, rivalry. This is natural enough. It describes the way many families live. Family quarrels may be intense precisely because the members of the family have so much in common that differences between them become sharper and are more marked.

Certainly the English irritate the Scots, often acutely. There are more of them, and we resent this. They are inclined to equate the United Kingdom with England, and we resent that. Sometimes they appear to patronize us. At other times they ignore us or take us for granted. They assume an air of superiority. They remind us too often of their, occasional, sporting triumphs. All this is intolerable, to be put in perspective only by remembering that it is how many of us, Scots and English coming together as British, feel about the Americans.

Dislike of the English, resentment of certain English attitudes and assumptions, even anglophobia, may be found sprouting up, from time to time, at all levels of Scottish society. At its crudest it is expressed in the football chant, 'If you hate the fucking English, clap your hands.' This is on a par with the insults London-based tabloids hurl at Germans, whenever England and Germany come up against each other in competition. There is this – and this only – to be said for the Scots' chant as for other expressions of vulgar anglophobia: it shows an unwilling respect for the English, engendered by the confidence that they will not be unduly offended, as people of more delicate sensibility and less self-assurance – say the Irish or the Welsh – unquestionably would be. In insulting them, the Scots treat the English as equals.

Often it is this very English self-assurance that irritates, their certainty that God is an Englishman, even if many of them no longer practise any religion. Even the English ability to laugh at themselves – something the Scots are not good at – seems like an expression of their sense of superiority. Scots may rail against Scotland, but seldom indulge in light-hearted self-mockery like Noël Coward's 'Mad Dogs and Englishmen': 'it seems a pity when the English claim to rule the earth, / They should give rise to / Such hilarity and mirth'.

Strange as it may seem, dislike of the English is as common among Scottish unionists as among nationalists. Committed to the United Kingdom, they resent anything which suggests that the English either do not regard us Scots as equal partners, or forget that this is what we believe ourselves to be. Intelligent nationalists may even be less critical of the English than some unionists, and not only because any English assumption of superiority inadvertently serves the nationalist cause. They are also able to put forward the argument that we would be more agreeable neighbours to each other if the political Union was dissolved, and only what the SNP leader Alex Salmond calls 'the social union' survived. That, despite Ireland's history of subjection to England, there may now be less antipathy to the English in the Republic than in Scotland lends some weight to this argument.

Scots' dislike of the English rarely extends to individuals, with the exception of a few public figures such as Margaret Thatcher and some TV pundits, especially on sports programmes. Most Scots have English friends and acquaintances; a good many have English relatives. English people who settle in Scotland are rarely made to feel unwelcome. There are a lot of them now, especially in Edinburgh and in Aberdeen and the north-east. Generally, they settle in Scotland as easily and uncontroversially as Scots settle in England. Only a tiny number complain of suffering verbal abuse or discrimination. There is, admittedly, some dislike of English incomers in the west Highlands and Islands where they are known as 'white settlers', more energetic and enterprising often than the locals, and so viewed with some suspicion and resentment.

One curiosity: when Scots express dislike of an English accent, they mean what they identify as an upper-class one. English regional accents, and even the class-neutral Estuary English, attract little opprobrium. Margaret Thatcher might have been less resented if she had spoken as prime minister in the Lincolnshire accent of her childhood. Her remodelled voice made her sound patronizing. Egalitarian Scots, who will quote Burns's lines about the brotherhood of man, are often more class-conscious than English people today.

Hostility to the English was a twentieth-century development. There was less of it a hundred years ago. Scotland was then, or could then think itself, a successful country, contributing disproportionately to the greatest empire the world had ever seen. The resentment festered as Scotland grew comparatively poorer, and the Empire crumbled. By the second half of the twentieth century awareness of economic decline and inferiority affected the Scottish temper. Compensation was found in an assumption of moral superiority. The

English were richer, but the Scots were better, their income lower but their standards higher. The Scottish journalist John Lloyd, born in Fife but long resident in London, recalls that the Labour leader John Smith was 'among those who believed that "the Scots are a more moral people" (as he once told me) than the English whom he aspired to govern'. This conviction was perhaps the last flicker of historic Presbyterianism, of the certainty that the nation had made a Covenant with the Almighty, that the Scots were a Chosen People, like the Jews.

This sense of moral superiority sat uneasily with what has been called the 'Scottish cringe', evidence of a lack of self-confidence manifested in the reluctant or hesitant unionism which for long responded to the prospect of independence with the line, 'Aye, it would be grand, but we could never afford it.' The Tory Party, shamefully, played on this fear, emphasizing Scotland's economic dependence on England and stressing that, financially, we got more out of the Union than we put in. More robust unionism might have argued that, whatever its origins, the United Kingdom had long worked to the benefit of both Scots and English, and that Britishness was essentially a Scottish creation, and that our influence on the politics and culture of the UK was, and had been, disproportionate. But intellectual robustness was out of fashion in both Scotland and England. The Scots, led by the lacklustre and defensively minded Labour Party, opted for the halfway house of devolution, semi-detached but eschewing the risks and opportunities of independence. Far from opening the way to a 'new Scotland', devolution, representing a retreat from whole-hearted participation in the United Kingdom, may be seen as an example of the 'Scottish cringe' in action, just as the recoil from the European Union is evidence of a loss of confidence – an English (or British) cringe.

For most of the three centuries of Union, the English have been more aware of the Scots than the Scots have been of the English. This is not surprising. The Scottish presence in England was hard to ignore. Scots had been flocking south as immigrants since the first Union, that of the crowns. We have seen that, like immigrants in all countries and all ages, they were often resented: accused of clannishness, of taking English jobs, of being parasites. The accusations are standard –

though, interestingly, the Scots escaped the charge of debauching English womanhood.

Animosity was keenest, as we have seen, in the eighteenth century, when Scots could still be the object of distrust as Jacobite rebels, and English Tories, though themselves often, like Johnson, sympathetic to Jacobitism, classed the Presbyterian Scots with English Dissenters as ready to undermine the Church of England. The Bute ministry provoked the sharpest outbreak of Scotophobia from poets like Churchill and pamphleteers like Wilkes.

It died away, and animosity was replaced by admiration early in the nineteenth century as the extent and value of the Scottish contribution to Britain and Empire became apparent. There was another reason for the change of temper. Irish immigrants were now arriving in great numbers in both England and Scotland, and resentment of incomers was directed at them. They were after all far more deplorable objects of suspicion than the Scots, being mostly Roman Catholics and reluctant partners in the Union.

England has long, perhaps always, been open to immigrants (as, to a much smaller extent, has Scotland). Most were assimilated comfortably; within a couple of generations the French Huguenot refugees for instance became English men and women, only their family names recalling their immigrant origin. Many Scots likewise lost, even chose to lose, their connection with their forefathers' native land, and became English; the Waughs, as related earlier, being only a characteristic example. Jews too became Englishmen, especially if they were rich or talented. Many did so even while continuing to adhere to the Jewish faith. Others converted. Disraeli's father had him baptized in the Church of England, and so the young Disraeli was able to enter Parliament where eventually the country gentlemen of the Tory Party accepted him as their leader. (Only Bismarck refused to accept him as English, describing him as 'der alte Jude'.)

The second half of the twentieth century saw immigration on an unprecedented scale. After the waves of refugees from Nazi Germany and the Soviet Empire in eastern Europe, these immigrants came first from the vanishing British Empire, and their skins were black or brown. The character of England was changed. There were urban districts where the native population was soon in a minority. Yet, for the most part, despite the dark prophecies of Enoch Powell and a few others, the newcomers were accommodated with less strain than had been predicted. Once again the English showed themselves tolerant and easy-going.

There was however one interesting development or difference. The English found it easier to accept these coloured immigrants and even their children and grandchildren born in the United Kingdom as British rather than English; and they also tended to use the word British as a self-description. It was as if immigrants could be accommodated and assimilated more comfortably into a multi-ethnic Britain than into Enoch Powell's rooted community of immemorial England. It was certainly easier to become British than English. Curiously, in Scotland, where there were far fewer immigrants, the SNP promoted the description 'New Scots'. But, if the Union should break, then black and brown British would have to be accepted as English, for the option of a British identity would have been withdrawn.

Scottish devolution has not yet brought the English to the point of seriously questioning the value of the Union. They are more concerned with that other union, the European one. There is admittedly some resentment of the role that Scots, or rather Scots MPs, now play in the politics of the UK. It is provoked partly by the suspicion that Scots have engineered a political settlement that gives them the best of both worlds, enabling them to enjoy the advantages of membership of the UK while managing their own affairs, to some extent at the expense of the English; partly by the realization that Scots MPs vote on matters that pertain only to England, while the English have no say in comparable matters affecting only Scotland. (The Scottish answer is that this is a problem for the English themselves to deal with.)

English discontent with the new political arrangements has so far been restrained. They accept for instance, with only the occasional grumble, the presence of several Scots in the Cabinet, even the anomalous position of John Reid, MP for a Scottish constituency, in charge of the Health Service in England, though he has no responsibility for the Health Service in Scotland, not even in the town he represents in Parliament. But there has been no serious suggestion that this is in some way unconstitutional or improper. The English seem content to muddle through. Likewise the Chancellor of the Exchequer, Gordon Brown, who is a Scot returned to Parliament by a constituency in Scotland, is accepted as the heir presumptive to Tony Blair. Few suppose that his Scottishness will debar him, even though the former Cabinet secretary Lord Butler has spoken of Brown's 'ignorance of England'.

There is some evidence of a stirring of English patriotism, if not nationalism, in response partly to the EU, partly to the constitutional changes within the UK. The proliferation of St George's flags at sporting events has been remarked; it is not long since English football supporters waved the Union flag, as if England was indistinguishable from Britain. Inasmuch as there is now a realization that the two are distinct this may point to a revised understanding of the meaning of the United Kingdom, rather than to a wish to tear up the Treaty of Union. Certainly it is a development which no Scot can intelligently complain of. It is indeed rather one which Scots should approve. It may lead to a new and more satisfactory definition of Britishness.

This has always allowed for diversity, as T. S. Eliot recognized in his essay 'Notes Towards the Definition of Culture'. He wrote: 'It is to the advantage of England that the Welsh should continue to be Welsh, the Scots Scots and the Irish Irish . . . If the other cultures of the British Isles were wholly superseded by English culture, English culture would disappear too.' If now Englishness is reasserting an individual identity, Scots, Welsh and Irish should welcome this.

In the mid-nineteenth century the English historian H. T. Buckle concluded that the mentality of Scots and English was so different that it was as if they had never had any influence on each other. This opinion, odd at the time, is now surely untenable. Scots and English have always had more things in common than things that divide them. If both now feel the need to establish, or re-establish, a distinct identity, this is partly because in the twentieth century the differences between them diminished still further. In both countries the national Church lost much of its influence as society became more secular.

People watched the same films and television programmes, read more or less the same newspapers, and listened to the same popular music. They shared the same tastes in holiday destinations, and in eating and drinking. Indian restaurants, Chinese restaurants, pizza houses, burger bars proliferated in towns and cities all over the United Kingdom and the same stores were to be found in high streets and shopping centres. A supermarket in Edinburgh or Aberdeen stocked the same goods as one in Oxford or Manchester. Uniformity smothered old distinctions. The way of life of early-twenty-first-century Scots and English is most accurately described as British. Rebelling against uniformity both Scots and English have felt the need to assert an older, more narrowly national, identity. Yet this very identity is unavoidably contained within a wider British one, for it is the experience of 300 years of Union that has formed us all. The political Union may some day be dissolved, but the new Scotland that would then come into being would itself be the child of the centuries of Union, a product of the British experience. England may discover an English nationalism that has long lain dormant; but the England it would champion would be an England shaped in some measure by the centuries of association with Scotland and the work and influence of Scots who have settled in England and whose descendants have become English.

Bibliographical Notes

'A man will turn over half a library to make one book' (Johnson to Boswell). I don't make so bold a claim. Nevertheless this book is the result of wide and various reading over a great many years. To list all the works that have contributed to its making would be tedious and pretentious. It's enough to state that they fall into two categories: books by classic authors and more recent ones from which I have drawn.

Classic authors include: Burnet, Johnson, Boswell, Scott, Carlyle, Macaulay (and Hugh Trevor-Roper's introduction to the abridged Penguin edition of the *History of England*), Stevenson, Buchan, Mackenzie, Trevelyan.

Among more recent books I have used are:

Neal Ascherson, *Stone Voices: The Search for Scotland*, Granta Books, London, 2002

Melvyn Bragg, *The Adventure of English: The Biography of a Language*, Hodder & Stoughton, London, 2003

James Buchan, *Capital of the Mind*, John Murray, London, 2003

Linda Colley, *Britons: Forging the Nation 1707–1837*, Yale University Press, London, 1992

T. M. Devine, *The Scottish Nation 1700–2000*, Allen Lane, London, 1999

T. M. Devine, *Scotland's Empire 1600–1815*, Allen Lane, London, 2003

Michael Fry, *Patronage and Principle: A Political History of Modern Scotland*, Mercat Press, Edinburgh, 1987

Michael Fry, *The Scottish Empire*, Tuckwell Press, East Lothian, 2001

David Gilmour, *The Long Recessional: The Imperial Life of Rudyard Kipling*, John Murray, London, 2002

Christopher Harvie, *No Gods and Precious Few Heroes: Scotland, 1914–1980*, Edward Arnold, London, 1981

Christopher Harvie, *Travelling Scot: Essays on the History, Politics and Future of the Scots*, Argyll Publishing, Argyll, 1999

Simon Heffer, *Moral Desperado: A Life of Thomas Carlyle*, Weidenfeld & Nicolson, London, 1995

Arthur Herman, *The Scottish Enlightenment: The Scots' Invention of the Modern World*, Fourth Estate, London, 2002

Ludovic Kennedy, *In Bed with an Elephant: A Personal View of Scotland*, Bantam Press, London, 1995

Bruce Lenman, *The Jacobite Risings in Britain 1689–1746*, Eyre Methuen, London, 1980

Bruce Lenman (ed.), *Integration, Enlightenment and Industrialization: Scotland 1746–1832*, Edward Arnold, London, 1981

Michael Lynch, *Scotland, A New History*, Ebury Press, London, 1991

Karl Miller (ed.), *Memoirs of Modern Scotland*, Faber, London, 1970

Karl Miller, *Cockburn's Millennium*, Duckworth, London, 1975

Alistair Moffat, *Arthur and the Lost Kingdoms*, Weidenfeld & Nicolson, London, 1999

Tom Nairn, *The Break-up of Britain: Crisis and Neo-nationalism 1965–75*, New Left Books, London, 1977

Sonia Orwell and Ian Angus (eds), *George Orwell: Collected Essays, Journalism and Letters*, Secker & Warburg, London, 1968

Jeremy Paxman, *The English*, Michael Joseph, London, 1998

Francis Pryor, *Britain AD: A Quest for Arthur, England and the Anglo-Saxons*, HarperCollins, London, 2004

Paul H. Scott, *Walter Scott and Scotland*, William Blackwood, Edinburgh, 1981

Paul H. Scott, *Scotland Resurgent*, Saltire Society, Edinburgh, 2003

A. N. Wilson, *The Laird of Abbotsford*, Oxford University Press, Oxford, 1980

Other citations, especially those of authors of political biographies and of memoirs, will be found in the text.

Index